the way of the cocktail

THE WAY

OF THE

COCKTAIL

JAPANESE TRADITIONS,
TECHNIQUES, AND RECIPES

JULIA MOMOSÉ

with Emma Janzen

PHOTOGRAPHS BY KEVIN MIYAZAKI
ILLUSTRATIONS BY YUKO SHIMIZU

CONTENTS

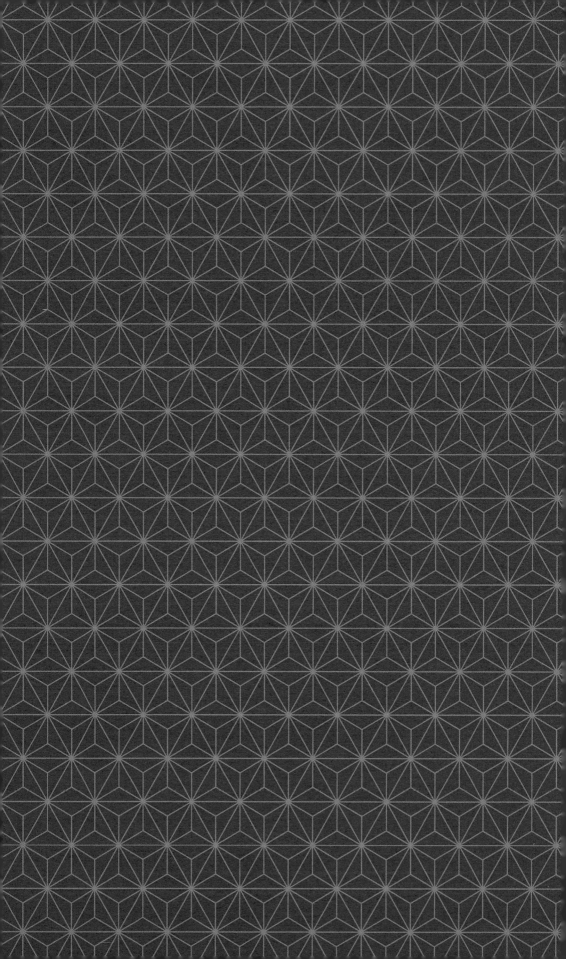

INTRODUCTION AND INTENTIONS

The spirits of the past and present commune in Kyōto. Their voices lilt together within the imposing bamboo forests of Arashiyama, fluttering through the leaves and playing percussion on bending boughs. They dance in the sunlight filtering through statuesque torii, the vermillion gates that lead to the shrine of Fushimi Inari-taisha, where wishes are implored and granted. They alight in Gion—enchanting Gion, where temples tower over the city from their mountain perches, and narrow paths lead to a labyrinth of meandering cobblestone streets flanked by weathered machiya, the traditional wooden townhouses that date back to the 1600s. Every turn beckons a new adventure. It is my favorite place in Japan.

Before leaving my home to study in America, I worked mostly in this historic district, famous for its geisha culture. I preferred to walk the winding route to work, so I would take the train to the Sanjō station, one stop beyond what was necessary. As I ascended the steps to street level, the electricity of the bustling intersection greeted me with a wild breeze blowing from the nearby Kamo River. Rushing against shopping bags clutched in the hands of eager tourists, the wind added to the musical cacophony of the birds chirping loudly from the trees—an invigorating welcome no matter the season.

Gion attracts people from all walks of life—artisans, families, young lovers, fire dancers, and salarymen alike flock to its small bars and shops for both work and repose. Its ancient roadways wind through the grid of the old city like vines pulling against their trellis, making it easy for visitors to get lost. I let my nose guide the way, following the sultry scent of the waffle shop, the tang in the air from nukazuké (rice bran pickles) at Nishiki Market, and the caramelized tinge of roasting coffee coming from the old café. At night, hanging lanterns brighten the rows of stores, teahouses, and eateries that flank the cozy passageways. Elegant women in formal kimono usher guests through the discreet entrances and barely marked doors of kyō-ryōriya (traditional Kyōto restaurants), while thirsty crowds spill out of lively izakaya, where there will often be a waiting list to get inside for the best highballs and otsumami (snacks).

My first time in a cocktail bar was in this captivating city. Time stood still as I bore witness to a completely different side of the place I thought I knew so well. To get to the bar, my friend and I descended a moss-laden concrete staircase. We rang a doorbell and looked up into the camera. A voice crackled through the speaker. He waved and the door slid open to reveal a narrow, unadorned hallway that led to a heavy red velvet curtain. The soft lilt of a sweet jazz riff floated to our ears, intimations of another time and place; the source, a woman in a scarlet red dress poised like a goddess near the piano in the corner. To the left, dramatic lighting illuminated the long wooden bar, where a stately bartender worked quietly in a white suit jacket. The way he moved was mesmerizing. Carrying himself with an elegance I had never before envisioned, he gave every moment his full attention. It was my first time in a real cocktail bar, so every detail of the experience felt sharp and new. The ice clinking in the glass softly, the low murmur of conversation from the other guests, the sweet ripple of the piano keys—it felt special to witness a secret world hidden beneath the bustling streets of Kyōto.

I didn't know what to order, so I asked for a martini. The bartender smiled and with a knowing nod began his studied ritual of mixing. He selected an exquisite, cut crystal glass and filled it with perfect shards of ice, like a slippery jigsaw puzzle, and set it aside to chill. After measuring the gin and vermouth into a weighted mixing glass, he wiped droplets off the mouth of each bottle before positioning them on the bar before me, like a proud display of the quality within. His stir swirled silently with evenly measured rotations; he cast a spell across the room with the glimmer of the barspoon. When he poured the cocktail into the glass, the sight was like a moonstone melting into its setting. With a flourish, lemon oils were expressed over the glistening jewel, and with a look of approval, the martini was nudged toward me across the bar. It was then I knew I wanted to be a bartender. I wanted to provide that experience for other people.

I left home for Cornell University in Ithaca, New York, to study design and environmental analysis. With visions of bartending in mind, I immediately sought work to pay for school, but it was not as easy as just showing up ready and eager. One bar manager believed college girls weren't serious enough to work as bartenders. It was a different time for gender politics in America, and coming from Japan, where gender discrimination was the norm, I was not surprised. I asked to prove myself, and I worked my way from host to cocktail server, finally getting behind the bar as a barback.

In this role, I carried with me behaviors I observed in Japan, without recognizing that was the case at the time. I would anticipate the bartender's needs, lining up the bottles and glassware as orders were yelled across the bar, cleaning up spills as the liquid was hurriedly poured from spout to glass. The endless hustle to place drinks into the hands of thirsty college students pushed me to learn by watching, listening, and polishing glassware. I memorized as many recipes as I could—staples of their day, like the Long Island Iced Tea, Fuzzy Navel, and Mudslide, and garish shooters like the Pineapple Upside-Down Cake and Surfer on Acid. Eventually, I became a bartender and I made it my mission to perfect the drinks I could. It wasn't poetry—not like what I found in that Kyōto jazz bar— but for the moment, it was enough.

Extenuating circumstances led me to leave school and return home to Japan to recalibrate. One night, a friend and I wandered the streets of Kōbe after a luxurious dinner, in search of a nightcap. We came upon a chic bar where charcoal gray walls framed a long, live-edge wooden counter, dark like cherrywood. The floor dipped behind the bar so the owner could stand as we sank down into midcentury modern dining chairs. The only sound that punctuated the room was the *chk, chk, chk* of an ice pick as the bartender expertly chipped spheres to order. Without skipping a beat, he lowered the tool for a brief moment to acknowledge our arrival, offering a set of menus featuring classics like Manhattans, gimlets, and French 75s. To follow suit, I chose an uncomplicated option, a gin and tonic, and was instantly reminded of the painstaking care bartenders in Japan put into each drink as I watched him complete his initial task.

Under the glow of a spotlight, he finessed the slick globe of ice with reverence—each curve and divot carefully considered before easing the sphere into an old fashioned glass. Then he began again, shattering tiny flecks of frozen ice into the air as he shaped two smaller spheres for my gin and tonic. Every order got the same amount of care, whether it was a fancy cocktail or what would be considered a standard highball in America. It felt refreshing to see how, in his eyes, they all deserved to be magnificent. Every drink *should* be made this way, I thought. Every interaction and every guest deserves the same amount of care. I left feeling both inspired and grounded, with a sense of reinvigorated passion for the craft.

When I returned to America, this time to Baltimore, I worked at a bar that served mostly classic cocktails. To learn the ins and outs of America's rich cocktail history, I studied what made the old fashioned so beloved and why a perfect Manhattan benefits from a split of two types of vermouth instead of merely sweet. I was hooked, and there was no looking back. Eventually, I moved to Chicago to work at The Aviary. I was the first female bartender to work behind the copper bar at The Office, in the basement of The Aviary, where we had conversations with guests about drinks instead of offering a menu. Then, I served as head bartender at the Michelin-starred GreenRiver and subsequently as the cocktail creative at the Michelin two-star Oriole. At each place, I leaned toward making approachable but technique-driven creations with subtle Japanese influences.

In time, I realized I wanted to own and operate a cocktail bar with Japanese sensibilities—something well beyond implementing Japanese elements to complement a Western vision. A place where we honor the way of the cocktail and the way of hospitality. Chef Noah Sandoval from Oriole approached me around this time with an offer to bring this vision to life. I could feel the puzzle pieces falling into place. For the next few years I conceptualized and designed every tiny detail of the space, traveling home frequently to stay in touch with my roots. We officially opened our doors in January 2019, welcoming in the New Year and new beginnings.

Kumiko is a place where I embrace two cultures: my culture of birth and my culture of residence. The word *kumiko* represents a Japanese woodworking technique where hand-cut pieces of wood are intricately pieced together to create panels of symbolic patterns. Though the finished work is breathtaking, what is deeply inspiring is the journey required to achieve the final product. This philosophy speaks directly to my heritage and the culture of cocktails in Japan, which we have implemented at Kumiko—everything we do at the bar is about the process, not just the results.

Many people call Kumiko a Japanese-inspired cocktail bar, but that doesn't fully capture its spirit. It is not a true Japanese bar because the physical space exists outside of Japan. Nor is it merely "Japanese-inspired," because I am from Japan and that informs how the business is managed. Instead, it is a place that lingers somewhere between the two worlds, the cumulation of my experience behind the bar in America and my upbringing in Japan, fitting together in perfect harmony, like the small pieces of wood that lace the fabric of a kumiko panel.

There is a word in the Japanese language called *wa,* which translates to "harmony" in English. Taken literally, it illustrates the way people in Japan value tranquility and cooperation over individual pursuits. It is about coming together to create peace and unity for the greater good, a moral code that sprang from Japan's agricultural past when farmers had to work closely together to make the most out of the country's available land.

Today, this philosophy is fitting for a country of over 126 million people living on an island only slightly larger than the UK, which has about half the number of residents. We wait for the green pedestrian signs to light up before crossing the road so traffic accidents don't happen. We don't litter, so everyone can enjoy clean streets. At restaurants, we eat at a reasonable pace so the next person in line doesn't have to wait too long for a seat. Keeping the peace ensures everyone lives comfortably, even in crowded conditions.

Wa resonates on a deeper cultural level, too. It is the old word for "Japan," used to express a sense of place, culture, and elements that are Japanese in spirit— what makes something from Japan *Japanese.* For example, *wa*shitsu are rooms designed with sustainability in mind, with elements like tatami floors made from rice straw left over from the harvest. Or *wa*gashi, which are Japanese confections made from ingredients like rice, agar-agar, arrowroot, yomogi (mugwort), or adzuki beans, sculpted into edible works of art representative of the seasons. The term *wa* applies to everything: art, design, architecture, business, and beyond. I believe it also applies to cocktails.

A Japanese cocktail is not just a drink that was invented in Japan—though some do exist, like the cerulean Sky Diving (page 306) or the historic Million Dollar (page 313). Nor does its definition come just from the ingredients that go into the glass: Including saké or shōchū in a drink does not make it a Japanese cocktail. A cocktail can only truly be "Japanese" if it reflects the broader sense of harmony and interconnectedness that defines Japanese culture at large. It is about intention, mindset, and technique. About ceremony and concentration, refinement, precision, and elegance. It is the crafting of an experience where every element dovetails seamlessly, a process that is celebrated as much as the final product. It is, quite simply, about *wa.*

For cocktails, the journey to *wa* begins at the fountainhead of the supply chain. A master bartender considers the thought and care farmers infuse into growing sugarcane, barley, or rice for the spirits; the mastery of the distillers who transform those natural agricultural products into the rum, whisky, or shōchū; the dexterity and expertise of the artisans who make the tools used to shake or stir—these components inspire the way of cocktail making long before any liquid flows from the bottle. It is the bartender's job to respect the craftsmanship of each element from origin to glass and then use those components wisely and with practiced technique honoring each moment along the way to creating a drink.

Then, more intentions align—the design and architecture of the bar, how that space comes alive when the lights are turned on, and the personality of the master bartender when the curtains rise for service. Glassware gets chilled until frosted. Bottles placed on the bar with labels facing the guest. The music adjusted to a precise volume—not too loud, not too soft. The shake, an intentional choreography developed over decades of practice. A hot towel, calibrated to the ideal temperature, placed on the bar top just within reach. These pieces are niceties in isolation, but when woven together they create an art of cocktail-making that is purely Japanese.

As a bartender, I think of the concept of *wa* in all aspects of my profession and life. It is the way I hold my tools with intention, anticipating every next move and adjusting so that one movement flows seamlessly into the next; the way ingredients layer and align to create balanced flavor. *Wa* is what I strive for in every interaction with a guest and what I weave into every practiced motion while mixing a cocktail. It is about creating something greater than the sum of its parts, both in the overall experience and in the glass.

Throughout this book, we will delve into the soul of Japanese cocktails, covering everything from how tradition and philosophy impact drink-making to more cocktail-specific fundamentals like technique, tools, and elements of hospitality. We will examine how modern Japanese cocktails are a product of both Japanese *and* American bartending history, as the two cultures have been in recurring dialogue since the 1800s, then journey into the realm of Japanese spirits, saké, and wine.

Naturally, there are also recipes. Within these pages are cocktails that capture the spirit of Japanese cocktail culture, offered through the lens of a young Japanese woman now living in Chicago. You'll find drinks inspired by flavors I loved growing up, riffs on classics that have long been embraced by Japanese bartenders, and my interpretations of drinks invented in Japan. The cocktails have been designed around Japan's seasons and their star ingredients; you can use that part of the book with seasonality in mind. Or not! Because making a cocktail can so often be an escape, you can dip into whatever section you feel like at any given time. And because drinks are so often accompanied by food in Japan, I welcome you to explore the snacks and small plates suggested throughout the book to round out your cocktail experience with delectable pairings.

I hope that within these pages, you gain an understanding of the layered elements that make Japanese cocktail culture so specialized and significant. I invite you to be mindful of each step on the path to your goals, for it is as much about the process as the achievement.

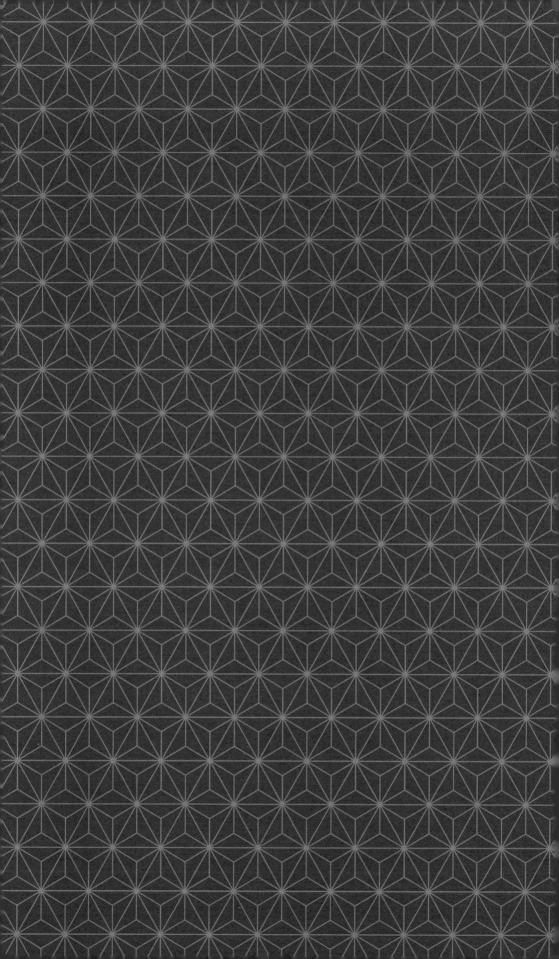

PART I

THE JAPANESE

WAY

日本の飲食文化

EATING AND DRINKING IN JAPAN

Growing up in Japan, I was never aware of the significant place the food and drink of my childhood held within a larger global context, but after living in America I have gained an appreciation for the specific nature and rich history of Japanese foodways. Every region has distinct culinary and beverage traditions, thanks to the farmers, chefs, and vendors who have spent centuries developing, perfecting, and protecting a deep culinary heritage. From the ubiquitous earthy sweet potato shōchū of Kagoshima to the salty, squishy tako-yaki (fluffy dough balls often filled with octopus) made famous by street vendors in Ōsaka, Japan offers a national tapestry of cuisine so profound in its pure and honest presentation that it is considered some of the best in the world.

Aside from the people and overall culture, what I miss the most about living in Japan is not just the variety and quality of food and beverages made there, but how much enjoyment comes with eating and drinking. We even have a special word for the occasion: *itadakimasu*. The phrase literally translates to "I humbly receive," but more generally conveys a feeling of thankfulness for the meal or beverage we are about to enjoy. Whether it is an intricate multicourse kaiseki dinner or a quick standing meal at the train station soba stall, we say this without hesitation because we recognize the amount of care that goes into the preparation of every bite or sip.

This sentiment also translates to the Japanese cocktail scene, where bartenders consider every element of a drink within the scope of the larger picture. Maybe they chose a specific gin for your martini because it is infused with botanicals that grow in the town where you are from; or they chose a cobbler shaker instead of a Boston shaker for your gimlet because they understand how to use the tool to achieve optimal chill and dilution every time. It can be as simple as opting for a lemon peel garnish instead of a cherry in the old fashioned because they wanted to offer a ray of sunshine on a gloomy evening. Itadakimasu is a verbal acknowledgment of the entire package—a special pause in the experience for both you and the bartender.

There are other cultural factors that influence the way food and drink are experienced in Japan. Specifically, there are three essential principles you need to know to fully understand why Japanese cocktail culture stands so distinct from others around the world: First, living habits and rituals are largely driven by shun (seasonality) and, more specifically, by sekki (microseasons). Second, the Japanese philosophy of monozukuri, the way the culture puts a premium on craftsmanship, experience, and expertise. Finally, omotenashi, the fastidious sincerity that distinguishes Japanese hospitality from other parts of the world. These pillars touch all aspects of Japanese life, from schooling and business to daily practices. As you get to know these philosophies, you will have a better understanding of why Japanese cocktail culture is so unique.

shun

SEASONALITY

Our home in Tomio, a small town in the Nara prefecture of Japan, was surrounded by a small garden. Stretched like a pretty ribbon around a gift box, each corner was dedicated to growing seasonal fruits and vegetables. In spring, the umé blossoms arrived, while summer sprang forth in the canary yellow fruit of the biwa (loquat) tree. In autumn, momiji (Japanese maple), kaki (persimmon), and kinmokusei (osmanthus) erupted in a mosaic of color, and winter welcomed the pretty pink buds of the tsubaki (camellia) tree, which always stood tragically beautiful against a backdrop of fresh fallen snow.

Unlike many Western countries where central heat and air conditioning create even-keeled indoor climates year-round, in Japan, many homes do not have these amenities, so people feel the characteristics of each season more dramatically. That is in part why the shift of the seasons inspired what we would eat and drink growing up. Everything was intrinsically tied to the rhythms of the earth and its ever-changing moods, and these moments were often cause for celebrations and gatherings of friends and families. There is a word for this attention to seasonality as it pertains to food: *shun*.

The Japanese calendar features spring, summer, fall, and winter, as is the case in most temperate countries around the world. But there are also twenty-four more specific microseasons, called sekki, that transition every two weeks to mark celestial events, solstices, and equinoxes. The organizational system was originally inspired by one from the Han dynasty in China, and many Japanese calendars still honor the scheme. Each season and microseason arrives accompanied by different events in nature, such as when the rivers thaw or when the caterpillars turn into butterflies. These in turn inspire food- and drink-driven rituals.

eating and drinking in tandem with the seasons helps us live in the moment. we appreciate everything when it's meant to be enjoyed and stay careful not to force things out of their natural state. thus, balance is maintained.

For example, when the blooms of the sakura (Japanese cherry) tree greet the world in the spring, friends and families gather over Japanese saké, shōchū, and beer at cherry blossom festivals. They say that if a sakura blossom falls into your saké glass, you will be blessed with good fortune. Summertime, on the other hand, means exhaustion from the intense heat and humidity. That is when the kakigōri (shaved ice) trucks sing through the streets as a harbinger of icy-cold relief, the markets fill with cucumbers, melons, and tomatoes, and we find liquid relief in thirst-quenching cups of mugi-cha (barley tea) and shiso no jyūsu, the juice of the redolent herb.

In the fall, when the maple leaves morph from vibrant green to shades of gold, orange, and crimson, festivals draw crowds with sweet potato snacks and roasted chestnuts paired with shōchū (often cut with hot water). Days grow shorter, and as a chill enters the air in the mornings and evenings, we warm up over mugs of hot bancha (tea of the second harvest and beyond). In the winter, we seek ways to fend off the cold, so we snuggle in layers of blankets under the kotatsu (a low, heated table) and drink comforting hot saké alongside sunny Japanese citrus. In December, people get swept up by the holiday spirit as Western traditions like

Christmas are embraced. Cakes decorated with bright red strawberries and white whipping cream appear in confectionery windows, and at the end of the year, I look forward to one of my favorite seasonal pairings: Kentucky Fried Chicken and Champagne.

monozukuri

CRAFTSMANSHIP AND SPECIALIZATION

At Suntory's Yamazaki Distillery in Ōsaka, former chief blender Seiichi Koshimizu is famous for his inspiring dedication to the craft. Blending whisky demands a meticulous technique, a gentle touch, and subtle finesse to bring different batches together in a way that creates the best possible expression of the spirit. As such, to keep his palate as consistent as possible, Koshimizu-san would eat a very light breakfast alongside green tea, and for lunch, tempura udon from the cafeteria every day when working at the distillery. Additionally, he avoided eating garlic or smoking cigarettes—even outside of work. He maintained this rigorous approach every day for ten years, because only through this constant repetition was he able to distinguish new flavors and elevate the blends year after year.

This respect for craftsmanship and specialization is called *monozukuri,* a word used to express a profession or practice that takes an extreme amount of dedication and consideration to master, translating directly to mean "the making of things." It sounds simple, but the word carries a weight that resonates deep within the Japanese psyche. Monozukuri is about single-minded commitment and devotion, usually to a craft such as woodworking or ceramics, farming, bartending, or cooking. From a young age, one is taught to seek this singular path and continuously hone the skills required to do that job perfectly. It is not always without sacrifice. Sometimes it means you have to eat the same lunch every day so that your palate remains consistent.

We say it takes at least ten years to get to the point of mastering a craft. To reach this level, one must humbly follow the path of master bartender and apprentice. In Japanese, the terminology is *masutā* (referencing the proprietor of the bar—master of the craft) and *minarai* (the person who watches and learns). The apprentice observes the masutā and works slowly, step by step and with continuous practice, to become proficient in a single task before moving on to the next. Typically there is little direct training, and the apprentice's skills are put to the test with a gradual increase in responsibilities, counting on their ability to watch and learn. This cycle continues until the apprentice is skilled enough to be deemed a master bartender, and then it starts anew with another generation.

In the bar world, the process is slow, each step followed with a sense of patience and gratitude. If the apprentice dives into drink-making too quickly they might miss a crucial element of the process, so they begin by analyzing how to polish glassware, clean efficiently, when to offer hot hand towels to guests, and how to keep them entertained while the bartender mixes the cocktails. Eventually, they might start practicing with a jigger or shaker, and further down the path, they will finally make drinks (and then usually still only under the watchful gaze of their teacher).

Monozukuri is also part of the reason so many bars and restaurants in Japan specialize in a certain style of food and drink. For example, an izakaya that concentrates on yakitori will make better flame-kissed skewers of chicken livers than one that focuses on fresh seafood. In the cocktail realm, some bartenders specialize in a cocktail they love the most, like Masayuki Kodato of Bar Shake in Tōkyō, who will beam with pride as he mixes you his perfect version of the Campari Soda (page 171). At nearby Bar Orchard Ginza, Takuo and Sumiré Miyanohara built an empire on fresh fruit cocktails, so the "menu" at the bar is represented by a platter piled high with grapes, bananas, yuzu, and other delicacies. Sumiré refers to her partner as "Mr. Blender" because of his knack for transforming nature's bounty into delicious cocktails.

A decade of studying and practice may qualify you in name as a master bartender, but the quest never really ends, because the Japanese attitude toward perfection is unique in and of itself: There will never be a point where you are so good at your profession that you don't have to try anymore. Instead, you always take care to pursue a high standard of excellence, finding satisfaction in the hope that you will continue to learn and grow. This is one reason why Japan has some of the best cocktail bars in the world. When a bartender has dedicated their life to perfecting the dry gin martini, that dry gin martini is transcendent compared to one made in a bar with a "something for everybody" mentality. Monozukuri allows for exceptional specificity, and when applied to cocktails, that means insurmountable enjoyment for guests.

omotenashi

HOSPITALITY

When I worked in the restaurant business in Kyōto, I also held a job at a bagel shop in a high-end department store. Every day, the staff would line up and bow to customers as they entered in the mornings. We would do the same at the end of the night. The owners taught me to always have a smile on my face, even if I was taking out the trash or cleaning up a spill. That philosophy lingered and influenced the way I have worked ever since. No matter how bad of a day I'm having, the guest must never know.

This level of consideration springs from a general sense of respect and the desire for the well-being of the group above the individual. From a young age we are taught to leave our classrooms looking better than when we arrived. As adults, we show up early for the trains and line up single file to board after exiting passengers have left the car. There is no eating, drinking, phone calls, or music spilling out of headphones allowed on the train—and people respect these rules, for the most part, because thoughtful observation of the rules keeps society functioning efficiently.

In the hospitality world, this selflessness manifests in a much larger commitment to customer service called *omotenashi*—an unbridled hospitality that stems from the desire to make our guests or customers feel happy, comfortable, or at ease. At bars in big cities like Tōkyō or Kyōto, omotenashi reveals itself in many small, subtle ways. If a guest is left-handed, the bartender might place the glass on their left side; if someone heads outside for a smoke break or a visit to the restroom, an attentive bartender will keep their cocktail in the freezer so the drink stays ice-cold. Many times, the bartender or owner will physically walk the guest to another bar or restaurant after their visit. That is something we also do at Kumiko, because these small gestures also build relationships with other bars and restaurants in our neighborhood. If we know a guest is going to a nearby bar, we will call ahead for them to make reservations when possible, sharing pertinent information such as water preference (still or sparkling), allergies, and celebrations. Oftentimes, either I or a bartender or server will personally escort them to the next destination—we keep large umbrellas on hand in case of rain—or call them a car to make sure they get home safely and comfortably.

There is no manual to learn how to best express omotenashi. It must come from a genuine desire to make others happy, and is adapted to suit every individual, because a gesture appreciated by one person might seem overbearing to another. The goal is to anticipate what every guest needs and deliver before they know they need it, without making anyone uncomfortable. When done right, this dedication to great hospitality can bring joy to both the people at work and the guest—the ultimate achievement of harmony.

TYPES OF JAPANESE BARS

Just as other countries have dive bars, piano bars, cocktail bars, pubs, cafés, and other types of bars, Japan also offers an array of different types of establishments for drinking. Here are some of the main ones to know.

ōsenchikkubā | AUTHENTIC BAR

The ōsenchikkubā bar, which translates literally to "authentic" bar, is the Japanese equivalent of a proper cocktail bar. The terminology came about after the Great Kantō earthquake struck in the Chūō ward of Tōkyō in 1923, a time when many bars offered female companionship as the main draw. By using the name ōsenchikkubā, cocktail bars distinguished themselves as places that served cocktails and not other forms of entertainment. These bars are the Japanese cocktail bars we know and love, tucked away in the alleys and high-rises of Ginza, or down cobblestone streets in Kyōto, where the bartenders are trained experts in the craft of cocktail making, and standard (or "classic") recipes reign supreme, though signature offerings are not totally uncommon. Cocktails may be ordered here, and bottle service is not typical.

izakaya | GASTROPUB

Before we had cocktail bars, we had izakaya. This style of bar dates back to the Edo period, when saké merchants would set up tasting corners in their sakaya (saké shop). As the story goes, one merchant began to serve simple home-cooked dishes to accompany the local brews, and before you know it the sakaya became an izakaya—a word combining sakaya and the verb *iru,* which means to be or to stay. So, an izakaya is a saké shop where you stay for a while for eating and drinking. Today almost every izakaya will have a specialty, either of food or drink; some specialize in a particular dish, like yakitori, seafood, or regional cuisine, while others can be shōchū-focused, saké-focused, or specializing in beer or simple cocktails such as highballs.

shottobā | SHOT BAR

While the name may sound a bit like a club or college bar, shot bars are not a place where people go to throw back small pours of liquor until they reach oblivion. Instead, they are where spirits are served neat or on the rocks, ordered by the glass rather than by the bottle. It is not typical to order cocktails at a shot bar, though some have a small list of simple drinks like highballs. The name came about in the 1960s as a way to differentiate these bars from snack bars (see below), where bottle service is typical.

sunakku bā | SNACK BAR

Sunakku bā are so called for the light snacks they serve, a custom that started in the late 1960s as a way to legally remain open after midnight. At most of them, women in the employ of the mama-san (the female owner of the bar) float about the room, lighting cigarettes, making small talk, and encouraging men to drink through their bottles of whisky or shōchū. "Bottle keep" service is typical—most sunakku have rows of bottles on shelves with little placards of the patron's name hung around the neck of the bottles, to encourage repeat business. In a sense, the sunakku is like a second home for lonely salarymen. These bars typically bear the name of a woman and are recognizable by the word スナック (sunakku) on their sign.

risuningubā • rekōdobā | LISTENING BARS • RECORD BARS

These bars evolved from the jazz kissa, a special type of kissate, which is a tearoom–coffee shop hybrid where you can also get yōshoku (a Western-style meal). Jazz kissa opened after World War II as cafés where people could listen to music that was not easily accessible at the time. Over time, these establishments evolved into idiosyncratic places, each with its own specific identity and sense of decorum. Today, listening bars and record bars both offer music and drinks, though there is a slight difference in the culture of each: Record bars are relatively relaxed places with a personality to match the style of music they play, while listening bars tend to be more strict in nature and are not for chitter-chatter and rambunctious drinking.

kyabakura • hosutesu/ hosuto-kurabu | CABARET CLUB (AKA HOSTESS CLUB/HOST CLUB)

Cabaret clubs offer the fantasy of companionship. There is no sex or nudity at kyabakura—the purpose is to provide a sense of intimacy through conversation and companionship alone. Some are membership-based, and have ratings for their top hosts or hostesses. The basic role of the host is to sit with clients, pour their drinks, make conversation, and ultimately guide them to spend money.

kurabu | CLUBS

While there are nightclubs and dance clubs throughout Japan as well, a kurabu is a specific members-only, restricted-access version of the kyabakura (see above). These bars do not take walk-ins and are by reference only. Sometimes they even refuse service to members if the hostess who typically takes care of the member is not working.

tachinomiya • sutandingubā | STANDING BARS

Tachinomiya and sutandingubā both mean "standing bar." These are bars where there are no seats. The choice to call a bar a tachinomiya or a sutandingubā comes down to how the owner wants the bar to be perceived and enjoyed, like two sides to the same coin. In general, both are no-frills, typically very small spaces. Tachinomiya are more casual. There may or may not be a bartender; sometimes it is a few tables set up by vending machines beneath the train tracks where salarymen gather after work—more of a locals-only spot. Sutandingubā typically have a bar you can cozy up to, with a bartender serving a range of drinks, and some offer food as well, though at a tachinomiya this food is likely coming from a vending machine. Both serve as a perfect pit stop for an after-work treat on the way home or to another bar.

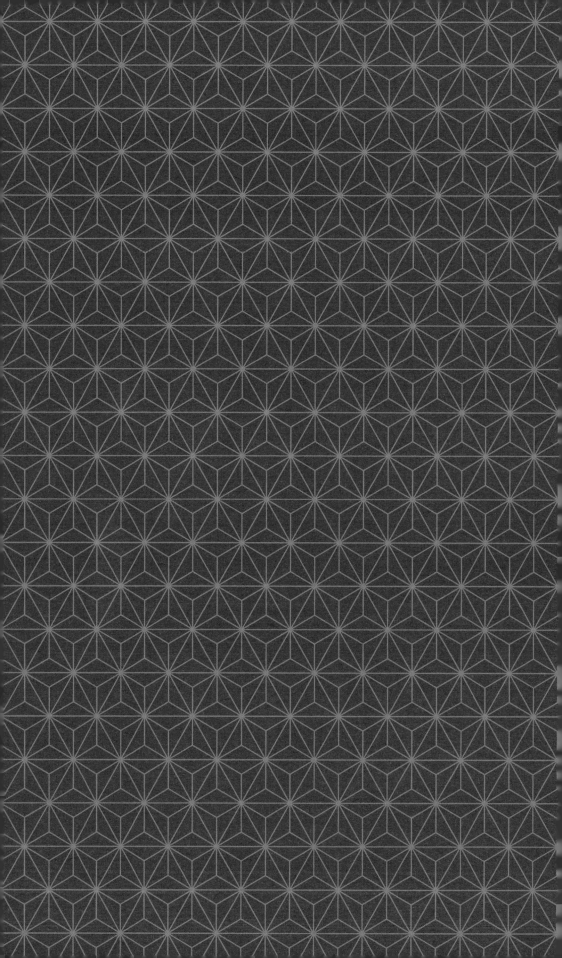

A BRIEF HISTORY OF COCKTAILS IN JAPAN

For as long as the islands of Japan have been inhabited, its people have adopted influences from abroad. For example, the logographics we use today, called kanji, originated in China, altered slightly to work with the existing language. Portuguese soldiers brought lasting culinary treasures like peppers and tempura when they arrived in 1543. Around the same time, distillation techniques were introduced to the southern parts of Japan via China, Thailand, and other countries, laying a foundation for shōchū to emerge. And later, in 1853, United States Navy Commodore Matthew Calbraith Perry brought whiskey to Japanese shores during his campaign to open Japan's borders to the West, setting the course for the country's passionate appreciation for aged spirits.

The stage for global influences expanded significantly in 1868, when Japan entered the Meiji Restoration, a great political revolution that embraced Western influences in everything from politics and economics to social practices. Universal education was installed, the government put a priority on industrialization, and the first railroads were built. New fashion trends such as men's suits and hairstyles (many cut their top knots and started to wear hats) spread, as did sports like cricket and baseball. European-style hotels opened during these years and with them came new styles of music like military tunes and Christian hymns.

Meanwhile, across the Pacific Ocean, cocktail culture was entering a golden age in America. In his aptly titled book *Imbibe!,* author and historian David Wondrich paints a spirited picture of this time: "In the century and a half between the American Revolution and Prohibition, this art [of mixing drinks] was born, reached maturity, and spread to every corner of the globe, in the process establishing the principles, techniques, and even a surprising number of the tools and formulas that still characterize the art today."

With Japan's acceptance of global influences seeping into all aspects of society, the path was clear for cocktails to make their debut. Drinking culture was already strong in Japan thanks to established traditions of saké and shōchū, so it was a natural evolution. When cocktails finally arrived, Japanese bartenders integrated cocktail culture into Japanese society in a way that was anchored firmly within the overarching sentiment of the time, by fusing Western novelties with a grounded Eastern approach. From the first flicker of mixed drinks to today's explosive landscape of tradition mixed with ingenuity, Japan's cocktail history starts in Yokohama, just south of the capital city of Tōkyō.

A GRAND ENTRANCE FOR COCKTAILS

A small fishing village near Tōkyō, Yokohama served as the gateway to Japan for America, Europe, and other Western countries when it was established as a port in the mid-1800s. The Official Visitor's Guide calls it "the city of firsts," rattling off an impressive list of accolades, including Japan's first iron bridge, first dress shop, and the original site of bread, ice cream, and beer. Like other notable port cities in the nineteenth century, the streets buzzed with exciting new sources of commerce, culture, and innovation.

Yokohama was one of the first places to permit foreigners to live within city limits, but this allowance came with constraints. To keep cultures from intertwining too deeply, newcomers were required to isolate from the locals per Shogunate policy, and when tourists and merchants came to visit they had to comply with restrictions on when and how far they could venture outside of their designated area. For these reasons, hotels became one of the prominent gateways for the mingling of cultures. One in particular ascended as *the* place to visit for foreign celebrities, dignitaries, and those of general affluence: the Grand Hotel, which opened in 1873. With celebrity visits from the likes of Charlie Chaplin, Douglas Fairbanks, Rudyard Kipling, General Douglas MacArthur, and Babe Ruth, it was the hotel bar that naturally became the place to see and be seen.

The barkeeps likely only served wine and beer for the first fifteen years or so, until a charismatic gentleman by the name of Louis Eppinger arrived with cocktail culture in tow. Born in Germany, Eppinger established quite a reputation for himself in the American hospitality industry by owning and operating saloons and hotels in Indianapolis, San Francisco, Portland, and Salt Lake City. In *The History of the San Francisco Stock and Exchange Board,* author Joseph L. King gives us a glimpse into his personality: "He was very popular, and a genial, jolly barkeeper, holding your attention while preparing a mixed drink," he writes. "In his white coat, with his bullet-shaped head, with a little hair on the top, and a black mustache, always laughing and telling a joke, he appeared to be just the man to succeed in keeping a bar."

Eppinger's charm made an impression on all his guests, and also introduced a new and exciting trade for locals (and a dose of nostalgia for Western guests). With the spirit of the Meiji Restoration in full swing, it is no surprise that everything Eppinger brought with him from the world of American bartending—the ingredients, tools, techniques, and recipes—eventually took root within Japanese drinking culture.

Two of the many cocktails he introduced during this time are now considered icons in the realm of Japanese cocktails. The first, the Bamboo Cocktail (page 206), might not have been an original invention of Eppinger's, but it was the one he became widely associated with, even to this day. With its contemplative mix of sherry, vermouth, and orange bitters, many Japanese bartenders embraced the drink as a national treasure, perpetually refining their interpretations to inch it closer toward the point of perfection. Even today it remains on the menu at the Grand Hotel (now called the Hotel New Grand) at Bar Sea Guardian II, where it is a sherry-heavy concoction made with a splash of Noilly Prat Original Dry vermouth and orange bitters. In recent years, contemporary bartenders in other global cities have also embraced variations on the cocktail, making it one of the most internationally recognized Japanese cocktails of all time.

Eppinger is also credited with creating the Million Dollar (page 313), a cocktail made of gin, sweet vermouth, pineapple, grenadine, and egg white. The drink would go on to earn great fame when one of his protégés, Shogo Hamada, took the cocktail to Tōkyō when he left Yokohama to work at Café Raion (Lion), a bar in the posh Ginza neighborhood. There, a bar regular, journalist and playwright Hiroshi Kikuchi, fell in love with the drink. He went so far as to promote the cocktail in a 1926 advertising campaign for his magazine *Bungei-shunjū* with the slogan, "If alcohol, then a cocktail; if a cocktail, then a Million

Dollar; if a magazine, then my *Bungei-shunjū*." The fruity concoction never quite found fame on other shores, but it is still considered a classic in Japan and can be found on menus everywhere (especially in Yokohama, where local pride for historic cocktails remains strong).

In 1907, Eppinger died at the age of seventy-seven in Yokohama, leaving behind the legacy of ushering cocktails into Japan. Fifteen years after he passed, a great earthquake destroyed the Grand Hotel, prompting many of its staff to seek brighter opportunities in bigger cities. Some of Eppinger's mentees moved to Tōkyō, where many built on the foundation of knowledge Eppinger instilled to open their own bars in the Ginza neighborhood.

GINZA EMERGES AS THE HEART OF COCKTAIL CULTURE

After surviving a fire that razed the neighborhood in 1872, Ginza eventually became the center of modernization in Japan. By 1875, the area had been completely rebuilt (with the help of an English architect who smartly decided to use nonflammable materials), and by the early 1900s the neighborhood had developed into quite the cosmopolitan hub. Locals would make a day out of wandering around the bazaars that opened during this time, to the point where the practice earned a name—*gin-bura*, which means "wandering around Ginza." It was a fashionable neighborhood where trends were set—a thriving social scene that welcomed contemporary cuisine and customs. For the locals eager to embrace change, Ginza was a desirable and distinctive vision of avant-garde Japan.

Most notably, the cultural underpinnings of European café society started to seep into Ginza in the 1910s, attracting flocks of glamorous and liberal Modern Boys (*mobo*) and Modern Girls (*moga*) to its cinemas, theaters, and bars. Just as in Europe, these cafés sold beer and liqueur-based concoctions in addition to coffee and tea, offering a bit of escapism for these internationally minded patrons. It was also in these storied salons where former bartenders from the Grand Hotel planted the seeds of what would become Japanese cocktail culture.

A GLIMPSE INTO THE PAST In the book *Tōkyō: A Cultural and Literary History,* author Stephen Mansfield paints a vivid picture of what the Ginza scene looked like in the early 1900s: "Flapper girls in bobbed hairdos and Eton crops strolled under the willow trees of the boulevard in the company of foppish, lank-haired young men sporting bell-bottom trousers and round spectacles (*roido* eyeglasses) in imitation of the silent film actor Harold Lloyd."

In the last years of the Meiji Era, writers and artists gathered in these European-style cafés, sipping cordials and cocktails while discussing politics and poetry. Their writings represent some of the only documented mentions of

cocktails from this time period, so it's not entirely known which cafés were the first to open with cocktails on the menu, or how many places were offering such drinks. There are most certainly many places that went unrecorded, but here are a few notable ones that contributed to the growth of cocktail culture in Japan.

MAISON KŌNOSU

Opened in 1910, Maison Kōnosu is often credited as the first European-style bar in the area, with a reputation for good cocktails. Located in present-day Nihonbashi, just north of Ginza proper in the Chūō ward of Tōkyō, the bar launched under the guidance of Komazō Okuda. Originally from Kyōto, Okuda first trained in the French culinary arts, but at the café he created a drinks program known for punches and a cocktail called Goshiki no Saké, which translates to "alcohol in five colors." (You may know a similar French invention, the pousse café, which traveled to the US by way of Jerry Thomas's 1862 cocktail book *How to Mix Drinks*.) At a time when cocktails were simple and straightforward, this unique art of layering ingredients demanded a lot of skilled technique—a great example of the uncompromising level of monozukuri and omotenashi practiced by Japan's first bartenders. It also speaks to the ability and the desire of Japanese people to adopt customs and drink culture from abroad.

CAFÉ PURANTAN

Following Maison Kōnosu, Café Purantan (Printemps) opened a year later, in 1911. Japanese artist Shōzō Matsuyama imbued the parlor with an atmosphere designed to imitate the specific look and feel of Parisian cafés, which he fell in love with during trips to France. It was also one of the first café-galleries and membership-based hospitality institutions in Japan. Novelists, artists, musicians, politicians, and others were among the first clientele, showing up thirsty for Western-style cocktails, coffee, and stimulating conversation. The membership requirement was eventually dropped and the space opened up for all people, but nevertheless the model was notable in that it set the template for members-only bars we see throughout the country today.

CAFÉ RAION

Shogo Hamada, bartender at the Grand Hotel in Yokohama from 1912 to 1923, was recruited to work at the grandiose Café Raion (Lion) in Ginza in 1924. The three-story café, which was known mostly for its food, has been described as a "fashionable and imposing sight whose trend-setting modernity attracted people seeking something new in Western restaurants." The establishment employed women as drinking companions and did not require a membership fee—strategic moves to bring in all sorts of patrons beyond the typical artists and thespians.

TRADITIONS ARE CEMENTED

When America entered into Prohibition in 1920, countless cocktail traditions were lost over the course of the thirteen years that followed before the act was repealed. In Japan, that pause never happened. Instead, there was a line break, a fresh start if you will, when the Great Kantō earthquake struck in the Chūō ward of Tōkyō in 1923. Yet again the district of Ginza fell, but from the ashes came a revitalized metropolis, complete with fancy department stores and a stop on the subway line that ferried eager visitors to the heart of the leading shopping district.

Restaurants and cafés re-emerged, along with a set of new bars that placed a sole focus on cocktails. To clearly differentiate these establishments from other types of bars, these were called *ōsenchikkubā*, a term that translates to "authentic bars." At places like Bar Lupin and Café Line, the owners abandoned the tactic of luring customers in with female staff. Instead, the draw was cocktails, executed largely by returning Japanese navy men who had spent time as cabin bartenders during trips abroad. These men brought home with them an intense and regimented style of apprenticeship training, much like the French brigade style of kitchen management we still see across the world today. While remaining faithful to the techniques, ingredients, recipes, and practices of cocktailing learned abroad, these bartenders made Ginza the stronghold of a new way of bartending, setting a firm foundation of technique and tradition for future generations to build upon. This intensely structured approach to bartending lives on today, albeit less militaristically perhaps, in the authentic bars of Ginza like Four Seasons, Tender Bar, and JBA Bar Suzuki.

Tatsuzō Maniwa, member of the Japan Bartenders Association (now Nippon Bartenders Association) and published author, shared his experiences working as a bartender apprentice in the 1920s in a memoir published by the Japan Hotel Association:

I worked from the time the sun was full in the sky even though business hours weren't even until the evening. Continuing with sorting from the night before, wiping each bottle, polishing the counter, of course, as well as the floor, and scrubbing the deck with a wire scrubbing brush. I was sent running to clean the senior bartender's clothes and carried out all kinds of roles by myself. When it came to the real job, washing glasses and dishes was my specialty. If I were to touch a shaker tin or one of the Western spirits, though, I would be scolded loudly, "It's too soon. In two or three years."

An intriguing case study from this era comes from the Imperial Hotel in Tōkyō. Originally a modest wooden structure built in the late 1800s, American architect Frank Lloyd Wright was hired to create a modern iteration of the hotel, which opened the same day the great Kantō earthquake struck in 1923.

Miraculously, the hotel remained standing, and the bar subsequently became home to one of Japan's historic cocktails: the Mount Fuji. Made with Old Tom gin, maraschino, lemon, pineapple, simple syrup, egg white, and fresh cream, it is a decadent number that falls right in line with other Japanese cocktails created during this time.

Several versions of the recipe for the Mount Fuji float around within the ether of Japanese cocktail history—in 1933, the Japan Bartenders Association exhibited a version at the World Cocktail Competition held in Madrid, made with vermouth (there is debate whether it was prepared with rosso or bianco vermouth), Bacardi white rum, lemon juice, and orange bitters. A version appeared on the menu at the Fujiya Hotel in 1937, believed to have been created by former Imperial Hotel manager Shōzō Yamaguchi, featuring gin, pineapple juice, lemon juice, sugar, and egg white. It is thrilling to see how even early on the template of a Japanese-made cocktail was going through various iterations, inspiring bartenders to create drinks based on the original.

MOUNT FUJI

Spirits writer Ishikura Kazuo shares a theory that the Imperial Hotel recipe was likely created around 1922, the result of a collaboration between manager Shōzō Yamaguchi and chief bartender Noborifumi Ōsaka. The following recipe was first printed on the Imperial Bar menu in 1924, and lives on at the Imperial Hotel, where it is celebrated as an original classic.

1½ ounces Old Tom gin

1 teaspoon maraschino liqueur

½ ounce lemon juice

1 teaspoon pineapple juice

1 teaspoon simple syrup

1 egg white

2 teaspoons fresh cream

In a shaker tin, combine ingredients with ice and shake. Strain into a chilled cocktail glass and garnish with one red cherry on the rim, like the rising sun over the snow-capped peak of Mount Fuji.

Another interesting milestone that took place during this time was in 1924, when two Japanese books were published on the subject of cocktails. The first was *Kakuteru (Kongōshu Chōgō-hō)*, or *Cocktail (Mixed Saké Formulas)*, written by Tokuzō Akiyama. Known as the "Japanese Escoffier," for his French training and work as chef to Emperor Taishō, Akiyama first published a 1,600-page book on French cuisine in 1923 and a year later released the book on cocktails, featuring 209 recipes.

The second book, *Kokutēru* (Cocktail) came out a month later, written by Yonekichi Maeda, a 27-year-old bartender who worked at a bar called Café Line. In the preface, Maeda laments how in the wake of the earthquake many cafés were without bartenders who knew how to craft cocktails to the liking of their guests. In his view, cocktails would be just the thing (outside of other modern luxuries) that would give workers a little pleasure after the labors of a hard day, so he created the book to spread the gospel far and wide.

The text features around 287 recipes, some "standard" from abroad and some Japanese originals, such as the Line Cocktail (page 229). In accounts from his research, Eiji Arakawa, a modern cocktail historian and owner of Bar UK in Ōsaka, hypothesizes that Maeda likely discovered many recipes during his global travels, when he worked aboard an international passenger ship. This theory seems to carry weight, as many are also recorded in Harry MacElhone's *Harry's ABC of Mixing Cocktails* from 1919, and in *The Savoy Cocktail Book* from Harry Craddock in 1930. Some are identical, such as the Morning Cocktail (except that Maeda's is stirred while Craddock's is shaken). Others, such as the Thistle cocktail, have slight twists—in Maeda's *Kokutēru*, rye whiskey appears in place of the Scotch as featured in *The Savoy Cocktail Book*.

SAIDĀNEKUTĀ

Some of the recipes in *Kokutēru* are completely unique to the book, like the Line Cocktail (page 229) and this recipe made with brandy, sherry, and Mitsuya Cider, a carbonated beverage reminiscent of lemon-lime soda and ginger ale, developed in 1884. *Saidānekutā* translates to "cider nectar," a nod to the key ingredient, which you can still find in Japan (and online) today.

½ ounce brandy

½ ounce sherry

2 ounces Mitsuya Cider

Fill a punch glass halfway with crushed ice and a spoonful of sugar. Measure ingredients into the glass, stir with a barspoon, and top with still water.

According to Arakawa, Maeda left his post as a bartender at Café Line after publishing the cocktail book to open a liquor store in Ginza called Maeda Yonekichi Honten. There, he sold Western spirits and bottled cocktails for over a decade before passing away at age forty-two due to acute alcohol poisoning. He left behind a great legacy with *Kokutēru*—arguably the most notable historic text on Japanese cocktails—in part because it was written by a bartender about his

MOUNT FUJI

(page 34)

SAIDĀNEKUTĀ

(page 35)

YUKIGUNI
(page 40)

KAIKAN FIZZ
(page 39)

craft, but also because in the decades to follow his documentation became integral to the development of authentic cocktail bars.

Like a slow wave, cocktail culture continued to solidify throughout the course of the late 1920s and early 1930s, giving rise to bartending associations such as Nippon Bartenders Association (NBA), which was established in 1929. Subsequently, companies like Suntory (then called Kotobukiya) sponsored the first cocktail competitions in the country (1931) and released mixing spirits such as Hermes gin (1936). Drinking culture remained strong—that is, until WWII disrupted every aspect of Japanese life and culture in 1939.

WARTIME DEVASTATES

Many articles describe Japanese bartending culture romantically, as an uninterrupted saga of dedication, focus, and growth. However, that rose-colored dispatch does not tell the entire story. Japan did not go through a prohibition like America, but WWII swiftly and brutally dimmed the lights of Ginza. Bars and restaurants were placed on strict curfews and in some cases forced to close completely. By 1944, limits on sales of luxury items like alcohol were imposed, and though the government did not make women enlist to fight, they were pulled from their jobs in hospitality to work in factories. If these factors didn't spur closures of bars across the city, the firebombings that came in 1945 determined the end of the rest.

Remarkably, whisky consumption remained somewhat strong during the war years, despite government-imposed rations on food and other agricultural products. US occupying forces came with a strong thirst for liquor, which is likely why a select few bars actually remained in operation during this dark era. One of these bars was Ginza's Bar Lupin, which debuted in 1928 and stayed afloat by buying liquor on the black market and discreetly serving their loyal patrons.

Another memorable story comes from the Main Bar of Tōkyō Kaikan, an event hall that opened in 1922. It was damaged during the war and then seized by American soldiers immediately following Japan's surrender in 1945; the building functioned as the American Club of Tōkyō for US troops until the occupation ended and Japan regained its sovereignty in 1952. The chief bartender during these years was Haruyoshi Honda, who tapped into the elements of expertise and omotenashi to create cocktails for foreign patrons. Of his creations, the Kaikan Fizz stands out as particularly interesting. The cocktail was popular among officers who wanted to drink alcohol in the morning without being detected—occupying forces referred to the Main Bar as the American Club, where they could eat and drink as much as they wanted.

KAIKAN FIZZ

The Kaikan Fizz from Tōkyō Kaikan is a delightful drink—stately yet nostalgic, bearing a striking resemblance to the sweet yogurt drink called Calpis (pronounced *karupisu*), whose exported version is known as Calpico. While eggs were commonly found in food and drink through the early 1900s, dairy products were a luxury commodity, so it is likely that the GIs were responsible for stocking the bar with milk and otherwise rare spirits, making this cocktail possible.

1½ ounces gin

½ ounce lemon juice

1 teaspoon sugar

1 ounce milk

Club soda (to top)

Shake well (really well, so the milk doesn't curdle) with ice and pour into a highball glass over fresh ice. Fill the glass full to the top with more ice and top the mixture with club soda poured over the back of a barspoon into the glass.

DRINKING CULTURE RETURNS

Many cocktail bars remained shuttered during the immediate postwar years because the overall sentiment of the time was that high-end drinking dens were places of escape and luxury, and in a postwar society, there is little room for such things. The country was devastated, so it wasn't until the mid-1950s that drinking culture reappeared, this time with an attitude centered around drinks that were easygoing and affordable.

In 1955, Shinjirō Torii of Kotobukiya (now Suntory) opened a series of casual "Torys Bars" across Ōsaka and Tōkyō as a way to advertise his products, specifically whisky in the form of highballs. Welcoming people from all walks of life, these relaxed drinking establishments helped boost whisky sales and encouraged Japanese drinkers to get back to the bar. Some say this casual drinking trend put a damper on cocktails, but I see it a different way: While some people leaned into simple pleasures like whisky highballs, chū-hi (shōchū highballs), and beer, this pause offered a ripe opportunity for those who were interested in rebuilding the authentic bar.

Throughout the postwar rebuilding, bars like Bordeaux in Ginza (1927 to 2016) reopened, as did Tōkyō Kaikan, and places like Ginza 1954 debuted with fresh fruit cocktails and katsu-sando (fried pork sandwiches). In cities outside of Tōkyō, bars began opening with Western spirits, cocktails, and the strong traditions of the authentic bar. One bar of specific note is Kern in Sakata city in northern Japan: It was run by Keiichi Iyama, who in 1955 left his job teaching dance in Tōkyō to return home to Sakata and open the bar. Three years later, he entered Kotobukiya's national cocktail competition—his cocktail Yukiguni (snow country) won first prize in 1959 after several rounds of competition and is now considered a standard, or classic, cocktail in Japan. Born in 1926, Iyama-san is one of the oldest working bartenders in Japan.

YUKIGUNI

As is commonly seen with classic cocktails worldwide, the Yukiguni recipe has undergone some changes to match the palate of the current drinker. Think more spirit, and less sugar. The recipe below comes from Suntory's database, reflecting the original specifications. Ilyama-san has since shared an update on the recipe, which suggests 1.5 to 1.85 ounces vodka, 0.24 to 0.27 ounce Hermes white Curaçao, and 0.10 to 0.14 ounce Suntory lime cordial. It is the mark of a true hospitality professional when they can look at their award-winning cocktail after sixty years and continue to acknowledge the need to adapt for the sake of the guest. I respect Iyama-san's humility and precision.

1 ounce vodka

½ ounce white Curaçao (triple sec)

½ ounce lime*

Prepare your cocktail glass by giving it a snow-style sugar rim; to do this, cut a lemon (or other citrus) in half and rub the juice side of the fruit along the outer rim of the lip of the glass. Dip the moistened rim in a dish of sugar so the grains stick to the surface of the glass like snowflakes. While the glass remains upside-down, tap lightly against your palm to shake off excess sugar. Turn the glass upward, slowly, so as to not cast any sugar over the surface of the bar. Set aside.

Shake the vodka, white Curaçao, and lime juice in a shaker tin with ice to chill, then strain into the rimmed cocktail glass and garnish with a green maraschino cherry.

* Originally this was not made with fresh juice, as bartenders were not able to get their hands on fresh limes in the 1950s. Suntory makes a lime cordial called Suntory Cocktail Lime.

In 1962, the Hotel Barmen's Guild, Japan (HBG), started in Tōkyō. What began as a group of nine hotel bartenders seeking to establish a forum for discussion and education, expanded to a full-on "Barmen's Club" in 1970, hosting competitions, distillery tours, and educational programming. Associations like these cultivated many bartenders who would go on to open their own successful businesses, and helped solidify national standards and philosophies surrounding cocktail culture.

Today, the HBA (in 1977 the name changed again to Hotel Barmen's Association) has branches as far north as Hokkaidō and as far south as Kyūshū.

While the authentic bars of the postwar years regained firm footing, they became a training ground for many of today's most notable legacy bartenders. When Tōkyō Kaikan shook off the chains of US occupation, its legacy of producing legendary bartenders continued with personalities like Tatsurō Yamazaki, who became instrumental in developing the authentic bar culture in Sapporo when he moved there in 1953 at the behest of his mentor, Haruyoshi Honda. At the event hall, Mr. Honda was also the mentor of Kiyoshi Imai, who became known as "Mr. Martini." Imai worked alongside Honda, Shogo Hamada, and other historic bar figures, becoming a luminary himself by the time he passed away in 1999 at the age of seventy-five. Imai is known primarily for his mastery of the martini, but he was also the first to design the backbar in such a way that the glassware was at eye level to the guests, a design element that has since spread to bars all across Japan and even to my bar, Kumiko, in Chicago. Tōkyō Kaikan has undeniably left a mark on the landscape of Japanese bartending, as evidenced by the craft that continues to live on throughout the country.

TODAY'S AUTHENTIC BARS ARE BORN

In the 1990s, a new wave of cocktail bars sprang forth in Ginza, generated by an intertwined family tree of bartenders begat by the age-old system of teacher and apprentice. Traditional recipes, design, and hospitality were carried respectfully into these hallowed spaces, where a cadre of master bartenders continued their deliberative practice of standard cocktails while at the same time worked ardently to create new signature inventions.

Many of the bars that opened during this time continue to stand as the most emblematic of Japan's cocktail scene today. For example, in 1993 Yūichi Hoshi opened Little Smith, a moody, architectural bar with undulating curves and a mysterious recessed lighting scheme that casts a soothing glow on the polished wooden bar top. Hoshi won the International Bartender Competition Japan Cup Grand Prix in 2001 with a drink called Sakura Sakura, made with dry gin, peach liqueur, sakura liqueur, and lemon juice. He went on to open Bar Hoshi in Ginza in 2004, and now owns multiple bars between Tōkyō and his hometown of Fukushima, though Little Smith remains one of the most well-known bars in Japan.

Another authentic bar whose reputation has risen to prominence is Mōri Bar, which opened in 1997 under the ownership of Takao Mōri. Widely considered one of the original Ginza bartenders, he is perhaps best known for his martini, which guests call the Mōri Martini. He free-pours the drink with great skill: one drop of orange bitters, followed by Boodles British gin (it must have weight to it, he says) and a splash of dry vermouth, and garnished with a light misting of oils from a lemon peel. (In 2007, his martini notoriety expanded with the publication of his book *Martini-ism.*) Mōri is also the "M" in Y&M Bar Kisling, which he opened in 2004 with Mitsugi Yoshida. Yoshida-san has since passed away, but the bar carries on in the capable hands of his former apprentice, Nobuo Abé.

One of the most well-known Japanese bartenders internationally is Kazuo Uyeda. With a resumé that includes time spent bartending at Tōkyō Kaikan and Bar l'Osier in Shiseido Parlor, he opened Tender in Ginza in 1997. Perched within one of the neighborhood's many high-rise buildings, every element of Uyeda-san's bar speaks to a steady quest for precision and monozukuri. (The gimlet, shaken and served over a glistening hand-chipped ice sphere, is a majesty to behold to this day.) With steady focus and intention, Uyeda constantly works on self-improvement as a bartender, remaining focused on his commitment to Japanese cocktail culture and techniques with little to no regard for other global trends. In 2000, he published the book *Cocktail Technic,* and a decade later the English translation, *Cocktail Techniques,* was released, helping bring recognition to Japan's cocktail scene. American bartenders flocked to the text, praising it for its honest and open look into the mind and methods of the soft-spoken master of bartending.

Westerners focus on results. While the Japanese have been influenced by this focus to a certain extent in recent years, we, at heart, respect the process . . . I believe that the effort put into mixing the cocktail contributes to its ultimate flavor.

—KAZUO UYEDA, *Cocktail Techniques*

Another wave of new (but still authentic) bars opened throughout Tōkyō in the early 2000s with the arrival of Star Bar Ginza (2000), Bar Ishinohana (2003), and the aforementioned Y&M Kisling (2004). At each bar, talented bartenders continue to uphold traditions for new audiences. Some have left an even bigger mark on Japanese bartending as a whole, like Hisashi Kishi, who opened Star Bar Ginza in 2000. In 1996, he had become the first Japanese bartender to win the Bartender Association's World Cocktail Championship, and together with apprentice Hidetsugu Ueno (who would go on to open Bar High Five), he developed a shape of ice specifically for an old fashioned glass called "brilliant-cut," or ice diamond (see page 62). Now, bars around the world aim to replicate this shape, which is favored for its ability to keep dilution rates slow while glistening in the glass like its namesake stone.

The way of the past remains alive and well outside of Tōkyō, too, at cocktail bars that similarly opened with a respect for tradition: In Yokohama, places like Bar Noble (2011) put forth a ritualistic style of drink-making inspired by the form and practice of the Japanese tea ceremony. At Bar Rocking Chair in Kyōto (2009), Kenji Tsubokura uses pinpoint precision to make classic and signature cocktails in a cozy space with dim lights and wood panels. (Tsubokura won the NBA National Cocktail Competition in 2015 and the IBA World Cocktail Championships in

2016.) And in Fukuoka, at Bar Oscar, Shuichi Nagatomo (who also worked at Bar l'Osier in the Shiseido Parlor with Kazuo Uyeda) has provided a relaxed setting for international drinkers for the past twenty-three years. There, his gentle and welcoming nature creates a safe haven for tourists and locals alike.

CUSTOMS AND CULTURE AT THE AUTHENTIC BARS OF TODAY

Today, Japan is dotted with cocktail bars that capture and perpetuate the true spirit of traditional cocktail culture. These can be found all over the country, though the concentration remains strong in Ginza, where over three hundred bars remain hidden in skyscrapers and apartment buildings. What unites many of these programs is a set of prescribed customs. Here are some of the specific practices that define the traditional experience, highlighting what continues to set Japanese cocktail culture apart from others established around the world.

senmon

SPECIALIZATION

Many American cocktail bars aim to be everything to every kind of customer, but in Japan a razor-sharp specialization is looked upon more favorably. Oftentimes a bar or master bartender will be recognized for one specific cocktail or style of drink, like the Mōri Martini at Mōri Bar; visitors to Ginza should also try the sidecar at Star Bar, and the Campari soda at Bar Shake for this reason.

Sometimes an entire spirit category or broader themes come into play. In Yokohama, The Bar Casablanca specializes in fresh seasonal fruit (as is the case at Bar Orchard Ginza in Tōkyō). There, a drink as simple as golden berries with Champagne explodes like a firework of fresh flavor when consumed during the slight chill of early winter. Other times the inspiration goes beyond the ingredients: Bar Le Parrain in Tōkyō is named for *The Godfather* movie series (*parrain* is French for godfather), and inside the moody cocktail den you will find framed photographs of scenes from the movies as wisps of smoke waft from the occasional cigar. The martini there is, naturally, quite exceptional.

To honor the place, time, and intent of the master bartender, I encourage visitors to research a bar's specialty before venturing in for the first time. Many bars have a website or Instagram presence, and some also have blogs, where you can get a sense of what they specialize in and how to best enjoy your time there. The purpose of visiting cocktail bars in Japan is to experience the work of the master bartender and not just pop in for a quick shot or beer, so for the best experience, pay attention to what they have spent decades perfecting and choose your drinks accordingly.

omakasé

DEALER'S CHOICE

Formal menus are not always printed and displayed at authentic bars. Instead, the bartender will ask questions about base spirit, style of drink (shaken, stirred, bubbly), and alcohol percentage (low, medium, high) to find the best match. Another question sometimes asked, especially of regulars, is: "How many drinks have you had tonight?" In this case, the bartender aims to make sure the guest can comfortably enjoy more than one drink while ensuring no one gets overserved.

sutandādo kakuteru

STANDARD COCKTAILS

When menus do exist at the cocktail bar, most feature classic cocktails like the gin fizz, martini, White Lady, and daiquiri. Classic cocktails, which in Japan are called *sutandādo*, or standard cocktails, are those that have stood the test of time and hold a place in history and cocktail culture. Japanese bartenders are expected to commit to memory these "standard" recipes (often determined by the Nippon Bartender's Association) to qualify as a master bartender. In addition to straightforward classics, you also sometimes see the master bartender's award-winning recipes called out in a special section on a menu to highlight their original creations. There is enormous prestige attached to various bar associations and the competitions they hold in Japan, and those awards are held in high regard.

It is also interesting to note how most Japanese bartenders (in traditional bars) are not using homemade ingredients as is common in Western bars. In America, many bartenders make their own versions of syrups, liqueurs, and other ingredients to prove creativity and set their programs apart from others. That practice isn't as prevalent in Japan, likely because there has always been an inherent respect for commercial products like syrups and liqueurs. The value of the bar program lies in the thoughtful use of those ingredients.

omotenashi

HOSPITALITY

A sense of omotenashi, or limitless hospitality, guides the guest experience from start to finish. Without it, the bar is frankly not reflective of Japanese cocktail culture. While there is no official rule book for omotenashi, there are some acts of above-and-beyond hospitality that have become common among bartenders in Japan. Here are a few that I particularly appreciate.

- *If a bar is full when a guest arrives, the bartender will briefly leave their post at the bar to accompany them to an alternative destination.*

- *If a guest leaves for a smoke break or restroom visit, the bartender will store their cocktail in the freezer to keep it cold.*

- *When a guest returns, the bartender will come out from behind the bar to pull out the guest's chair and offer a fresh, hot (or cold if appropriate) oshibori, or hand towel, for freshening up.*

- *If a guest pulls out a phone to snap a picture of their drink, sometimes the bartender will move a candle closer to the glass to better illuminate the shot. (Before testing this, please ask for permission to photograph, and don't use a flash.)*

- *The bartender will keep track of the guest's favorite glassware or cocktail pick and make an effort to use these items for the drinks served throughout the course of the evening and on future visits.*

- *Smoking is still common in Japanese bars, though recent laws are changing that, and sometimes if a guest orders a cigar the bartender will move that person farther away from other guests so the smoke does not interfere with anyone's drinking experience.*

- *At the end of a visit, bartenders (or the owner or master bartender) will walk guests to the elevator to thank them and wish them a safe journey. Some bartenders have even been known to race down flights of stairs to catch the elevator at the ground level so as to send off their guests with a second farewell of gratitude.*

oshibori

HAND TOWEL

The first thing offered to guests at authentic bars when they sit down is an oshibori, or hot towel. They come in many colors, sometimes chosen to reflect the season or the mood the bartender wishes to evoke on a certain night. Sometimes they are scented. The oshibori often stays on the bar or at the table for the duration of the visit so the guest can use it as they snack on finger food or to wipe condensation from the cocktail glass if it sweats as it warms. I have also experienced another level of oshibori hospitality where a fresh oshibori is presented whenever the guest returns to the bar, either after a trip to the washroom or stepping out for a cigarette.

otōshi

SEATING CHARGE

Because space is limited in Japanese cocktail bars, a seat charge, or otōshi, is often added to the tab at the end of service. It can range from a flat fee of $10 to $20 per person. In return, the bar offers snacks to nibble on as soon as you arrive, like a small bowl of mixed nuts, crackers, dried fruit, wasabi peas, or fancy chocolates. These snacks are also called otōshi, and the phrase *otōshidegozaimasu*—"Here is your otōshi"—is uttered as they place the dish before you. This implies that there will be a seat charge at the end of the evening so that the guest is not surprised when the bill arrives.

Some places choose to get creative with the offerings: At The Bar Casablanca in Yokohama and Little Smith in Tōkyō, heated drams of consommé stimulate the appetite with essences of umami and salt; and at a tiny whisky bar called Shu-Ha-Li in Saitama, just north of Tōkyō, one of the most memorable I've had was a halved avocado toasted in the oven and sprinkled with melting cheese. With a small dose of thoughtfulness added to the ritual, these owners have lifted the simple otōshi into an *experience* that creates potent memories for guests.

ABOKADO NO CHĪZU-YAKI (AVOCADO BAKED WITH CHEESE)

This—*this!*—is how otōshi is done! Here is a recipe I created in honor of Shu-Ha-Li's avocado with cheese. *Serves two*

1 avocado

Kosher salt and freshly cracked
  black pepper

Handful of shredded cheese, such as a
  mozzarella blend

¼ teaspoon shichimi tōgarashi,
  or to taste

Halve the avocado lengthwise and remove the pit. Cut a crosshatch pattern into the flesh without piercing the shell. Slide a spoon under the flesh to make the sections easier to scoop out later.

Line a small baking sheet with foil. Place the avocado halves flesh side up on the foil and season with salt and pepper. Sprinkle a layer of cheese over the surface. Place in a toaster oven (or in an oven preheated to 350°F) until the cheese is melted and golden, 5 to 10 minutes. Garnish with a sprinkling of shichimi tōgarashi and additional salt and pepper to taste.

A NEW ERA FOR JAPANESE COCKTAILS

As cocktail culture continues to globalize, Japanese bartenders of all generations are traveling more than ever, finding inspiration in drink traditions around the world and bringing those new customs back to their home bars in Kyōto, Ōsaka, Sapporo, and beyond. Like the founders of Japanese cocktail culture before them, these forward-thinking barkeeps are expanding the vision of what it means to be a Japanese cocktail bar.

In Tōkyō, the latter half of the 2000s welcomed places like Bar Shake (2007), Bar Orchard Ginza (2007), and Bar High Five (2008). Many of these establishments hold tight to the tradition of the authentic bar while also introducing personal touches. Hidetsugu Ueno's diamond ice at Bar High Five is a prime example of his contemporary thinking, paired with the strong foundations learned as an apprentice of Hisashi Kishi at Star Bar. At High Five, Ueno breaks away from the hushed reverence and stoic ambiance that pervades many authentic bars by infusing moments of playfulness into his craft. When he's not casting a serious eye toward the technique of one of his apprentices, he can often be found sending a subtle wink and small smile to guests as he oversees the making of exceptionally modern Bamboo Cocktails or dealer's choice configurations.

Other guardians of the craft represent a new wave of energetic, passionate, and creative bartenders, including Hiroyasu Kayama of Bar BenFiddich (2013) and Gen Yamamoto of Bar Gen Yamamoto (2013), who introduce their guests to one-of-a-kind experiences completely different from any other bar. These are authentic bars in visage—suited bartenders artfully concocting drinks in the manner of master craftsmen—but they are doing something no one else is doing. For example, Kayama-san grows and harvests botanicals for housemade absinthe, bitters, and Campari. And no other bars conduct a tasting menu of petite cocktails made with produce at its peak of seasonality with a focus on Japanese spirits like Yamamoto-san. They are truly unique bars within the global cocktail landscape.

More and more of these singular bars are opening up around Japan. Kyōto especially has a thoroughly contemporary and exciting cocktail scene, with bartenders like Tomoiki Sekiné pushing the boundaries of gin cocktails (and use of Japanese ingredients) at nokishita711. Hidenori Yasuda crafts an artist's wonderland at Cinematik Saloon, where cinema meets live music and cocktails. And at Hakata Yatai Bar Ebi-chan in Fukuoka, Akio Ebina moved the bar out of a brick-and-mortar setting to a yatai (a small mobile food cart), breaking down and reassembling the entire bar for service each night.

While so many of today's cocktail bars continue to uphold the tenets once established by previous generations, almost every aspect of cocktail culture—from the interior design to the music, ingredients, and recipes—is changing. Here are a few examples of how things are evolving as we head into the future.

COCKTAILS

Now, bartenders are deliberately experimenting with original concoctions, at times using unconventional craft spirits or contemporary techniques from around the world. Some inventions are merely slight modifications to classic cocktails, like at Bee's Knees in Kyōto, where the namesake drink is made with a yuzu tea in addition to the standard gin, lemon, and honey. At Bar Trench in Tōkyō, recipes fly further from home in drinks like the mezcal milk punch, made with mezcal, brandy, chamomile, green tea, clarified whole milk, and cardamom bitters. Mezcal is not a traditional ingredient used in Japan, so that is notable in itself, but when clarification techniques are used to create a translucent cocktail packed with flavor, it drives home the novel element of surprise.

These contemporary places also use spirits and liqueurs indigenous to Japan as bartenders look to invent drinks that speak to the same sense of place as the ingredients. At The SG Club in Tōkyō, cocktails showcase shōchū, saké, and Japanese whisky in addition to hōjicha (roasted green tea), shisho, and yuzu. In appearance, sentiment, and staffing, it is a very international cocktail bar, but the ingredients speak to how its identity remains rooted in Japanese culture. A similar mentality can be found at Bar Rocking Chair in Kyōto, where Japanese rums like Nine Leaves are used in the signature daiquiri. The Kyōto Martini is an especially powerful example of this, with a base of fresh green tea, wasanbon (a fine-grain Japanese sugar), and dried orange peel combined in a mortar and pestle. Ki No Bi Kyoto dry gin is added to the mix and muddled again before the liquids head into an AeroPress, where Dolin Dry Vermouth de Chambéry is added. The drink is stirred and strained into a cocktail glass—which speaks to the history of Japan's adoration for classic cocktails like the martini while tweaking the formula using local ingredients.

In this new era, bartenders are also modernizing flavors through more bespoke ingredients. At nokishita711, cocktails like the Fungus Negroni feature shiitake-infused gin, amaro, mirin, soy sauce, umami bitters, and fermented mushroom syrup to speak to familiar Japanese flavors. At Bar BenFiddich, Kayama-san takes the idea of housemade ingredients to the next level by using herbs, spices, and other ingredients to re-create popular commercial liqueurs and spirits from scratch. Trying one of his original "Campari" concoctions offers a quick reminder that Japan's contemporary guard has a wealth of creativity to offer.

dezain

DESIGN

Many contemporary bars are updating their interiors to speak clearly to modern sensibilities. Gone are the long, low bars with dark wood cladding and bright overhead lighting. Now we see stylish touches in places like Bar Juniper, where a sleek but cozy mix of copper piping, subway tile, plush teal barstool tops, and softly glowing matte white pendant lights brings gin drinks into a more current setting. There, a custom refrigerator for bottles anchors the backbar like a stormworn old submarine, complete with portholes. At nokishita711, dried flowers and a tangled web of tree branches hang from the ceiling, creating an otherworldly canvas for guests to leave business cards, handwritten notes, metro tickets, shopping receipts, and international currency as love letters to the establishment. More art installation than anything else, it is a whimsical setting where guests are encouraged to pay what they wish for the drinks.

Also in Kyōto, Cinematik Saloon takes design inspiration from its name—the bar is housed in a large warehouse-like loft, oriented to showcase a large screen onto which vintage films are projected. Dim lights drive the theme home while owner Hidenori Yasuda selects tunes from a collection of over two thousand vinyl recordings. A cinematic experience, indeed. Meanwhile, at nearby L'Escamoteur Bar, a steampunk vibe fuses French and Japanese sensibilities in the tiny attic-like nook, which is cluttered with knicknacks lining shelves, wiry Edison lightbulbs casting a glow through the room, and vintage books hanging from the rafters like bats. When the music is loud and the barstools are full, it can be hard to recall whether one is drinking in Paris or Kyōto, a terrific sleight of hand thanks to owner (and trained magician) Christophe Rossi.

ongaku

MUSIC

The musical soundtrack plays a pivotal role at the Japanese cocktail bar. Most, if not all, traditional places will choose either classical or jazz, almost always played at a very soft volume so as not to interfere with the guest experience. Like a quiet companion, it is woven subtly through the fabric of the experience. In contrast, contemporary bars like BenFiddich in Tōkyō take a more dramatic approach with cinematic soundscapes that undulate at a louder decibel level, infusing a sense of drama into the graceful movements of Kayama-san. When underscored by the expressive musical sentiments of film and television composer Ludovico Einaudi, for example, every detail of the experience feels heightened.

The types of music found in Japanese cocktail bars are also changing as more bartenders travel around the world and become inspired by other cocktail cultures. At Bar High Five in Tōkyō, jazz singers such as Ella Fitzgerald croon through the speakers, bookended with other Western artists from the '30s and '40s, like the Andrews Sisters, to create an upbeat but vintage atmosphere that feels akin to the type of soundtrack one would find in today's American speakeasy culture. At other places like nokishita711 in Kyōto, the music sits firmly within today's hip-hop and R&B world—an unexpected but fitting scheme that encourages visitors to let go of preconceived notions of the Japanese cocktail bar. A similar sonic tapestry exists at Bar Trench in Tōkyō, where Rufus Wainwright covers intertwine with Frank Ocean tracks.

Sometimes only silence pervades. At places like Bar Gen Yamamoto in Tōkyō and Bar Bunkyu in Kyōto, there is no music at all. At the latter, the tiny cavelike room echoes with the sounds of Naoyuki Sakauchi's shakes and pours, each action amplified in volume thanks to the lack of ambient music. For many Western drinkers who are used to bars sounding loud and chaotic, this can feel jarring. But in many ways, it merely underscores the purpose of visiting cocktail bars in Japan: You don't go to the bar to listen to music; you go to converse with the bartender, pay attention to how they mix, and enjoy the cocktails. Sometimes that means sitting in reverent silence and allowing the reverberations of clinking ice or the invigorating sizzle of the soda to float through the room.

WOMEN BEHIND THE BAR

"Harmony is to be valued, and an avoidance of wanton opposition to be honored." So states Japan's first constitution of 604, established by Empress Suiko, the country's first recorded empress regnant, who is said to be responsible for the initial spread of Buddhism through the country. Evidently, Japan was not always a patriarchal society. This shift happened during the Meiji era, starting in 1868 and culminating in 1912, a time period we often speak of as one of growth and change, though now we know not all of that development was for the better.

Ryōsai kenbo, a phrase which translates to "good wife, wise mother," was an idiom taught in schools during the Meiji era. These teachings held that women were to be subject to their husbands, bear children, and train their sons so they would grow to better the nation. For a woman, to not have children was considered to be a failure not only to the family but to the country as well. Until the Meiji Constitution was abolished in 1946, women were not allowed to vote, own or inherit property, or choose their spouse. After WWII, a new constitution was written, and in the years following, from a legal perspective, women were allowed many of the same rights as men. However, the notion of men as the breadwinners and women as the caretakers perpetuates in Japanese society, which has led to the largely male-dominated workplace.

Cocktail bartending has long been considered work for men. The majority of the bars owned by women are companionship-focused, not cocktail-focused, like at sunakku (snack bars), where you will see a woman, the mama-san, presiding over the bar and operations. One can find unquestionable female bartending talent in the authentic bars of Japan (such as head bartender Kaori Kurakami of High Five, master bartender Hiroko Hasegawa of Bar Tsubomi, and Sumiré Miyanohara, co-owner of Bar Orchard), but if you look at the majority of famous bars, you will see a distinct and familiar gender bias permeating the industry as most, if not all, are owned and operated by men.

In Japan, there is a double standard perpetuated by social constructs of how women are supposed to make men feel. Women are expected to be sweet, kind, friendly, cute, soft-spoken, but when a female bartender at an authentic bar is perceived as too friendly, she is criticized, told she is too flirtatious and that she's acting as if she doesn't want to be a serious bartender. Men are placing limitations on which parts of professional hospitality women are able to succeed in by trying to keep women in neat little boxes that suit their own views on the world.

Snack bars with the mama-san are such a Japanese staple, and hostess bars have set a tone for the way men expect to be treated by the women working in the service industry. It is very difficult for a woman to break into the world of the authentic bar without going above and beyond to prove herself. As women, our presence behind the bar will always be questioned and our influence viewed as lesser than our male counterparts.

In an online forum, a Japanese man recently asked what he should call a female bartender. He was confused because he had been at a bar where there was only one bartender—a woman. He wasn't sure if she was the owner or just a bartender, but in any case, he wasn't comfortable calling her "masutā" (master bartender). This was interesting to me, because if that bartender had been a man, undoubtedly the customer would have called him "masutā" without hesitation. But because she was a woman, the customer did not feel comfortable calling her by the customary title. Several women responded to his comment: "Why shouldn't we have the same title? We are qualified and we do the same work."

In my view, this is an area of the culture of the Japanese bar scene, nay, the global bar world, that needs to change. Antiquated notions of harmony in the workplace, built upon the opinion that men hold authority, must be abolished. Though uncomfortable for some, it is time for women to genuinely have the same opportunities as men—to own and operate authentic bars and hold the title of masutā. Whatever you do, please, do not call us mama-san.

TIMELINE

MEIJI ERA

1868-1912—A pivotal time in which Japan steps away from a feudal society and begins to open for global trade and industrialization.

1899—Louis Eppinger arrives at the Grand Hotel in Yokohama, establishing the first Western-style cocktail program in Japan.

1910—Maison Kōnosu opens in Ginza, the first European-style bar in the area with cocktails and food.

1911—Café Purantan (Printemps) opens as the first café-gallery and membership-based hospitality institution in Japan.

TAISHŌ ERA

1912-1926—A moment of growth for the cocktail community. Quietly and steadily, foundations are set as the moga and mobo embrace Western wardrobe and activities, squeezing beside literaries and artists in bars and cafés.

1923— The Imperial Hotel, where the Mount Fuji cocktail was invented, opens in Tōkyō. The same year, the Great Kantō earthquake strikes in the Chūō-ward of Tōkyō. As bars reopen, many set out to distinguish themselves as cocktail bars. The Grand Hotel in Yokohama is destroyed in the earthquake, prompting Eppinger's protégés to take their craft to Tōkyō.

1924—Two Japanese books are published on the subject of cocktails—*Kakuteru (Kongōshu Chōgō-hō)*, or *Cocktail (Mixed Saké Formulas)*, written by chef Tokuzō Akiyama, and *Kokutēru (Cocktail)*, written by bartender Yonekichi Maeda. Eppinger disciples such as Shogo Hamada make Tōkyō home at Café Raion (Lion) in Ginza.

SHŌWA ERA

1926-1989—A time of great change in Japan. Strong foundations are built for the Japanese cocktail community prior to the war—which allow the bar community to not only survive, but rebuild stronger than ever in the years to come.

1928—Bar Lupin opens in Ginza as a cocktail-focused bar, and is one of the oldest bars still in operation today.

1929—Nippon Bartenders Association (NBA) is established.

1931—Suntory Whisky (then called Kotobukiya) sponsors the first cocktail competition in the country.

1939—World War II starts.

1945—Following the war, Tōkyō Kaikan and the Main Bar within it are seized by American soldiers; the Kaikan Fizz is invented during this time.

1952—Japan regains its sovereignty, and with that, there is movement throughout the country as people leave rural areas for the Tōkyō metropolis.

In other cases, bartenders who spent the occupation years in Tōkyō bars return home to open bars of their own.

1953—Tatsurō Yamazaki, a protégé of Haruyoshi Honda from Tōkyō Kaikan, moves to Sapporo; he becomes instrumental in developing the authentic bar culture there.

1955—Shinjiro Torii of Kotobukiya (now Suntory) opens a series of casual "Torys Bars" across Ōsaka and Tōkyō. Keiichi Iyama opens Kern (pronounced Kerun) in Sakata.

1962—The Hotel Barmen's Guild, Japan (HBG), starts in Tōkyō, expanding to a full-on "Barmen's Club" in 1970, hosting competitions, distillery tours, and educational programming. In 1977, the name will change to Hotel Barmen's Association (HBA), which is how it is known today.

HEISEI ERA

1989-2019—A time when many of today's bars of great renown open.

1993—Yūichi Hoshi opens Little Smith in Ginza.

1996—Hisashi Kishi becomes the first Japanese bartender to win the Bartender Association's World Cocktail Championship.

1997—Mōri Bar opens under the ownership of Takao Mōri. Kazuo Uyeda opens Tender Bar in Ginza.

2000—Uyeda publishes the book *Cocktail Technic (Cocktail Techniques)*, which helps

bring recognition to Japan's cocktail scene when the English translation is released a decade later. Hisashi Kishi opens Star Bar Ginza.

2004—Y&M Bar Kisling opens under Takao Mōri and Mitsugi Yoshida in Ginza.

2007—Masayuki Kodato opens Bar Shake in Ginza. Husband and wife team Takuo and Sumiré Miyanohara open Bar Orchard Ginza.

2008—Hidetsugu Ueno opens Bar High Five in Ginza.

2010—Co-owner and head bartender Rogerigo Igarashi Vaz opens Bar Trench in Ebisu.

2013—Hiroyasu Kayama opens Bar BenFiddich in Nishi-Shinjuku. Gen Yamamoto opens Bar Gen Yamamoto in Azabujuban.

2018—Shingo Gokan opens The SG Club in Shibuya.

REIWA ERA

2019-PRESENT—Starts on May 1, 2019, with Emperor Emeritus Akihito's son Naruhito taking the throne, as his father becomes the first Japanese monarch to abdicate the Chrysanthemum Throne in 200 years. Reiwa characterizes a hope for order and harmony in the years to come, a sentiment that aligns with my hopes for the success of my fellow Japanese bartenders and their beautiful establishments as they navigate this ever-changing world with passion, humility, and sincerity.

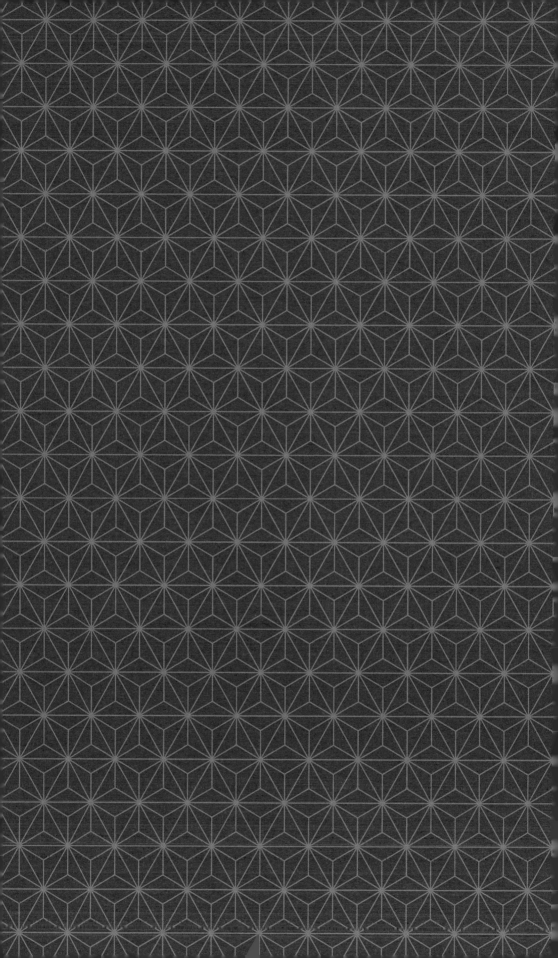

道具と手法

TOOLS AND TECHNIQUES

In his 1896 essay "The Tall Office Building Artistically Considered," architect Louis Sullivan coined the phrase "form ever follows function." In his assessment of modern architecture, Sullivan suggests the shape and layout of a building should naturally be informed by its purpose. Embellishments for the sake of embellishment are meaningless, but a special character that illuminates the function of a thing is divine. The theory (often condensed to read "form follows function") cemented quickly within the paradigm of architecture and has been echoed by countless professors and practitioners in the decades since. I believe the concept also applies to Japanese bartending.

Japanese-made bar tools are lauded for their balance, aesthetic, and precision. In Japanese bar culture, the tools also inform the style and technique of the bartender. The form of the bartender springs forth from the function of the tool. There is significance in the way a seasoned bartender wields their tools in harmony with their own physicality, ever ensuring the tool serves its function in creating a better drink.

Consider what many Westerners understand as the "Hard Shake," a technique developed by Kazuo Uyeda of Tender Bar in Tōkyō. Using a cobbler shaker, Uyeda-san developed a certain style based on the way his own body moves paired with an intended goal: to achieve the right temperature, balance (through dilution), and texture (through aeration) in his cocktails. When he came to America to demonstrate his technique with stateside bartenders, many took his style to be emblematic of *all* Japanese bartending and a misconception spread throughout the country that if you use a cobbler shaker "as they do in Japan," you have to shake it super hard and voilà, a better cocktail! That is a complete misunderstanding of the point. Uyeda-san's hard shake is not solely about the velocity of the movement; it was a shake specific to *him*. You cannot shake a cocktail hard and make a drink like Uyeda-san because the technique only works properly if you are in the same bar with the same ice, the same tools, and have the same stature, rhythm, and balance. That's why every bartender should have their own unique style and technique. Every bartender is different!

Style and performance are rooted in decades' worth of patient study and practice as tools and techniques get passed down from teacher to apprentice. Like the conductor of an orchestra leading a musical number with their wooden baton, or a chef chopping vegetables with their favorite French knife, a physical and emotional relationship develops between jigger or barspoon and bartender. This rapport is personal and its importance cannot be overstated, because in Japanese bartending every motion should be graceful and flow seamlessly from one movement to the next. Harmony should be found through the entire process, not only in what ends up in the glass.

Because technique is informed by the tools, the bartender, and the environment, I believe it is important to consider them all in tandem to get the full picture. I realize it is difficult, if not impossible, to learn bartending technique by reading a book; instead consider this a stepping-stone or foundation to build upon and you should walk away with a deeper appreciation for what makes the motions of Japanese bartending so alluring. Please also note that I do not cover every single type of tool you might find in a Japanese cocktail bar in this chapter. Instead, I spotlight ones unique to my style of Japanese bartending.

THE BACKSTORY OF BAR TOOLS

As cocktail culture first came to Japan by way of America, so did the bar tools. The jigger and cobbler shaker specifically were first patented in America in the late 1800s, and companions like the Hawthorne strainer and barspoons were promptly embraced by Japanese bartenders.

Within the last decade or so, as interest in Japanese bartending culture has spread around the world, Japanese bar tool makers are revitalizing the industry with new high-end inventions. Tetsuya Yokoyama's Birdy cocktail shaker was one of the first to challenge the status quo with its launch in 2013. Made using technologies adopted from the automotive industry, the three-piece shaker looks like most three-piece shakers on the outside but has a high-polish interior finish to elevate the texture of shaken cocktails. While most people were thinking about shakers in terms of only shape and size, Yokoyama tapped into an element of the tool that would offer a technical improvement. A superb collision of science and art. Yokoyama says he was inspired by watching bartenders dedicated to their craft, and wanted to create an enhanced tool to match their skills.

Today, one of the most interesting things about the bar tools industry in Japan is how regional traditions have sparked concentrations of specialization across the country. There is a heavy focus on steel work in Nīgata, fine forging and metal work in the Kansai area, and ceramics in central and southern Japan. Traditional tools that have been adopted for the bar, like knives, graters, and strainers, still come from the areas of Kansai, Tōkyō, and Nara, while the heavier stainless-steel tools inspired by the West, like jiggers, shaker tins, and Hawthorne strainers, come from Nīgata.

And as Japanese bartenders increasingly travel to other countries to learn new techniques, updated styles are emerging as well. Yukiwa released a shaker in 2015 with a higher polish similar to that of the Birdy, in addition to a Parisian-style two-piece tin that stands out as a statuesque anomaly in a culture where the three-piece shaker still represents the norm. It is exciting to see how Japanese toolmakers are getting inspired by other global traditions, bringing them home, and making devices that are reliable and rooted in Japanese craftsmanship.

gurasu • tōki

DRINKING VESSELS

GLASSWARE

Many cocktail bars around the world have a large volume of uniform glassware at the ready, but Japanese bartenders prefer to assemble a small and curated collection of unique pieces that match their specific aesthetic because that makes every drink special. Most often, the glassware is made of high-quality crystal—the type you would not find in a busy American cocktail bar because it is too fragile to withstand high-volume use—etched with ornate designs or featuring hand-cut patterns, known as kiriko. True kiriko glasses cost over $100 and are handled with the greatest amount of respect and care.

The best cocktail glasses elicit a moment of pause and appreciation for the artistry that went into making the cocktail, but not all glassware must be traditional. At Bar Orchard Ginza, Takuo and Sumiré Miyanohara compiled an array of fanciful drinking vessels with the element of surprise in mind. One of their most famous is a white clawfoot bathtub-shaped "glass" that comes garnished with a salt foam and miniature rubber ducky. At Bar BenFiddich in Tōkyō's Shinjuku neighborhood, unexpected curves and lines grace the geometric glassware to heighten the sense of drama that Hiroyasu Kayama has worked so hard to establish. That creativity, meant to spark joy and delight, is part of what makes these bars extra special.

CERAMICS

Earthenware, stoneware, and porcelain pottery represent Japan's oldest art forms, and many consider the ceramics born of the ancient craft to be some of the best in the world. Historically, ceramic cups have been reserved for tea or shōchū, with vessels like the chawan (teacup) used to make and serve matcha, but as more contemporary bartenders seek to anchor their programs in a deep Japanese sensibility, some are using ceramics for cocktails, too.

One of the elements I look for in Japanese ceramics is how the pieces represent the maker and the region where they are made. Ceramics look and feel different depending on local customs, with distinct signature glazes based on how the type of soil fires. For example, in Kyōto, the glaze on Kyō-yaki pieces have a dappled appearance with little starbursts; from the mountains, Shigaraki-yaki is a more rustic style with green and brown hues; then as you move east toward Tōkyō, Tokoname-yaki (made in Aichi prefecture known for its teaware) is made of very soft red clay.

While ceramics may appear sturdy, they require the same gentle touch as glassware, with additional considerations. Those that remain unglazed will pick up the aromas and flavors of what you put inside, so you should only serve one kind of tea or liquid from the vessel or it will absorb clashing personalities. And over time, as chips and breaks are bound to occur, they're pieced back together with lacquer and gold, a method called kintsugi; the resulting vessel can look even more exquisite after it's been broken and repaired.

kōri

ICE

Ice serves many functions in the Japanese cocktail bar. The most obvious—dilution and chilling—is already a universal understanding among bartenders around the world. What makes ice important to the Japanese cocktail bar is also its aesthetic role. Bartenders spend a seemingly infinite amount of time perfecting the presentation of their drinks in addition to ensuring they are delectable, which is why ice has brought Japanese bars notoriety within today's global bar scene more so than any championship-winning recipe. It is an element of technique that some people never considered until photographs and reports from visitors to Japan began to circle the web in recent years. It is an expression of both subtlety and glamour in the glass.

Most bars in Japan are too small to house ice machines, so they rely on daily deliveries of large, crystal-clear blocks of ice to stock the bar for each service. The clarity of cocktail ice is of the utmost importance, because it impacts both the look and flavor of the drink. Cloudy or opaque ice, the type made in a typical home freezer in which the cube freezes inward, thus trapping unwanted air bubbles, is not pleasing to look at. Many spirits purists and bartenders sense an unwanted flavor that is imparted by such ice as well, either from the freezer itself, or the minerals in the water, or the trapped air that escapes from the ice and into the drink.

Additionally, this porous ice melts more rapidly than solid, crystal-clear ice, which also creates unwanted effects. When ice isn't concrete to its core, it is prone to water down the drink more rapidly and does not retain its temperature very well, so the cocktail will not be as cold to begin with and will get watered down faster than what is considered optimal. The lifespan of the cocktail as a whole is shortened by this lesser-quality soft ice.

To avoid these unappealing characteristics and outcomes, many bartenders (and specialty ice companies) use a method called directional freezing, in which the ice forms unilaterally. During this process, the crystals fall into a rigid structure, pushing minerals and air bubbles out of the way as they form their hexagonal structure. This may be achieved in any freezer (see box on page 64) or through the use of a Clinebell machine, most commonly used to make the building blocks for ice sculptures.

The bar takes these large blocks of ice and breaks them down with various tools such as saws, mallets, knives, and ice picks. This is the ultimate form of customization and kodawari, an unwavering focus on perfecting the task at hand. Many bartenders will spend years learning how to tap and break down ice into the right size and shape for shaking, stirring, and building cocktails.

TYPES OF ICE

LARGE CUBES

One of the most basic shapes of cocktail ice, ranging in size from 2 to 5 inches. The 2-inch cubes are best for serving spirits over a single rock. The larger cubes will be cut or chipped into different shapes, such as diamonds or spheres.

SPHERES

Globe-like balls in various sizes, this shape dates back to American cocktail culture in the late 1800s and has remained a feature of Japanese bartending since. Spheres are most commonly used for stirred cocktails, highballs, or pours of spirits. They are desirable for their low melting rate and striking appearance. Spheres may be chipped, cut, pressed, or even formed in special ice machines.

HIGHBALL OR COLLINS PRISMS

Cut into a long, narrow rectangular shape, single highball prisms should fit neatly within a highball or collins glass. In Japan, it is common to see two rectangular pieces of ice used in cocktails like this, rather than the single uniform spear sometimes used in America.

DIAMONDS OR BRILLIANT-CUT ICE

When Hidetsugo Ueno worked at Star Bar Ginza as an apprentice in Tōkyō, he and master bartender Hisashi Kishi took ice to a new level by carving the edges in an angular design, echoing the look of a sparkling diamond. This type of ice brings beauty to the glass while keeping dilution rates relatively slow. They are commonly used in stirred drinks and for rocks pours of spirits.

MACHINE ICE: PRISMS AND ASSORTED SHAPES

This is basic ice used for shaking and stirring cocktails and sometimes for serving simple highballs. Many Japanese bars have these cubes delivered from ice companies, or will purchase a bag of clear cubes from the nearby convenience store in case of unanticipated shortages. Some bars, especially the more recently opened cocktail bars, have Hoshizaki machines, which create 1 × 1¼ × 1-inch cubes. Hoshizaki also makes machines that create large rocks, hearts, spheres, and star-shaped ice, adding an element of delight to traditional whisky highballs and chū-hi (shōchū highballs).

MACHINE ICE: SHAVED OR CRUSHED

Used for frappé-esque cocktails, swizzles, and some tropical cocktails, most Japanese bars make this ice using a small crushed ice machine or by saving the shavings of ice from ice prep earlier in the day. All of the small shavings and pieces from diamonds and spheres may be used for other cocktails throughout the evening. For a more modern presentation, some bars employ the type of ice shaver used to make kakigōri (shaved ice).

Like sculptors, Japanese bartenders will often finesse the final shape of a piece of ice at the very last moment before delivering a drink to a guest. This maintains the utmost freshness and highlights another moment of beauty in the drink-making process. First the bartender removes the ice from the freezer to temper it, sometimes placing it in a cedar wood hangiri (a vessel used for cooling and preparing sushi rice), while the rest of the drink comes together. As tempered ice cuts more smoothly, this contributes to a process that's both pleasing to watch for the guest and more flawless to execute by the bartender.

HOW TO MAKE CRYSTAL-CLEAR ICE Start with filtered water, filling an insulated container (like a thermos or styrofoam box) three-quarters of the way full. Cover the top with plastic wrap so as to protect the water from any odors circulating in your freezer. Remove the container from the freezer before the block has frozen completely. This prevents ice crystals from forming on the bottom of the container and shooting air bubbles back up through your clear block of ice. This resulting block can be broken down into manageable sections using an ice pick. Store your ice in airtight bags or containers to protect from any impurities in the air and to preserve the shape and smoothness of the ice.

Here are some of the tools you might need for a reputable Japanese-style ice program.

kōrinoko

ICE SAWS

Japanese cocktail bars usually order crystal-clear ice blocks from local companies and use kōrinoko to break them down swiftly and efficiently. Many different brands exist in Japan, and within some brands there will be many options, allowing bartenders to pick out the perfect blade. When working on breaking blocks down into smaller cubes, the key is to use a saw with relatively wide teeth, because they catch on to ice better—if the jagged edges are too fine, it will feel like you are trying to cut wood with a butter knife. The blade also needs to be long enough to hang over the edge of the block so your hand doesn't knock against the side with every motion. Stainless-steel saws won't rust over time, and high-quality saws are always a good call because they are safer to use than cheaper saws.

The cutting process is simple. Temper the ice first—you will know it is ready when it has a glistening sheen of water on the exterior. Lay down a plastic tarp or mat to protect your workspace, and a cutting board upon which to work. Score the block first using a knife and a ruler, so you have precise marks to hit. I work from the center outward, which helps facilitate even cuts (and if you mess up, you will still have plenty of salvageable ice left). If you chip from the end, there's a chance the saw might slip, miscut, or break off end pieces, which is not ideal. Once the ice is 4 to 5 inches thick, the time is right to break the rest down with a pick or knife.

aisupikku

PICKS

The ice pick is a critical tool not only for the Japanese bar but for many home bars as well. It can be wielded for the simplest of tasks, from breaking apart cubes of ice clumped together in an ice bucket to chipping cylinders and spheres from larger blocks, or cracking long, single rectangular prisms in half for highballs. Japanese bartenders use either a single-prong, three-prong, five-prong, or six-prong pick— sometimes one of each for various tasks. Super-long single-prong picks are good for big blocks, while the shorter ones are good for scoring and other finishing. A three-prong pick will require fewer scratches and strikes on a large block of ice but will require more energy to disperse force—they are also typically lighter in weight, so easier to wield. The six-prong pick is best for splitting a large block in half if you allow the ice to temper fully and use enough strength.

At the pinnacle of the mastery of the ice pick is the ice sphere. You can tell when a sphere has been made by hand because it looks dimpled from the strikes of stainless-steel prongs, each divot like a crater in the moon. To chip ice into a sphere using an ice pick, use your wrists to make small brisk whipping movements, because you will have more control over where the pick lands. Pointing the pick downward will yield bigger chunks to fall off the cube, while angling it upward will shave off little parts of the ice. A combination of both techniques will result in a dazzling final product, so use strong downward strokes against the eight corners first to remove large chunks, then softer strokes against the sides to refine each edge. Move the ice in your hands at an even pace, almost every second, so the cube doesn't melt quickly. For safety, make sure you hold the ice from the base beneath the path of the ice pick, and chip at the top so you don't stab your hand, and always hit the ice with the pick, and not the other way around. Eventually, you should be able to do this process by feel, without looking at the cube, as it becomes a sense memory.

naifu

KNIVES

Just like a reliable chef's knife, a bartender's knife is a versatile and important tool. There are many shapes and sizes of knife suitable for working with ice, so most bartenders choose several to keep for various purposes. For breaking down full blocks, bartenders reach for a basic chef's knife, soba-cutting knife, or my preference, a nata (a flat-edge gardening knife). Working with large blocks can dull and damage knives, but nata are sturdy and economical, built to undergo many sharpenings, which makes them ideal for the task.

Once the ice block is cut into a more manageable size, such as a large cube, it can be manipulated further into various shapes like diamonds and spheres. Honetsuki, a boning knife, is well-suited for these tasks because it is sturdy with a relatively short blade that rests flat on level surfaces so you can bring the blade down evenly all the way through the ice. It can swiftly shape a cube into a diamond, or continue to shave the ice down into a sphere.

Many Japanese bartenders will use a weighted rubber mallet in conjunction with a long flat-bladed ice knife to split large blocks of ice. Use your blade to score the ice block by running it back and forth over the tempered block. Hold the knife perfectly straight against the block and then tap gently along the blade from center to handle to tip until the ice splits in half. Repeat this process, cutting each piece in half until you have the desired size and shape.

Knives are fantastic finishing tools as well. A paring knife may be used to shave away dimples formed from chipping with an ice pick. Another knife that is popular for finishing is a serrated blade, like a bread knife. Such a knife leaves wave-like ridges, which will be polished away instantly with a pour of spirit, or if that initial dilution is not required, wiped away with a clean cloth prior to use.

CARVING DIAMOND ICE: USING A CUTTING BOARD Position the cutting board along the edge of a table or the bar so you can cut all the way through without hitting your hand on the edge of the board. Shave away frosty or irregular edges, then, working quickly so the ice doesn't overly soften, bevel the four edges of the top portion of the cube, turning the cube on its side for each cut while taking care to keep the angle of the knife even to ensure efficient, symmetrical cuts. Once the beveled top is formed, turn the cube upright so that all 4 of the beveled edges face upward. Start at one of the beveled corners and slice down to create another face of ice. When you do this with each corner, you transform the 4-faced prism to one with 8 facets, like an octagonal shape, or a diamond. To serve, place the carved cube with the beveled top facing upward in the glass and pour your ambient-temperature spirits down the side of the glass rather than over the top of the cube in order to retain the sharp edges of the beveled top.

CARVING DIAMOND ICE: USING YOUR HANDS You can cut diamonds in your hand, but I do recommend practicing extreme caution when using this method because there are increased safety risks as the ice melts and becomes more slippery. Holding the ice like an apple, pull the knife toward you as if peeling the fruit to create the beveled top. Working quickly, turn the ice and continue with the same swiping cuts to bevel the edges along the body of the cube. As you are practicing this technique, I recommend returning to the freezer as you go, taking breaks in between, until you can complete the diamond in under a minute.

aisu-kurasshā

ICE CRUSHERS

In Japan, there are a few different types of equipment used to shave or crush ice for cocktails. For crushed ice, modern electric ice crushers can be found easily in restaurant supply stores, but these tend to break easily. If you can, find a vintage piece that is hand-cranked, which will likely prove more reliable. These machines process about one scoop (8 to 10 ounces) of textured crushed cubes per use, so they are perfect for Japanese bars where drink-making happens at a steady pace and not at high volume. For shaved ice, some bars will use a kakigōri shaver, a mechanism traditionally used to cut sheer sheets of shaved ice for the beloved dessert treats of the same name. Many tower over a foot tall and require effort to crank, but the thin, smooth folds of ice are worth the effort.

aisu-tongu

ICE TONGS

Handling ice is done with the utmost care in Japan, so most bartenders use tongs and shovels, commonly known as ice scoops in America, for the most efficiency (and to limit human contact). Because most Japanese bars are compact, large ice bins are not commonly used. Instead, ice is kept in smaller buckets, replenished from a small under-counter freezer as needed. This setup allows the bartender to marry efficiency with presentation as they can pick out individual pieces or scoop a few at once while standing upright. Some Japanese tongs are short and have curved claws, like a hawk's talons, which are lovely to look at and useful for transporting ice spheres. Longer rectangular tongs with serrated edges (like alligator teeth) are good for handling highball ice because the jagged edges latch firmly on to the slick surface. I love how deliberate I can be with this type of ice tong.

shitagoshiraé

MISE EN PLACE

Most bartenders know that creating an organized workspace is paramount to making sure service runs smoothly when doors open for the night. In large American bars, mise en place is organized so ingredients and equipment always stay within arm's reach. This minimizes the number of movements needed to make a cocktail, so the bartender can quickly and efficiently mix several drinks at a time while serving large crowds. In Japan, the goal is to create the best singular drink in each moment, slow and steady, so cocktails are almost always mixed one at a time, carefully and without the urge to rush. The mise en place follows suit.

There is a home for every ingredient and tool at the Japanese cocktail bar— not for the sake of speed, but for care of the products, respect for the process, and to maintain order and efficiency. While the setup changes from place to place, you can find certain commonalities. Because traditional Japanese cocktail bars are tiny, there is often not room for a large well or speed rail, so bottles are often stored on the backbar. When a drink is being prepared, each bottle is brought to the bar top, aligned in a clean and organized row with the labels facing the guest, so they can examine the information if they please. Afterward, the lips of bottles are always wiped clean before being returned to their home on the backbar.

Most bartenders in authentic cocktail bars also favor a clean bar top so guests have a full and unobstructed view of how the drinks are mixed (that, or they opt for a display of bottles, fruit, and knickknacks that overflows from the backbar to the front). Sometimes you will see a row of clean tins and mixing glasses ready for use alongside a narrow pitcher of water to keep barspoons clean, but for the most part storage happens underneath the bar, out of sight.

Similarly, glassware is either kept on the backbar at the same level as the bar top or out of sight, sometimes in a refrigerator with glass doors. This chills the glassware before use, and adds an element of delight to the experience—when a bartender selects the glass for a drink, the moment they reveal the vessel is surprising and special.

At Kumiko, I had drawers built into the backbar and I cannot emphasize how glorious they are for reducing clutter and hiding away loose items you need at your fingertips during service. In traditional Japanese homes, there are lots of sliding doors, cubbies, nooks, and crannies to store things, so bringing this concept to the bar setting works great for items like pens, cutlery, share plates, and more.

mejākappu

JIGGERS

Interestingly enough, what is known today as the Japanese jigger is actually an American invention that got mislabeled along the winding road of history. As the story goes, a Chicagoan by the name of Cornelius Dungan first filed a patent for a "vessel for measuring liquors," called a jigger, in 1893. The tool found its way to Japan thereafter and was quickly adopted for its accuracy. In America, Dungan's elongated version disappeared over time as designs changed to a shorter, squattier version of the jigger. Fast-forward to the 2000s and the return of cocktail culture in America: Cocktail Kingdom owner Greg Boehm started traveling to Japan and noticed the slender jiggers they used in cocktail bars. Inspired by the design, he started making "Japanese-style" jiggers, not realizing at first that the design was an American patent. Thankfully, he has since worked to clear up the confusion on both sides of the ocean.

Jiggers come in and out of fashion in the United States, but you will almost always see Japanese bartenders employing "measure cups," as they are called, to make cocktails with precision and consistency. (A notable exception may be the building of a house highball—a master typically knows their build by sight and feel.) The hourglass-shaped tool comes in various sizes, some with curved lips and others with a sharper, cleaner edge. Many hold different volumes on each side of the jigger, and some have marks on the inside of each cup to indicate measurements. With so many options available, every bartender tends to choose one that speaks to their individual sensibilities. Once the tool is selected the bartender works to develop a consistent grip and pour for that style—once that is determined, that jigger is the one they will always use.

MILLILITERS TO OUNCES

Japanese jiggers have inner measurements that do not quite line up with the American counterparts. With lines at 10, 15, 20, 30, 45, and 60 milliliters, conversions to fluid ounces can be difficult. There is no perfect translation, but here are my general guidelines for conversions:

½ ounce	= 15 milliliters	1½ ounces	= 45 milliliters
1 ounce	= 30 milliliters	2 ounces	= 60 milliliters

Japanese bartenders tend to use jiggers with a more fluid motion instead of a clunky dump from the side, as happens in most American bars. Almost all of them will place a jigger *behind* the mixing glass and move it forward in one slow and continuous arc to get the liquid into the mixing glass or shaker tin. The movement comes from the wrist and not the entire arm. Once done pouring, the jigger is brought back to the starting point to collect whatever droplets are left in the cup,

then poured one more time to make sure all the liquid gets into the drink. This is more elegant than holding the jigger upside down and tapping the drops to come out. By pouring once then pouring again, we are showing an awareness of the final drop and the importance it brings to the drink as a whole.

mikishingu gurasu

MIXING GLASSES

Mixing glasses serve the same purpose in bars all over the world, but in Japan the functionality of the tool goes hand in hand with its aesthetics, as most Japanese mixing glasses are adorned with absolutely stunning patterns. The most well-known is yarai, a crosshatch pattern etched into some of the first mixing glasses that came into the US from Japan (in Japan, yarai is the name of the pattern, not the mixing glass itself!). Others showcase etched florals, swooping blades of grass, spirals, and faceted bases that glimmer under dim lights.

Generally speaking, you will not see Japanese bartenders making more than one drink at a time in a mixing glass, so smaller vessels (350 to 500 milliliters) are common. When stirring a cocktail, start by stacking the ice almost two times higher than the liquid in the glass, the goal is to move the liquid around the ice, not the other way around, to properly chill and dilute. For drinks served up and on the rocks, reset the ice levels in the mixing glass after stirring and before straining, so the liquid is the only thing that escapes through the strainer. This creates a smooth, seamless pour with fewer air bubbles forming in the final drink. This technique is not a hard-and-fast rule, but attention to little details like this contributes to a more enjoyable drinking experience.

bāsupūn

BARSPOONS

There are a few things that set Japanese barspoons apart. Most have a weighted balance, a spiraled coil on the arm instead of a flat surface, and are often quite elongated compared to American ones. They also sometimes have flourishes on one end, like a teardrop shape, a masher, or a trident, which add extra functionality. The trident specifically is an excellent example of form following function as it is used to scoot the lime garnish deep down into a good gin and tonic.

When stirring, there should always be a fluid ballet happening between the ice and the spoon. To do this, pinch close to the center of the spoon for control, anchoring it against the inside of the glass. Support the mixing vessel at the base so you do not transfer any heat to the glass, then use the weight of the upper two-thirds of the spoon to swirl it around while utilizing a pull-push motion along the spoon. You want to feel the liquid moving softly, evenly, and quietly. If serving the cocktail on the rocks, aim for only 75 percent of optimal dilution so the peak moment of drinkability will happen in the second or third sip, or just after the drink sits for the common pre-sip photoshoot. For drinks served up, you have to hit perfect dilution before you strain it into the cocktail vessel because there is no ice to melt further after the drink is served.

shēkā

SHAKER TINS

For shaken cocktails, bartenders around the world prefer one of two types of shaker tin. The two-piece Boston shaker is common in American bartending because it is a workhorse: easy to clean, stackable, and virtually indestructible; and some bartenders in Japan will use a two-piece when working with fresh fruits or creams because the minimal shape is easier to clean. But for the most part, the three-piece, or cobbler shaker, remains king. Originally patented by New York inventor Edward Hauck in 1884, the design is timeless and reliable with three distinct parts—the tumbler-shaped body, the built-in strainer, and the cap—and a sleek, curvaceous shape. Because the form of the tin is more petite than a Boston shaker, it requires less strain to get the ice moving and the liquid flowing around in the tin, so you can get a perfectly aerated cocktail with less hassle. The simple cap releases easily so there is no need for brash banging of tins to open, and the built-in strainer allows small ice shards to float on top of the cocktail, which is a thing many Japanese bartenders prize for the message it delivers: The drink is as cold as possible.

A bartender's shake is personal, driven in part by the type of drink inside the tin, but also by the size of one's hands, shoulders, and the way they carry themselves. Everyone's shake will be unique to them, but speaking generally, Japanese bartenders almost always start out by shaking softly and then building up to a harder movement near the end, because it is more ergonomic and makes a difference to the overall ambiance of the room. Sometimes the cascading gallop of a shaker tin filled with ice can be deafening and break up conversation, so harmony is maintained when the bartender eases into the ritual instead. My personal shake, ingrained in my system now, is the result of years of experimentation and observation of Japanese techniques. I keep the movements close to my chest, with flicks of the wrist back and forth, back and forth, like the wings of a hummingbird, making slight adjustments for different ice and different ingredients. When a shake is controlled and practiced, it is mesmerizing, even peaceful, to behold.

sutorēnā

STRAINERS

COCKTAIL STRAINERS

Historically, two types of strainer have held a place at the American cocktail bar—the Julep strainer, a shallow cup-like tool with little round holes typically paired with a mixing glass, and the Hawthorne strainer, a flat but round head with a coil that commonly strains a shaken cocktail from a Boston-style shaker. Both were invented in America, but only the latter took root in Japanese cocktail bars, used to strain stirred cocktails from the mixing glass, as the three-piece cobbler shaker does not require such a device. The look of the classic Hawthorne strainer has remained mostly the same since the 1800s, though now brands like Yukiwa have started experimenting with contemporary designs. My favorite is a classic design from Yukiwa with a floral pattern on the frame and a small heart-shaped cutout at the tip of the handle. After nearly ten years of use, I find no fault with this beauty.

TEA STRAINERS/SIFTERS

These are commonly used in Japanese bartending for the same reason fine strainers are used in other cultures: to prevent unwanted bits and pieces of fruit and herbs from landing in a finished cocktail. Japanese tea strainers differ slightly from others, though—the materials range from bamboo and stainless steel to copper wire, and the mesh tends to be super fine. This is particularly helpful in cocktails that call for sifting matcha or straining loose tea. These strainers often require more intense cleaning than American ones, so having a good cleaning brush is important because you don't want residual ingredients getting in the way of your next cocktail.

bitāzu botoru

BITTERS BOTTLES

Precision is especially important in Japanese cocktail making, so most bartenders will use Japanese Bitters bottles to get a more accurate measurement with each dash. Japanese-style bitters bottles have a heavy bottom and tapered neck and come in all shapes and sizes, but the most important thread among them (and the element that differentiates Japanese Bitters bottles from other styles) is the specially designed precision spout, which regulates the amount of air displacement that happens when you turn the vessel upside down. This results in an accurate dash or drop every time. Find the size, shape, and design of a bitters bottle that best suits your needs and then stick to that exact type for optimal and accurate mixing.

madorā • masshā

STIR STICKS, MASHERS

In Japan, madorā are not the thick, baseball bat–shaped pounders we use to muddle ingredients in America. Instead, they are long, thin sticks used to stir a cocktail, almost like a straw (though you cannot drink out of them). Japanese stir sticks come in different shapes and sizes. Many have decorative elements to bring extra joy to the imbiber, and they are almost always light and easy to handle.

What we call muddlers in America are called masshā (mashers) or pestles in Japan. The technique is the same as it is in the US, where you use the thicker end of the stick to crush fruits, herbs, or vegetables into a drink.

gānisshu tsūru

GARNISH TOOLS

There is a word for when condiments or garnishes are added to Japanese cuisine in a way that is specifically intended to enhance the aroma and flavor of a dish: *yakumi.* The word is formed by two kanji: 薬 for "medicine" plus 味 for "flavor." Yakumi are selected with seasonality and a direct intention in mind, with attention to form and function. The same theory applies to Japanese cocktails—the garnish is selected with a specific aim and is never an afterthought. Whether to add a pleasing aroma, a caress of beauty, a lingering brush of dryness, or a salty contrast to sweetness, the garnish is the final ingredient of a beverage. For competitions, the NBA even has formal requirements for drink entries—every element of the garnish must be communicated to judges ahead of time.

When the presentation is pleasing, the drink will appear that much more delicious to the guest, which translates to flavor. Master the art of the garnish, and every drink will look *and* taste better!

PEELERS
A martini without an expression of glistening lemon oils, an old fashioned without the classic orange peel, or a horse's neck without the coil of a full lemon—so many cocktails would feel incomplete without a citrus garnish. The Y-peeler, or T-shape peeler as it is called in Japan, is most commonly used in Japanese bars.

The most bewitching part of garnishing happens when a practiced bartender expresses the oils of a citrus peel over the top of a cocktail in deliberate, strategic movements to make sure the drink gets the exact amount of coverage. To do this, hold the colorful zest side of the peel toward the glass and squeeze ever so slightly to cast the oils upward and over the drink.

SCISSORS

I use embroidery scissors for à la minute trimming of leaves from herbs; you want to make sure the garnishes look as fresh as possible.

GRATERS

Preground spices do not offer the same flavor as freshly ground, so most bartenders use a copper grater called oroshigané to grate on the spot. What I use specifically is a copper suehiro grater. Suehiro refers to the shape of the grater—wide on the bottom and narrow on top, like a triangle with the top clipped off. The surface is dotted with super-fine sharp teeth, which create an even shred, and the flat base allows for more control when rested on the cutting board. Most come with a small bamboo brush to sweep lingering bits into a cocktail or dish.

MORTAR AND PESTLE

The suribachi (mortar) and surikogi (pestle) are great for cracking spices for toasting and infusing into spirits, creating "dusts" to sprinkle on top of cocktails or use as a special seasoned rim, making fresh syrups, or pulverizing fresh fruit. Traditionally, the suribachi is made from earthenware with small ridges etched into the unglazed pottery within the bowl, while the surikogi is made of hardwood.

TONGS

In addition to the types of tongs used for ice, there are certain styles used for handling and placing garnishes on drinks. These are often lighter and thinner, with small arms and no teeth so they do not damage herbs and peels.

TWEEZERS

Useful for the careful placement of fragile garnishes like flowers and microherbs. The very best bartenders wield this tool with such agility you can barely tell if it was the tweezers or their fingers that deftly placed a paper-thin lemon wheel or dainty sprig of mint into the glass.

CHOPSTICKS

Japanese plating chopsticks, or moribashi, are good for fine garnish work like placing a single sesame seed on the white canvas of an egg white cocktail, because the balance and weight of the chopsticks leave little room for error.

KNIVES

I use two knives—a petty knife (4- or 5-inch blade) and a paring knife (2- or 3-inch blade). The petty knife is useful for breaking down larger ingredients like pineapples and mangoes. I like paring knives for detailed garnish work, like manicuring peels or cutting windows into leaves to make snowflake shapes.

JAPANESE COCKTAIL TOOL RECOMMENDATIONS

I could fill a whole Rolodex with recommendations for exemplary Japanese-made bar tools and glassware. For the sake of brevity, here are a few companies that I would be remiss to exclude as I turn to them most for my glassware, jiggers, shakers, and more.

KIMURA GARASU

Kimura Glass manufactured electric lightbulbs in Tōkyō before starting to make glassware in 1910. They currently make over one thousand unique drinking vessels. The glasses are especially popular in cocktail bars because of the diversity of options and elegance of each design, paired with the quality of mouth-blown, lead-free crystal. All of their etching is done by hand without the use of stencils or machinery.

TOYO SASAKI

The Toyo Glass company started making glassware in 1878, but merged with Sasaki Glass in 1957 and have since become famous for a wide range of brands. The extra-sturdy Hard Strong line is stackable and extremely resilient—good for restaurants and casual bars. The Fine Crystal-Ion Strong series of stemware is equally durable, and a series of kiriko called Yachiyo Kiriko (along with their Edo Glass line) showcases the talents of glassware artisans certified by the government.

SANPŌ SANGYŌ

Sanpō Industries, responsible for renowned cocktail tool brand Yukiwa, is located in Tsubame City in the Nīgata prefecture, an area known for fine metalwork of both traditional Japanese and Western-style tableware. Founded in 1950, they started with cocktail shakers and expanded the collection to include tongs, strainers, jiggers, barspoons, and in 2015, double-walled stainless mixing tins. Yukiwa is a brand that is built to last.

YOKOYAMA KŌGYŌ

This auto parts manufacturer entered into the realm of barware production in 2013 through a collaboration between bartender Erik Lorincz and Tetsuya Yokoyama, the company's New Business Developer. The famous Birdy shaker tins have a hand-polished interior that efficiently enables smaller, tighter bubbles to form. The mixing tin applies similar technology, but with the function of smoothing the stir, chilling drinks more effectively. Birdy will be an exciting brand to watch as they inspire others to dive deeper into the future—bringing tradition and technology together in harmony.

RAKURAKU KŌRI CHŌKOKU BEST KATAYAMA

Rakuraku kōri chōkoku translates to "easy breezy ice sculpting." Founded in 1955 in Miki City, a town in the Hyogo prefecture known for their knife production, Best Katayama produces a wide variety of ice chisels, knives, and saws. I recommend the Ice Saw No. 410 Pistol Grip 270, a blade 270 millimeters (10.6 inches) long that is well suited to breaking down large blocks of ice thanks to the sturdy steel blade and well-spaced teeth.

FUJITA MARUNOKO INDUSTRY CO. LTD.

A mere thirty-minute walk from Best Katayama is Fujita Marunoko, founded in 1940. In 1972, their sole focus shifted to saws. The deep ice teeth of their forged stainless-steel saws are carefully tempered, polished, and sharpened. The Yotsumé Jirushi Ice Saw Pistol Grip KN-270 is an ergonomic option for scoring and breaking down smaller sheets of ice, while the Yotsumé Jirushi Ice Saw KN-420, is available in varying lengths of blade starting at 300 millimeters (11.8 inches) extending all the way to 600 millimeters (23.6 inches).

TAKAKYU SANGYŌ

Takakyu Industries, founded in 1950 with factories in Ōsaka and Saitama, makes a series of ice picks. The economy line under the brand "Pilot" may be found in most households, izakayas, and even some hotels for breaking apart ice clumps for simple drinks. Their "Deluxe" 3-Prong Pick is my choice for chipping spheres, though this pick is not an investment piece—it is cheap and meant to be used until it wears out, a workhorse as some might say, reliable and easy to handle.

YAMACHŪ

This Nīgata-based producer is a luxury brand whose humble beginnings making knit socks started in 1958. Since then, they have vastly expanded their offerings to include collectible Japanese muddlers and a high-end line of ice picks with durable beechwood handles featuring stainless-steel prongs. The most classic is the Daiya pick, named for its diamond-shaped weighted steel end. The Ice Pickel has a stainless-steel handle fashioned after the axes used by mountain climbers, and the Marron is a rounded, ergonomic choice with a chestnut-shaped weighted stainless-steel-tipped handle that fits comfortably in the nook of a fist.

ARITSUGU

Aritsugu opened during a time of unrest and feudal warfare in 1560 in Kyōto, and is now under the ownership and care of an eighteenth-generation knife maker. Fujiwara Aritsugu was appointed as one of the swordsmiths for the imperial household, and as more peaceful times came to Japan in the 1700s, he moved away from making swords and started to forge knives for carving Buddhist sculptures. Aritsugu has come to be one of the most highly regarded knife and kitchen tool makers in Japan.

ŌTSUKA GARASU

Established in 1930, in Chiba, Ōtsuka Glass Company produces a popular brand of bitters bottles called Maru-T. Their stainless-steel tops are designed to release one exact drop, approximately 0.2 milliliters, when slowly turned upside down. To add a dash, a quick swoop of the wrist in an even motion will consistently release about 1 milliliter.

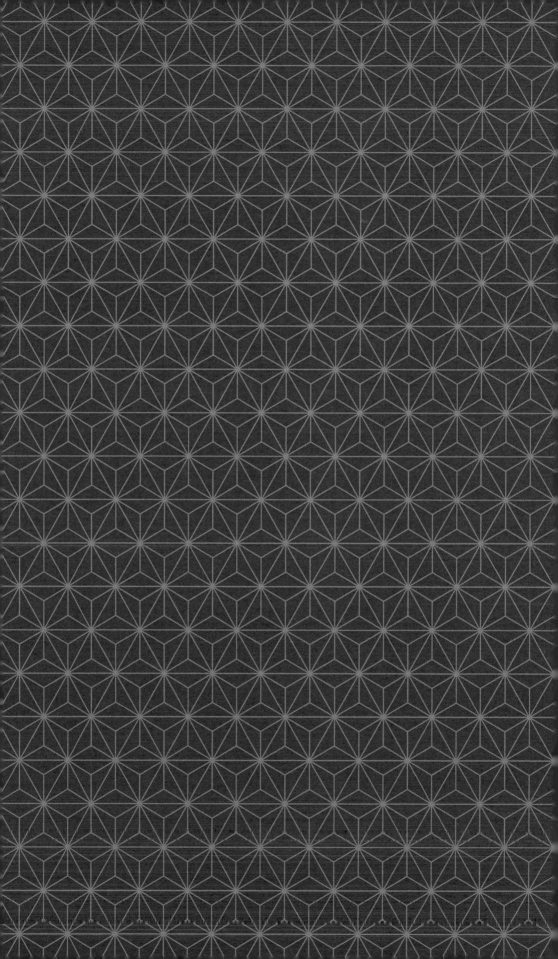

BEVERAGES
OF JAPAN

Nestled on the banks of the Kamo River, an artery of the Katsura River that runs through the city of Kyōto, sits the historic Tsuki no Katsura, a traditional kura (saké brewery) that dates back to 1675. Drawing upon the city's soft fushimizu, its renowned underground water source, the brewery was the first to make lightly sparkling unfiltered saké in the 1960s, and the first to purposefully age saké. Today, master bartender Masuda Tokubee oversees production with deep wisdom and a quiet graciousness. Representing the fourteenth generation of his family, he blends tradition with a modern sensibility to make saké that elicits gasps of wonder from around the world.

Set out from the kura on the narrow and winding Tobakaidō (a road built in the year 796) and about ten minutes later you will arrive at The Kyōto Distillery, a small operation in a nondescript industrial warehouse in the Minami-Ku neighborhood. There, an international assembly of spirits aficionados make gin with a distinctly Japanese sensibility. The portfolio is thoroughly contemporary, featuring a rice-based distillate and unique regional botanicals such as gyokuro from Uji and yuzu from northern Kyōto.

When the Kyōto Distillery needs water to bring the spirits down to proof, they turn to Masuda-san at Tsuki no Katsura saké brewery for their famed water. (Fushimizu is extremely soft, which means it opens up the characteristics of the distillate without drastically altering the flavor they work so hard to achieve, as harder mineral-laden water is apt to do.) But the historic saké house and the innovative spirits company are connected by more than just a water source—both producers embody the spirit of Japanese beverage culture. One by keeping old traditions alive while supporting innovation, and the other by helping usher homegrown spirits into a new era. In their own ways, both are part of the current cocktail conversation in Japan as well, as traditions shift and morph into a novel new drinkscape.

Historically, beverages like saké and its distilled cousin shōchū have been consumed neat, on ice, or cut with water, soda, or tea—not mixed into cocktails—as a way of honoring the heritage and craftsmanship that went into their production. Now, younger generations are looking inward to native flavors, spirits, and other beverages to create cocktails that have more of a Japanese footprint, giving these indigenous ingredients a fresh home within the cocktail world. Here are some of Japan's most illustrious beverages to know, with some details on production processes where applicable, and notes on how each is typically consumed or mixed into cocktails.

nihonshu

JAPANESE SAKÉ

Saké is the first recorded Japanese alcoholic beverage and is representative of Japanese culture in the way it is produced and served. Its roots can be traced back to when communities started cultivating rice in the Yayoi period (400 BCE–AD 200), and after fermentation was introduced years later, the standardized category of rice-based alcohol called nihonshu emerged. Made from a simple quartet of ingredients—rice, water, yeast, and kōji (a mold that facilitates the saccharification process)—the slow and methodical cycle of production goes hand in hand with the seasons as rice is planted in the springtime and harvested in autumn when the brewing season begins and runs through the winter. (Note: In Japan, the word *saké* serves as a catch-all for *all types* of alcohol; the rice-based fermented beverage is called nihonshu or seishu. For the purposes of this book, I use saké and nihonshu interchangeably to indicate the fermented beverage made from rice.)

There are just over fourteen hundred nihonshu producers operating in Japan today, with about 30 to 35 percent of all nihonshu falling into the category of tokutei meishō-shu (premium saké), which adheres to specific guidelines regarding ingredients and seimaibuai (the percentage of rice that remains after polishing). The premium category may be further broken out into junmai (pure rice) or arukōru-tenka or aruten, which indicates the inclusion of brewer's alcohol. Nihonshu with a seimaibuai of 50 percent receives the classification of a daiginjō or junmai daiginjō, while those at 60 percent seimaibuai qualify as a ginjō or junmai ginjō.

The other 65 to 70 percent of the market is represented by futsushu, or table saké. Futsushu is typically more affordable because the polish rates are lower and it is faster to produce. Sometimes people think table saké is of lesser quality compared to special designation saké, but I do not subscribe to that mentality. Premium saké sounds fancy—and it is exceptional—but, I will always love, drink, and share futsushu with anyone who wants to try something delicious as it is in its own right.

Within those designations, each region tends to have its own individual style of saké, dictated by local customs, rice varieties, and water sources. More important, every tōji (master brewer) brings their personal touch to the process to create one-of-a-kind saké with every batch. Some producers, like Tsuki No Katsura, have been walking the line of tradition and innovation to make a gentle Kyōto-style saké since the 1600s. Miho Imada, the tōji and president of Imada Shuzō in Hiroshima, evokes a sense of *wa* in her utilization of modern technology to revitalize traditions. She spent nine years cultivating a forgotten heirloom rice called Hattansō for her junmai, Forgotten Fortune. On a quest to create the perfect sparkling saké to pair with local delicacies from the sea, like oysters and octopus, she ferments with a combination of yellow and white kōji to make Seaside Sparkling, which is carbonated using secondary fermentation in the bottle. Most recently, Imada-san is using progressive milling techniques that allow for henpei (flat polish) and genkei (original form) polishing. In essence, the rice is milled to follow the shape of the rice rather than arbitrarily polishing the oval into a sphere. With this mindful precision, less polishing is required to get the shinpaku (the starchy center, or "white heart," of the rice grain), resulting in less waste. I am intrigued to see how this might affect labeling and categorizing in the future as more brewers adopt this ingenious process.

Others, like Amabuki Brewery, founded in 1688 in the Saga prefecture, work only with yeast cultivated from flowers. The Gin no Kurenai junmai-shu, featured in the Sakurazuké Martini (page 141), is fermented with flower yeast from the fringed pink nadeshiko (dianthus). Their rice is grown without pesticides,

KŌJI

Not many countries have a national microorganism, but in Japan it is kōji. This fascinating mold is a cornerstone of Japanese beverage and cuisine—an essential component of nihonshu, shōchū, amazaké, awamori, miso, and soy sauce—used to create striking layers of flavor that would not otherwise exist in these products. At its simplest, the process begins with a grain or legume such as rice, barley, or soybeans, which gets inoculated and propagated with kōjikin (kōji mold spores). The kōjikin produces special enzymes that convert the complex starches into simple sugars (glucose) and from this stage yeast transforms those sugars into alcohol and carbon dioxide. The amazing thing about this process is that the kōjikin and the yeast cells are working in tandem, a phenomenon called multiple parallel fermentation. This is a key element that sets nihonshu apart from wine and beer. Unlike wine grapes, there are no naturally occurring sugars in rice. And beer undergoes saccharification fully before alcohol production begins. It is only with nihonshu that multiple parallel fermentation occurs, all thanks to kōji.

There are a few different types of kōji used in food and beverage production—each has distinct characteristics that determine their use. *Aspergillus oryzae*, more commonly known as yellow kōji or saké kōji, is the most delicate of the three types with a gorgeous fragrance that reminds me of grapefruit flowers after rainfall. *Aspergillus luchuensis*, or black kōji, creates the most acid and is used for the production of awamori (a distillate made in Okinawa with black kōji and Thai rice). There are some nihonshu producers, like Ikékamé Shuzō in Fukuoka, who experiment with black kōji, as it brings a deep, savory, and tangy quality to the brew. The third type, *Aspergillus kawachii,* or white kōji, is a spontaneous mutation of black kōji most commonly used for shōchū production because it's cleaner to work with (black kōji is notorious for leaving a trail of black dust in its wake) and more tender in nature.

With kōji, you can make amazaké (a low- to no-alcohol rice brew; see page 302), ferment soybeans for miso, or set some aside for umami-laden cooking adventures. These days, chefs around the world are enjoying the virtues of the ingredient in the kitchen—sprinkle some into a marinade for grilled mushrooms or mix it with butter for a pop of umami.

protected by hungry ducks who oxygenate the fields with their paddling, and they use an heirloom black rice for their junmai, which yields a rose-tinged pour in the glass.

Another notable outfit is from Kumamoto. Chiyonosono Brewery was founded in 1896, and was the first to make a commercially available junmai-shu after WWII rations were lifted. Today, they work with heirloom varieties of rice to make gorgeous expressions like their junmai Shared Promise. The name reflects the oath the brewery made after the war to protect the tradition and legacy of saké in their region by producing only junmai-shu. It is a fruity, floral saké with an interesting saline character from the rice.

As a respected traditional beverage, saké is usually consumed in tune with the seasons. From spring's first fresh releases (shinshu) to saké served with chrysanthemum petals (kikuzaké) in the fall, it is almost always sipped in its pure form alongside food. Yet as contemporary bartenders embrace more indigenous Japanese ingredients in their bar programs, some are defying this tradition to great effect. At Bar Trench in Tōkyō, the Trench 75, made with Nikka Coffey gin, lemon, honey, and sparkling saké, serves as a Japanese twist on the classic French 75. The saké brings a sublime bubbly texture and subtle fruity temperament to the drink. Nihonshu can be mixed subtly, as in the Saké and Sonic (page 123), or to bridge flavors in more complex cocktails like the Kaki Flip (page 230). Try mixing it in drinks like the Spindrift (page 167), where nigorizaké practically sings when paired with grassy Brazilian cachaça and fresh honeydew melon juice.

shōchū

SHŌCHŪ

Many people refer to shōchū as the vodka of Japan, while others equate it to whisky, but these comparisons don't do the spirit justice, nor are they accurate. With roots that can be traced back to the 1500s, shōchū is a traditional Japanese distilled beverage made from rice, barley, sweet potato, buckwheat, sugarcane, or one of forty-nine other agricultural products, employing kōji for fermentation. This unique production process means shōchū boasts a deep and distinctive flavor that no vodka could come close to matching.

In all of Japan there are over 350 honkaku shōchū distilleries registered with the National Tax Agency (as of 2017), but nearly 45 percent of them are located in Kyūshū, the third largest island of Japan as well as the country's southernmost region. Production is categorized into three styles. Ōtsurui shōchū (also called honkaku shōchū) dates back to the fourteenth century and is single-distilled in a pot still, which allows the character of the raw materials to shine. The second classification—kōrui shōchū—is typically made in bulk from grains or molasses in large facilities and distilled multiple times in a patent still (also known as a column still or Coffey still) to strip away most of the flavor. Today, kōrui makes up most of the country's production by volume, and because it is cheap and easy to drink, you'll find it in canned highballs, izakayas, and as the base for fruit liqueurs such as umé-shu. A third type is konwa shōchū, made from a blend of ōtsurui and kōrui shōchū. This style is intended for people who want some, but not all, of the robust flavor that comes from a single distillation.

While producers can and do age honkaku shōchū in wooden barrels, they must soften the color by blending with a lighter-colored shōchū or filtering out the color entirely to remain classified as shōchū (the regulations dictate the optical density of the rested spirit must be less than 0.08 on a spectrometer). Some distillers bottle their aged shōchū without softening the color to sell it as "rice whisky" overseas (they cannot call it whisky in Japan because it is fermented with kōji), and there is talk of creating a new category specifically for aged kōji distillates like this, called "kōji whiskey." This style was first developed in the 1890s by Japanese biochemist Jōkichi Takaminé for a company known as the "Whiskey Trust," in Illinois. Though they went so far as to patent the technique, ultimately Takaminé's efforts did not come to fruition. Perhaps in the future, this historic category will be revitalized, and richly aged shōchū will be given an internationally recognized specification.

It is hard to picture any bar in Japan that doesn't have a bottle of shōchū at the ready, and of course many casual establishments like izakayas also specialize in the beverage. In most places, people drink it plainly—on the rocks or mixed with tea or water to open up all of the aromas and flavors. More recently, a movement has sparked among bartenders in Japan (and some in the US) to introduce shōchū to modern audiences through cocktails. Tōkyō bars Bar Orchard Ginza and The SG Club are both welcoming shōchū into the modern age—the latter released a signature line intended for use in mixed drinks called The SG Shōchū in February of 2020, a move that could change the backbars of many cocktail bars in Japan.

Shōchū is also a very versatile ingredient for cocktails, perfect for mixing with other spirits, citrus, and liqueurs, because the flavor profiles within the category are so distinct and diverse. Depending on the maker, you will find different expressions of the raw ingredient. For example, some sweet potato shōchū is robust and umami-driven while others are sweet like pecan pie or sweet potatoes dressed with butter.

For a more contemporary way of drinking shōchū, try the Midori Shōchū Sour (page 163), which takes the traditional pairing of green tea and lifts it with a layer of citrus. Barley shōchū brings depth to cold-brew coffee concentrate and apricot liqueur in the Apricots and Cream (page 197), while in my version of the Japanese Cocktail, sweet potato shōchū finds a match in Armagnac and cashew orgeat (see Japanese Cocktail #2, page 215). Or for something light and lovely, the bright side of sudachi shōchū sings in the Sudachi Shōchū Sour (page 225) with lime, grapefruit, and orange liqueur. A simple pleasure.

DRINKING SHŌCHŪ WITH WATER

In Japan, drinking shōchū with some form of water is the most traditional way of enjoying the spirit. Here are some of the most common ways shōchū and water is served:

rokusu | SHŌCHŪ ON THE ROCKS

There are no real rules for ratios, though I urge you to use good, clean ice that has been made with filtered water, ideally with the directional freezing method (see page 61) so that the flavor of the spirit is not muddied by the ice as it melts.

oyuwari | SHŌCHŪ WITH HOT WATER

There are three popular ratios when mixing shōchū and hot water. Before mixing, take note of the ABV of the shōchū and the temperature of the water. Honkaku shōchū is typically bottled between 24% and 25% ABV, and the following ratios are based on this percentage to reach the optimal and distinct levels for drinking. The recommended water temperature is just off the boil cooled slightly to 185°F. This is hot enough to warm the cup and the shōchū, while retaining heat for the serve. One of the rules of serving oyuwari is to pour the water into the cup first, followed by the shōchū. The weight of the shōchū pulls it downward, while the steam of the water casts the aromatics upward.

- *Gogo 5:5—equal parts shōchū and hot water, ideal for slow sipping and highlights the aromatics of the shōchū.*

- *Rokuyon 6:4—6 parts shōchū to 4 parts of hot water means a 15% ABV, right alongside that of nihonshu or some wines. The*
cooler temperature makes the comparatively higher proof easier to handle but still showcases the aromatics and the body of the shōchū. This is one of the more popular ways to serve oyuwari.

maewarI | PRECUT SHŌCHŪ

Though at first glance, the difference between oyuwari and maewari may seem slight, true aficionados can taste the virtues in premixing a blend of shōchū and water. Unlike oyuwari, which is presented as two separate ingredients mixed together, maewari offers time for the flavors to meld and evolve. Whether served at room temperature, chilled, or heated, this method allows the shōchū and water to become more than the sum of their parts. Mix the ingredients at least twenty-four hours before enjoyment.

mizuwari/chu-hi | SHŌCHŪ HIGHBALL

A highball made with honkaku shōchū over clear ice and a delicious mixer cannot be beat. The mixer may be club soda, mineral water, tea, or juice. Green tea and oolong tea are popular choices both in izakaya and at home, and these teas may be brewed from exquisite loose-leaf tea or even poured from a large jug of tea bought at the convenience store. Explore mixing silky rice shōchū with genmaicha (green tea blended with roasted rice) or a more robust barley or sweet potato shōchū with oolong tea.

COMMON TYPES OF HONKAKU SHŌCHŪ AND GEOGRAPHIC INDICATIONS

The National Tax Agency (NTA) of Japan, the entity responsible for the legal definition of alcoholic beverages, approves fifty-four ingredients (to be used with the kōji base) for making honkaku shōchū. From aloe and carrot to seaweed, lotus root, and chestnuts, the full list shows the breadth and depth of Japan's agricultural treasures.

Because the country's geography is so diverse, shōchū production is largely informed by what ingredients grow best in certain areas, which is why most distilleries tend to specialize in one particular ingredient instead of making many different kinds. To honor and protect these regional customs, the NTA includes four types of shōchū within the Geographical Indication (GI) system. Of the fifty-four approved ingredients for honkaku shochu, four ingredients (rice, barley, sweet potato, and Thai rice) have a Geographical Indication to reflect quality and tradition.

komé | RICE

Rice shōchū production happens mostly in the northern prefectures of the island of Kyūshū, but especially in Kumamoto. Subtle in nature, it is an approachable entryway to the category for people who like nihonshu, vodka, gin, or other unaged spirits. Depending on the producer and processes they may implement, the flavor profiles range from fruity, like melon or bananas, to citrusy, like grapefruit or lemon, to supple, like sweet grains.

- GI: Kuma. Produced, stored, and bottled in Hitoyoshi City in Kumamoto.

mugi | BARLEY

Barley shōchū production is fairly spread out around the country, but you will see a concentration of distilleries in Northern Kyūshū through the Saga, Fukuoka, and Ōita prefectures. Whisky and beer drinkers may find familiar flavors in a roasted barley shōchū that is nutty and toasty, while genatsu (vacuum distilled) barley shōchū is mellow and borderline floral, something an unaged-spirits drinker may find appealing. I sip on genatsu mugi shōchū on the rocks or in highballs alongside sashimi and salads, and like to mix a roasted barley shōchū in cocktails like the Neither-Nor (page 288).

- GI: Iki. Produced, stored, and bottled in Iki City in Nagasaki.

imo | SWEET POTATO

Kagoshima is the heart of imo shōchū production, with over 120 producers operating in the prefecture. With a super-earthy, soulful base, shōchū made from sweet potatoes is great for fans of terroir-driven spirits like mezcal because over fifty varieties of sweet potato can be used, allowing for a great diversity of flavor within the category.

- GI: Satsuma. Produced, stored, and bottled in Kagoshima (excluding Amami City and Oshima District).

soba | BUCKWHEAT

Soba shōchū came into existence in the beginning of the 1970s, and is now made primarily in Miyazaki and Nagano prefectures. Nagano has cold temperatures and extremely steep mountains, which makes rice cultivation difficult but is great for growing buckwheat. The whisky drinker or adventurous vodka drinker looking to branch out will find comfort in the grain and lemon notes found in this shōchū.

- GI: None at this time.

kokutō | BLACK SUGAR

Kokutō shōchū may only be produced in the Amami Islands of Kagoshima prefecture. While it does not have a GI as of yet, the category is protected by the NTA's Liquor Tax Act. Kokutō translates to black (or brown) sugar, the result of cooking down sugarcane juice. In the glass, it carries a distinct brown sugar note along with grassy and citric aromatics from the kōji, kind of like an agricole rum or Jamaican pot still rum.

- GI: Amami (technically not yet a GI).

kasutori | SAKÉ LEES

Around 33 percent of the ingredients that go into making saké are left as saké kasu (lees). The white cake-like pieces are ripe with active yeasts and enzymes. Saké kasu is used in beauty products, pickles, bread, butter, amazaké, and so much more. It may also be distilled to make a form of honkaku shōchū called kasutori shōchū. The resulting shōchū lees are sometimes then used to fertilize rice fields, for making kasutori shōchū. This is a prime example of the Japanese concept of mottainai, a sentiment that expresses regret over waste and finds ways to not only reduce, reuse, recycle, but to respect the environment as well. The rice is sown and harvested, fermented, brewed, and pressed. The saké lees are distilled, and then the shōchū lees go back to the earth to fertilize the soil for the next round of rice. There are two types of kasutori shōchū: seichō kasutori shōchū and ginjō kasutori shōchū. The first has a bitter flavor profile due to the inclusion of rice hulls, which help the fermentation process. The second is softer, made by adding yeast and water to ginjō saké lees and re-fermenting them. The profile is light and fruity like its namesake, ginjō-shu, with a crisp finish. Perfect for nihonshu drinkers.

- GI: None at this time.

awamori | THAI RICE AND BLACK KŌJI

Awamori is a type of shōchū distinct to Okinawa, with an Appellation of Origin Status by the World Trade Organization. Made from Thai rice and black kōji, awamori only goes through one fermentation process before distillation, which sets it apart from other forms of shōchū and contributes a deep and distinct flavor profile akin to apples, bananas, and mushrooms.

- GI: Awagamori. Fermented, distilled, stored, and bottled in Okinawa.

uisukī

WHISKY

In 1853, U.S. Navy Commodore Matthew C. Perry brought whisky to Japan during his attempts to open the country up to the West. This pivotal introduction inspired an industrious few to try their hand at distilling the spirit, but the attempts yielded nothing like the whisky Japan is celebrated for today. The first whisky distilling license in Japan was registered with Eigashima Distillery in Hyogo prefecture in 1919, but the distillery did not produce any whisky until much later, which is probably why most modern accounts of Japanese whisky history begin with the intertwined origins of Suntory and Nikka.

In the early 1900s, Masataka Taketsuru, the son of saké brewers, was working for Kiichiro Iwai of Settsu Shuzō, the distillery now known as Mars Hombo Shuzō. The president of the company, Abe Kihei, sent Taketsuru to Scotland in 1918, where he studied English and chemistry at the University of Glasgow and fell in love with and married a woman named Rita Cowen. Taketsuru also worked short stints at several Scotch distilleries, namely Longmorn in Speyside and Hazelburn in Campbeltown. When he and Rita returned to Japan, his employer was no longer able to invest in whisky production, so he signed a ten-year contract with Kotobukiya holdings, under ownership of Shinjiro Torii, to open what is now Suntory's Yamazaki Distillery in Kyoto, in 1923.

The first whisky produced by Taketsuru at Yamazaki Distillery was bold and peaty—the style of whisky Taketsuru fell in love with in Scotland. But the peat was too aggressive for the Japanese market. Differences in opinion and vision led to Taketsuru's eventual demotion from distillery manager to brewery manager for the remainder of his contract. Torii took over production, taking the brand in a more delicate direction.

During this time, Rita was working as an English and music teacher. Through her grace and industriousness, she won over investors for her husband to open a distillery in his location of choice: Hokkaido. Taketsuru founded the Dai Nippon Kaju Kabushiki Kaisha (The Great Japanese Juice Company) in Yoichi in 1934. He sold apple juice products until it was time to release his first bottling of whisky in 1940. Dai Nippon Kaju was abbreviated to Nikka, and with that, the two largest producers of Japanese whisky set their own distinct courses and the stage for others to follow.

Here are a few others to know:

- *Hombo Shuzō* has returned as a force to be reckoned with after nearly giving up on distilling whisky a few times over the years. Now, they are creating incomparable single malts and blends by utilizing aging facilities in their mountain distillery Mars Shinshu of Nagano as well as their new Tsunuki Distillery and the Yakushima aging cellar in Kyūshū.

- Master distiller Ichiro Akuto of *Venture Whisky* produces stunning single malts and blends from his curated collection of barrels in Chichibu in Saitama prefecture. He has been instrumental in pushing for transparency in production practices and is a driving force in upholding the quality and spirit of Japanese whisky.

- *Eigashima Distillery* started making whisky in the 1960s and have since come out with incredible blends for mixing and outstanding single malts for sipping. Within their brand of Akashi is a five-year-old single malt in ex-reposado tequila barrels that is probably the wildest I have tasted.

- *Akkeshi Distillery*, which joins Nikka's Yoichi Distillery in Hokkaidō, is intent on creating whiskies that demonstrate the terroir of the region, from locally grown barley and harvested peat to barrels made of local mizunara oak for aging.

Whisky drinkers in Japan tend to enjoy styles from around the world, so it is very common to find bottlings from Scotland, Ireland, America, and beyond on backbars and stowed in freezers for highballs. While whiskies of both domestic and foreign origins are often enjoyed served neat, on ice, and in the form of highballs—when a cocktail is ordered, it is the global brands that play the starring role in drinks like the old fashioned, Manhattan, and whiskey sour. This is the standard—the classic—way to make these cocktails, as written in the cocktail books and passed down from master bartender to apprentice.

The crisp, clean character of blended Japanese whisky comes through best in nuanced highballs, like the Kumiko Highball (page 107) or Ringo Highball (page 216), where the spirit sings together with an apple-forward aperitif. Japanese whisky also inspires old fashioneds, like the Umé Old Fashioned (page 112) or Yaki-imo Old Fashioned (page 255).

uokka

VODKA

A clear, unaged spirit made from practically any fruit, grain, or vegetable that has enough fermentable sugars to convert into alcohol (usually grains like wheat or rye, potatoes, and sugar beets), vodka has historically been a small and underdeveloped market in Japan, but that is changing as many distillers start to produce modern versions of the spirit. Now, signs are pointing to a vodka renaissance as the category experienced double-digit growth in 2019.

For the most part, it is our favorite whisky distilleries that have led the charge, making unique vodkas with clear Japanese sentiment. Both Suntory and Nikka experimented with vodka production in the '50s and '60s, respectively, but many of the early experiments did not take off and were subsequently discontinued.

Only within the last few years have notable bottlings emerged—in 2018, Suntory introduced Haku as a vodka for craft spirit enthusiasts and cocktail makers. It is a rice-based spirit fermented with kōji before it is distilled, and filtered through bamboo charcoal. It is very light and clean—characteristics that align squarely with the craftsmanship seen in Suntory's whiskies.

Nikka Coffey vodka was released to the market in 2017, prized because the distillate runs through a Coffey still, which allows for more flavor retention of the raw materials. The base is a blend of two separate distillates—one of corn and one of barley—the former adding a light sweetness, whereas the barley malt brings a deep round texture with hints of chocolate to the spirit. The final blend is then filtered through white birch charcoal. At 40% ABV, it is a luscious vodka that reflects Nikka's similarly calculated approach to whisky making.

There are a few other Japanese vodkas available on the market today, such as Okuhida rice vodka, a high-proof spirit made in the Gifu prefecture that is said to have been gifted to Vladimir Putin at the G8 summit in 2006, and the Wa Premium craft vodka made in Mito City with saké as the base. Kissui vodka, made by Takara Shuzō in Kyōto, is a rice vodka as well, and was the first Japanese vodka sold in America in 2007. While vodka is defined as an odorless, tasteless distillate, I admire how Japanese distillers are using rice to tie the spirit to Japan and to showcase the qualities of the base ingredient. There is a moment when a neutral spirit becomes a *nuanced* spirit, and I think that Japanese vodkas firmly encapsulate that sentiment.

Vodka has always had a home in Japanese cocktails, and I specifically like working with Japanese vodka when mixing certain drinks because of the excellent weight it carries. Try Nikka Coffey vodka in the Silken Chocolate Martini (page 116), which I invented based on the vodka's inherent chocolatey profile. With crème de cacao, Pineau des Charentes, Cocchi Americano Rosa, and a mint garnish, it's a simple but sophisticated take on the '90s classic. On the softer side of the spectrum, the crystal-clean flavors of Suntory Haku vodka harmonize with strawberry syrup, lemon, and dry vermouth in the Ichigo Sour (page 127), a frothy egg white cocktail with fresh strawberries.

jin

GIN

A spirit with roots that can be traced back to thirteenth-century Dutch texts (where it was cited for its medicinal properties), gin has been distilled in Japan for almost an entire century. Some of the country's earliest commercial options were not much to write home about—simple and affordable London dry styles with straightforward botanical profiles. It wasn't until more recently that the botanical-

JAPANESE GIN BOTANICALS TO KNOW

Gin has evolved into a spirit that can express a distinct sense of place, thanks to the way distillers around the world have started incorporating local botanicals in their base spirits. These are some of the most common botanicals used to make modern Japanese gins.

SANSHŌ

While cardamom is the spice of choice in many global gins, Japanese distillers look to the sanshō tree for a piquant component. Though technically in the citrus family, the tree produces green "berries," or peppercorns as they are often called, which have a Meyer lemon quality that evolves into an electric pepperiness. In gin, they bring a citrusy flavor to the bouquet. The leaves, called kinomé, are also sometimes incorporated for roundness and spicy aromatics.

GREEN TEA

It is natural and fitting that one of Japan's most precious natural resources has found a home in Japanese gins. Several international producers have tinkered with green tea in the botanical profile, but when Japanese distillers select green tea for their gins (most commonly Gyokuro and sencha), a more significant harmony is achieved between the sense of place and the spirit.

SAKURA LEAVES AND BLOSSOMS

Floral elements like sakura blossoms impart a perfumed note as one might expect, but the leaves' contribution is more surprising, imbuing the gin with a spiced, woodsy element akin to allspice and cinnamon.

HINOKI

Cypress is a wood historically used to build Japanese shrines, temples, and ryokan (traditional Japanese inns) in the Kyōto area. The wood is also used to construct the small boxes used for measuring rice and as a cup for drinking saké, so it is natural that distillers are reaching for cypress wood chips to bring a new dimension to Japanese gin. The elegant ingredient has surprisingly bright aromatics thanks to a high level of resin in the grain.

YUZU

Lemon and orange citrus peels are par for the course in traditional gins, but in Japan it is natural to see the country's most famous citrus fruit used instead. Yuzu brings a nuanced and complex personality to gin, with a flavor landing somewhere between a tart tangerine and lemon, plus hints of orange blossom.

SHISO

This Japanese herb bears a unique flavor; you have to taste it to really know it. In gin, shiso brings a rich mintiness and a warming cinnamon-spice quality. (For more information on shiso, see page 193.)

laced liquor found its footing in Japan and subsequently made waves of interest around the rest of the world.

Now, a growing crop of Japanese gins are available on the market, most of which use local ingredients to distinguish their style from other international gins, setting the stage for a distinctly indigenous flavor profile. The Kyōto Distillery is the first gin-focused distillery in Japan. They use a rice distillate for the base in addition to water sourced from nearby saké brewery Tsuki no Katsura. Their flagship Ki No Bi dry gin features yuzu, hinoki (cypress), bamboo leaves, gyokuro (shade-grown green tea), ginger, red shiso leaf, kinomé (the leaves of the sanshō tree), and sanshō berries, in addition to traditional gin botanicals such as juniper, lemon peel, and orris root. Other Kyōto Distillery gin offerings include a Navy Strength variety, an Old Tom gin made with Okinawa black sugar, and a green tea–based gin made with gyokuro and tencha leaves, the latter being the leaves that are ground into matcha.

Other gin producers also speak to a Japanese sense of place through their botanical profiles. The nuanced Suntory Roku gin features fourteen botanicals, six of which are Japanese, including yuzu zest, sanshō, and sakura leaves and flowers, along with two types of tea: gyokuro and sencha. Nikka Coffey gin is a bold explosion of flavors from sanshō berries and a robust complement of Japanese citrus like yuzu, kabosu, amanatsu, and shīkuwāsā, in addition to imported classic gin botanicals like juniper, coriander, lemon zest, orange zest, and angelica. The final ingredient, apple juice, is a nod to Nikka's history as the Dai Nippon Kajū Kabushiki Gaisha, or the Great Japanese Juice Company, when they sold apple juice as they waited to release their first bottling of whisky in 1940.

Sakurao Distillery in Hiroshima makes a dry gin flavored with bitter orange called daidai, with navel orange, sweet summer orange, yuzu, hinoki (cypress), red shiso, green tea, and ginger. The Sakurao Limited Edition gin plays with Japanese varieties of spicebush and juniper, sakura petals, kinomé (sanshō leaves), oyster shells, wasabi, and green shiso. The inclusion of oyster shells imparts an enjoyable salinity to the gin and the refreshing spice of the wasabi is a welcome note, melding well with the kinomé.

Beyond incorporating native botanicals, some distilleries have made gins with deeper ties to Japan by using shōchū or rice distillates as the base. Komasa gin, which comes in two versions (one infused with small fragrant oranges called *Sakurajima komikan*, and another starring hōjicha, a roasted green tea) employs honkaku shōchū as the foundation, as does Wa Bi Gin, which is produced just up the road from the Kagoshima distillery at Hombo Shuzō (the makers of Mars Whisky). Rice shōchū comes into the picture with barrel-aged Okayama Craft Gin from historic saké brewery Miyashita Shuzō, while sweet potato shōchū appears in Kyoya Shuzō Premium Yuzugin from Miyazaki. Another shōchū-based favorite, JuJu gin, is made at the Hamada Distillery in Kagoshima, which was founded in 1868. The rice shōchū base provides a supple canvas for bright cardamom, yuzu, and comforting cinnamon. I drink this in an extra-dry martini or topped off with club soda.

The hyperlocal approach to the category means many of these inventive versions of gin taste quite distinctive. Especially ones like Masahiro Okinawa gin, which features awamori, the regional spirit, as the base. Made with shīkuwāsā (Okinawa citrus), juniper, guava leaves, Japanese long pepper, roselle hibiscus, and Okinawan bitter melon, it is a true taste of the island.

As Japanese bartenders love to showcase the finesse of their craft through classic drinks like the martini and gin and tonic, the juniper-based spirit has long been a star of the Japanese cocktail bar. International brands such as Gordon's and Tanqueray still remain as reliable standbys, but in more contemporary places you will see Japanese-made gin also finding a home. Currently, a small but growing number of Japanese gins are available in America. Each one brings a unique personality to cocktails like the Vesper (page 265), White Negroni (page 248), Kinmokusei Cocktail (page 242), or the Sanshō Grasshopper (page 292).

ramu

RUM

Rum might be the last spirit people think of when considering Japanese distillation history, but reports date production back to the seventeenth century. Today, most Japanese rum production remains centered in the southernmost prefecture of Okinawa, where an abundance of sugarcane grows. There, about half a dozen rum makers use native species of sugarcane to produce the spirit.

Helios Distillery has been distilling rum since 1961 on the main island of Okinawa (though the distillery operated under the name Taiyou Distillery until 1969); today, the brand releases aged rums under the brand name Teeda. Ie Rum Santa Maria, made on Ie Island, comes in both aged and unaged versions—the former rests in ex-Nikka whisky barrels. There is also a smaller concentration of rum production on the island of Minamidaitōjima, where Yuko Kinjo produces several products at Grace Rum under the label of Cor Cor. Each one is made using desalinated ocean water and is distilled only once to retain as much of the personality of the cane as possible. This means each expression has a distinct individuality and range of exciting, sweet notes that deliver a drinking experience that is hard to forget.

Nine Leaves is another interesting case in the world of Japanese rum. The founder and master distiller Yoshiharu Takeuchi turned his attention away from the automotive parts industry for the chance to showcase monozukuri, or craftmanship, within another realm. Feeling drawn to the scientific nature of distillation, he now makes rum using kokutō (black sugar) from the Okinawa archipelago and soft water from Shiga, his home and the location of the distillery. Named Nine Leaves after the nine bamboo leaves that mark his family crest,

Takeuchi-san makes several expressions: an unaged version, an aged variety called Angel's Half that utilizes American oak barrels, and other experimental aged releases using barrels previously employed to make bourbon, sherry, and Cabernet Sauvignon from California.

As is the case with rhum agricole from Martinique, many of the Japanese rums made from fresh-pressed sugarcane leap from the bottle with the grassy and vegetal flavors of the terroir. With that comes a host of other unique characteristics—each pour from the bottle is like another wave of aromatic flair. I have tasted some with flavors that range from briny kalamata olives and overripe melon to dried grass dusted with cinnamon. This diversity also makes Japanese rum a good candidate for cocktail making. Most brands are hard to find in the United States right now since they are made in such small batches, but if you do pick up a bottle, I recommend bookmarking it for your favorite rum cocktails (and especially ones that call for rhum agricole). To get started, try the Kamakiri (page 179) if you can find a bottle of the Cor Cor Red label—its tropical notes make the subtle ginger shōchū and ginger beer sing bright.

rikyūru

LIQUEURS

FRUIT LIQUEURS

In Japan, we take care to preserve fruits and vegetables that aren't consumed during peak ripeness so they do not go to waste and may be enjoyed year-round. One way to do this is by making "fruit alcohol," called *kajitsu-shu.* You can infuse alcohol with almost any fruit (think kumquats, quince, Japanese pear, tomato, and beyond) and rock sugar to create a liqueur, but there are a few that are more commonly used than others, such as mikan and yuzu, and perhaps the most popular, umé.

The dense and petite umé is often called a Japanese plum, but that is technically not correct as umé are their own type of stone fruit, related more closely to apricots. Unlike both plums and apricots, umé are not readily edible straight from the tree. When preserved with rock sugar and shōchū or neutral spirits, the liqueur umé-shu materializes. Other uses of the fruit include the traditional method of pickling in salt with red shiso to make uméboshi (salt-cured umé), or layering with rock sugar and vinegar to make umé-su. Umé-su is used primarily as a nonalcoholic base for a refreshing umé soda or in more complex spiritfrees like the Azalea (page 301).

These days, some companies also make commercial umé-shu—Suntory produces a Yamazaki whisky cask-aged version that is rich and flavorful. Meiri Shurui makes an umé-shu named after a garden of thousands of umé trees (called

Mito no Kairakuen) that is fortified with brandy, sweetened with honey, and aged for five years. Akashi-Tai, a historic saké brewery in the Hyogo prefecture, produces a variety that uses ginjō saké made from Yamadanishiki rice as the base, which highlights the fruity notes of the umé.

Izakaya, small mom and pop restaurants, and cocktail bars usually have their own housemade brew going every summer for use in simple highballs, too. Every place tends to have a somewhat different recipe from the next, so hopping from bar to bar to taste can be a delicious adventure. The layers of flavor found in the liqueur lends itself to mixing in cocktails as well. With traces of honeyed stone fruit, it is a natural match alongside Japanese whisky in drinks like the Umé Old Fashioned (page 112) or paired with lemongrass shōchū in the Umé Shōchū Sour (page 185).

DRINKING UMÉ-SU AND UMÉ-SHU

Making umé-su was always an all-hands-on-deck situation as my brothers and I would help my parents with the harvest. Sometimes we'd have to lean out of the second-floor window with long pruning shears to reach the last fruits clinging to the tallest branches of the tree. It was a rewarding annual family project because for as much labor that goes into the harvesting, cleaning, and preparation of the fruit, the anticipation of and pleasure from the final result was even greater.

Depending on the prevailing mood of the day, we'd drink it with either club soda, still water, mugi-cha (barley tea), or ryoku-cha (a type of green tea). The sweetness of the umé-su helps balance the roasted quality of the barley, whereas the more subdued elements of the umé-su resonate in the green tea. Cold-brew sencha is a standout pairing because the tropical passion fruit notes of the tea sparkle and send the tart umé into somewhat floral territory. This flexible template is a great companion for any hot summer day, especially since you can also bring in the alcoholic umé-shu for a spirited version of the drink. Choose your own adventure! *Serves one*

1½ ounces Umé-su (page 316) or Umé-shu (page 317) for an alcoholic version

4 to 5 ounces club soda, Cold-Brew Sencha (page 320) or Chilled Mugi-cha (page 320)

In a highball glass, combine the umé-su or umé-shu, your mixer of choice, and ice.

OTHER LIQUEURS

Beyond traditional fruit liqueurs, distillers and saké brewers also find inspiration in a wide range of other ingredients to turn into lush concoctions. From seasonal ones like shiso, matcha, sakura leaves and blossoms, and ginger, to traditional Japanese ingredients like chestnut, adzuki beans, and mugwort—everything is fair game. One particular favorite is yogurt liqueur. With offerings coming from Suntory and many other craft producers located in areas known for their dairy, each of these liqueurs has its own unique level of creaminess, sweetness, and tang. They are more commonly sipped on their own, or with soda for a quick and easy cocktail.

An interesting liqueur case study comes from Kamiya Bar, which was one of the first bars to open in Tōkyō, in Asakusa, in 1880. There, owner Denbei Kamiya launched a beverage called Denki Bran—some call it a cocktail, others call it a liqueur, but it is difficult to define because it crosses categories with a secret blend that includes brandy, gin, wine, Curaçao, and herbs. Kamiya Bar is still in operation to this day, and you can find bottles of Denki Bran in most liquor stores in Tōkyō as it has developed quite the cult following. The flavor profile is floral, pungent with woodsy herbs like rosemary and sage, sweet like caramel—and it burns like fire. Historically, the wild concoction was sipped next to a beer, and today that remains largely the case.

Another peculiar category can be found within the shōchū realm: Certain producers rely on the government's interpretation of liqueur as a way to sell their aged shōchū without stripping away any of the color. Gokujō Tsutsumi, for example, is a rice shōchū from Kumamoto rested in ex-sherry barrels for twelve years. The mahogany-hued distillate is too dark to qualify to be a shōchū, so the distiller adds a neutral dietary fiber, which allows the product to be labeled and sold as a liqueur. It bears the aroma of apricots, raisins, and vanilla enveloped by a round sweetness derived from the rice and sherry cask age. Despite being called a liqueur, there is no sugar added to this spirit, and in the United States it is sold as a sherry cask-aged shōchū.

PART II

RECIPES

I bought my first Moleskine notebook in college. Working as a barback in Ithaca, New York, I filled its crisp, clean pages with classic recipes and notes about bar regulars so I would remember every measured detail. In true Japanese fashion, I knew I had to master the classics first—the old fashioned, the Manhattan, the martini—but as I became more comfortable with those cornerstones of cocktail history, I started writing out ideas for my own recipes. Mostly, variations on classics incorporating ingredients I missed from Japan. This gave me comfort while living so many miles away from home, and eventually I realized this differentiated my style from other bartenders in America.

I have carried that sensibility with me since—my style of cocktail-making is Japanese in nature in that it bridges the gap between innovation and tradition. The interplay of old and new, sewn together deftly and with respect, is truly emblematic of the way cocktails are made throughout Japan today as modern bartenders build upon the foundation set by previous generations.

That's also the spirit I set out to capture with the cocktail recipes in this chapter. Here, you will find cocktails born of a wide range of inspirations, but all tied back to Japanese cocktail culture in one way or another. From ingredients drawn from my flavor memories growing up, to my interpretations of cocktails that have roots in Japanese bars and riffs on beloved classics, it is a collection of bespoke recipes that speak directly to the spirit of Japan.

I also include nonalcoholic drink recipes called "spiritfrees." Many people in Japan completely abstain from drinking alcohol, so one can always find delicious alcohol-free drinks in cafés, bars, and even vending machines there. American bars do not always have complex and delicious options, so I made it one of my missions to always develop sophisticated spiritfrees for adult palates. These are not merely zero-proof versions of existing cocktails, because by only subtracting the alcohol you are often left with a drink that is lacking or completely out of balance. Instead, I build on ideas from scratch, layering ingredients with inspiration coming from times and places rather than cocktails. These are for days when you are not in the mood to drink alcohol, or for friends who abstain regularly. I hope you find as much joy in these recipes as you do in the spirited ones.

To organize the recipes, I use the seasonal approach as an opportunity to pause and appreciate what's happening in nature around us. As I mentioned before, the Japanese calendar is broken into twenty-four specific microseasons called sekki, which transition nearly every two weeks to mark celestial events, nature's metamorphosis, and the comings and goings of flora and fauna. The specific dates for each microseason are approximate and ever-changing, so they are not noted here. Year to year, the climate shifts, but the heart of the sekki remains.

Follow your own path with these recipes and I hope that you will feel a little closer to Japan with each sip.

MIXING TIPS

If you want to practice the Japanese way of bartending and making drinks, remember that every minute decision made will have an impact on the flavor and personality of the finished cocktail. From chilling your glassware ahead of time to making sure your citrus is as fresh as possible, here are some of my learnings to keep in mind when embarking on the journey:

•

Only work with fresh citrus. Uncut citrus should stay fresh at room temperature for a week or two, or 3 to 4 weeks if stored in the refrigerator. Squeeze to order if you're making drinks for yourself or friends at home. If you are juicing in advance for a party or bar program, remember to agitate the juice before pouring into a cocktail, as fresh juice is prone to separate.

•

For every drink, start by chilling the glassware you intend to use. In most cases, this means filling a coupe or tumbler with ice and setting the glass aside, giving it time to frost while you shake or stir. (If you have room in the freezer for glasses, all the better.) Make sure you discard accumulated water from the ice used for chilling, or refresh the ice completely so the watery ice doesn't get in the way of the perfect balance.

•

Always pour bottles with the label facing out toward the guest, and wipe the mouth of the bottle right after pouring. This is to minimize the chance of getting the bottle sticky and the label stained from wayward drips.

•

When working with large pieces of ice, give them a moment to temper before handling to chip or carve, and before pouring your cocktail or spirit over the ice. Otherwise it will shatter from the core, like a broken mirror, cutting a harsh line through the piece that was once whole.

•

When working with citrus garnishes, I present two options: peels and manicured twists. A peel is a swath or disk cut from the fruit using a blade used only for the essential oils in the zest to garnish a cocktail with aromatics. A twist is a peel that is cut and maneuvered in a way that ornaments the glass. I call these garnishes "manicured" to indicate that the citrus has had its edges trimmed. During this process, many of the essential oils from the peel are expressed onto the cutting board, so I usually incorporate a second peel from the parts of the fruit with odd bumps or blemishes to express oils over the top of a cocktail, then discard. As with everything, there are exceptions to the rule: with lime garnishes, I find the zest to be overpowering so I do not use a secondary peel in that case.

•

Use a match for the flamed citrus peel called for in some cocktails. You don't want the aromas and flavor of lighter fluid to tarnish the cocktail. Strike a match (away from the cocktail and ice bin) and let it settle for a moment so the sulfur aromas evaporate. Then, holding the peel sideways over the top of the drink, pinch the peel slightly so it sprays oils through the top of the flame and over the drink.

SPRING

The two towers that define Suntory's Hakushu distillery rise out of the ambrosial forests of Mt. Kaikomagatake like a stoic fortress emerging from a rolling sea of trees. One spring my husband, Sammy, and I took the train there from Tōkyō—it was a cool and rainy day, and the air was so fresh and clean I could almost smell the grass growing. When we arrived, the distillery grounds were a sanctuary of blooming sakura blossoms, frilly and soft against the dark green and brown backdrop. It was toward the end of the season, so many of the petals had washed away already, but some still clung delicately to the branches, unwilling to float away.

When we stepped into the aging facility, where rows of sleeping wood barrels cradled young whisky into maturity, the temperature dipped a few degrees—a sensation matched by the intense aromas of the angel's share hanging in the air. Like diving too quickly into a dram, the initial heady shock of the redolence eventually melted into my bones like a hug. When I walked outside again, I was quickly reminded of how fresh the mountain air is, almost like I'd been holding my breath all winter. I inhaled deeply.

Spring is inherently full of new beginnings as the snow starts to melt and warm rains arrive. From the serene umé blossoms and darling pink sakura to golden daffodils and fragrant wisteria, the season is an abundance of flowers and new life. Saké brewers release the fresh nectar they've been laboring over all winter, which we enjoy paired with seasonal delicacies from the land and the sea. We celebrate the first tea harvests and gather young bitter greens, tossing them in salads with light vinaigrettes or using them in simple sautéed dishes. As a bartender, spring is such an invigorating time because it pulls me out of bed earlier and earlier every day. It is inspiring to see fresh herbs and produce arrive in markets after so many months of waiting—a swath of inspiration for cocktail making.

THE MICROSEASONS OF SPRING

RISSHUN | *spring begins*

Kumiko Highball
Umé Old Fashioned
Smoked Umé Margarita
Silken Chocolate Martini

SHUNBUN | *spring equinox*

Spiritfree: Shiozakura Highball
Sakura Collins
Cherry Blossom Cocktail
Sakurazuké Martini
Delicate Refusal

USUI | *snowfall turns to rain*

Hishimochi Bitters and Soda
Saké and Sonic
Rose Manhattan

SEIMEI | *pure sunlight*

Momosé Martini
Kinomé Martini
Kumiko Bloody Mary

KEICHITSU | *insects awaken*

Ichigo Sour
Kiss of Fire
Washitsu

KOKUU | *nurturing rains*

Gimlet
Ryūkyū Gimlet
Ryokucha-Hi
Wisteria Cocktail

risshun

SPRING BEGINS

east wind melts the ice, nightingales start
singing in the mountains, fish emerge

As spring starts to awaken, a warm wind blows in from the east and
the ice starts to melt. A dampness coats the grass and the air sits
in anticipation as plants start to grow. The first umé trees bloom.
Standing stark against a dead brown landscape, these cheerful pops of
fuchsia and white flowers represent resilience and strength, and serve
as a harbinger for the sweet-tart fruits that will follow in the summer.
Soon there will be first-harvest teas, but in the meantime we drink lots
of hot hōjicha and bancha, the end-of-harvest stem tea that offers a
sweet taste of dried earth.

KUMIKO HIGHBALL

In its most elemental form, the humble highball is a combination of spirit and soda, but in Japan, when we say highball, we almost always mean *whisky* and soda. A study in simplicity and a true labor of love, it is perhaps the most iconic Japanese "cocktail" of all time, with an interesting history that traces back to the rise of whisky in Japan.

Many say the highball was invented in the 1920s as a way for people to better enjoy whisky with food, but the drink really rose in nationwide popularity after WWII when Suntory founder Shinjirō Torii opened up Torys bars in Tōkyō and Ōsaka (Torys was the name of a whisky that launched in 1946). At the time, Torii wanted to showcase how highballs were as effortless to drink as beer, and because they were also affordable (a notable appeal in postwar times) this plan worked, helping lift the drink to countrywide fame.

When the whisky market started to decline in the '80s and '90s, the highball went underground for several decades, until in the last decade or so when Suntory started to promote the drink again. Their calibrated highball machines made it even easier for bars around the world to serve the drink, and when these came over to America within the last five years, bartenders took to them like moths to a flame.

Today, highballs remain pure and simple, and every kind of bar in Japan serves them, from casual izakaya to fancy cocktail bars; there are even canned versions that can be found in grocery stores, convenience stores, and vending machines! The type of whisky featured will vary by place, but as a general rule, highballs made with cheaper whiskies are treated with no less respect than those made with an expensive single malt, because it is a drink for every occasion and can be dressed up or down accordingly. I have derived as much joy and tasty delight from a Dewar's and soda as I have from a rare Japanese single malt highball. One thing that does unite most bars, though, is that they store bottles of whisky in the freezer for the drink because when the ice-cold spirit meets club soda and ice, the bristling chill illuminates the refreshing quality of the effervescent highball.

With the whisky left to personal taste, the real trick to making a great highball starts with finding the perfect ratio of whisky to mixer. For this you have to take the proof into consideration: If you're choosing 40% ABV (80 proof) whisky versus cask-strength (over 100 proof), the former will be more prone to overdilution, so keep in mind that not all highballs follow the same ratio of spirit to mixer. For the standard "house" highball at Kumiko, I use a 5:1 ratio of club soda (we do a 50:50 split of Fever-Tree and Q Mixers) to Suntory Toki whisky. Q Mixers club soda has an intense salinity to it which draws out the flavors of the whisky, and sharp bubbles which invigorate the drink as a whole. Fever-Tree club soda is softer and delicate, providing a second layer of carbonation for a multi-textural highball.

Before it became scarce, the Yamazaki 12-Year was my favorite whisky to suggest to first-time Japanese whisky highball drinkers. The sherry notes emerge in a soothing way when mixed with club soda. For myself, I like to pour a Hakushu 12-Year highball for its green yet still somewhat peated flavors. Many people think of the highball as refreshing and zippy, but with a single malt whisky it became a beautiful brooding combination. I wanted to re-create similar flavors for the first seasonal highball at Kumiko, so as an homage to the well-matured sherry-heavy whiskies that are becoming less and less available, I made a highball that paired blended Japanese whisky and oloroso sherry. The round richness of a VOS (*vinum optimum signatum*, a Latin term meaning "known as the best wine," or in colloquial English, "very old sherry") oloroso sherry brings a stroke of supple sophistication to the bright and bubbly drink. *Serves one*

1½ ounces chilled Japanese whisky

Club soda, to top

1 barspoon oloroso sherry (such as a Valdespino Don Gonzalo oloroso VOS)

In a chilled highball glass, add two pieces of ice large enough to fill the glass from top to bottom. Pour chilled whisky from the freezer into the glass. Add club soda, and gently nuzzle the ice upward with a barspoon to incorporate. Then drizzle the sherry over the top of the ice. This allows the sherry to layer on top of the drink, which makes the lovely aromas one of the first things you notice. No garnish.

HIGHBALL: THE MOMOSÉ METHOD

Making a memorable highball can be a labor of love. Because it is such a simple drink, there are a million tiny things you can do to make the most vibrant version of the drink possible. Here's how I assemble my best highball:

1.   Use a stylish highball glass, like the Compact series sold by Kimura Glass, a company crafting glassware in Tōkyō since 1910. The whisper-thin glass emphasizes the chill of the cocktail.

2.   Before you start making the drink, chill the club soda in the refrigerator and the whisky of choice in the freezer so they get perfectly cold.

3.   When ready, fill the glass with ice, stirring a couple times for a frosty chill. Pour off the ice and water and replace with two long rectangular pieces of ice. (If you do not have large pieces of ice, fill the glass three-quarters of the way with cubed ice, stirring a couple times to chill and melt away sharp edges. Strain the melted water from the glass, leaving the ice in.)

4.   Pour the whisky into the glass over the fresh ice. At this point, the drink calls for a couple stirs to introduce the spirit to the ice for chill and to even out any dilution. If you are mixing with whisky from the freezer, you do not need a long stir. Creating a chilled canvas is critical at this stage, as the colder the glass and the spirit, the better the club soda will retain its carbonation.

5.   Pour the club soda precisely and deftly into your chilled mixture, avoiding the ice and even the side of the glass if you can, because carbonated mixers only have so much sparkle to share. If you were to pour over the ice or alongside the edges of the glass, you are giving up effervescence before it has the chance to mingle with the spirit.

6.   Integrate the sparkling mixer and the spirit by using a barspoon to gently nuzzle the ice upward. This is not a traditional stir, but rather a small lift of the ice so it creates a vortex in the bottom of the glass where the spirit and mixer may socialize without interruption. You don't want to needlessly agitate the drink, so use a steady and gentle touch to guide the ice back downward and gingerly extract the barspoon.

7.   If you are building with smaller pieces of ice, at this point, the highball may need a final splash of sparkling water or a couple of additional pieces of ice so that the glass is satisfyingly filled from the base to the lip.

8.   If you prefer a garnish, add one here before serving. In Japan it is common to see the oils of a lemon cast over a highball, adding a unique contrast to the spirit. Even some of the canned whisky highballs are made with lemon essence to echo the stimulating combination. At Suntory's Hakushu distillery they suggest a mint sprig as garnish to the Hakushu 12-Year highball, a practice I have adopted at Kumiko. The mint plays up the green notes in the lightly peated whisky. Other than the mint sprig, I am a purist when it comes to a highball, and though I will happily garnish upon request, I prefer to keep the drink pure and simple: whisky and soda.

UMÉ OLD FASHIONED

The noble umé trees will not bear fruit until later in the year, but seeing the pink and white flowers blossom underneath late winter's cloak of snow always makes me crave a dose of Umé-shu (page 317). Because preservation techniques are so commonly embraced in Japan, most people will have a jar from the previous year's batch on hand in the spring, so it is not uncommon to see the liqueur consumed year-round. In this variation on the old fashioned, invented in homage to umé, the succulent flavors of umé-shu are amplified with the addition of the umé-flavored whisky from Eigashima Distillery. Powerful like the tree, but fragrant and bright like the flowers, the cocktail tastes of full-bodied malts, honey, and sweet stone fruit. *Serves one*

2 dashes Peychaud's bitters

1½ ounces Akashi Umé whisky

1 ounce Nikka Miyagikyo Single Malt Japanese whisky

¼ ounce Umé-shu (page 317)

¼ ounce Rich Honey Syrup (page 317)

1 barspoon Lionel Osmin Estela Tannat-Malbec vin de liqueur

GARNISH Lemon peel

Dash the Peychaud's bitters on top of a large piece of ice in a rocks glass. In a mixing glass, combine the umé whisky, Japanese single-malt whisky, umé-shu, honey syrup, and vin de liqueur. Add ice and stir to chill. Strain into the prepared rocks glass. Express lemon oils over the top of the drink (discard the peel).

SMOKED UMÉ MARGARITA

This margarita-like cocktail toys with expectations in subtle ways as the woodsmoke flavor of mezcal sits under a ribbon of dark sweetness from the umé-shu and oloroso sherry. Those earthy flavors perk up with zesty lime juice and a touch of anise from the Peychaud's bitters. On paper it reads somewhat intimidating with so many rich and brooding ingredients, but thanks to the fresh citrus, it is an evocative glass sprinkled with sunshine, ideal for a chilly spring evening. *Serves one*

1 ounce Fidencio Clásico mezcal

¾ ounce Umé-shu (page 317)

1 ounce El Maestro Sierra Oloroso 15-Year sherry

¾ ounce fresh lime juice

¼ ounce Simple Syrup (page 318)

2 dashes Peychaud's bitters

GARNISH Lemon peel

In a shaker tin, combine the mezcal, umé-shu, oloroso sherry, lime juice, simple syrup, and Peychaud's bitters with ice. Shake to chill, then strain into a chilled rocks glass over cubed ice. Express the oils of the lemon peel over the top of the drink (discard the peel).

SILKEN CHOCOLATE MARTINI

The first chocolate martini I learned to make featured the notoriously rich Godiva chocolate liqueur. At the time I found it delicious, but these days my palate calls for a more minimal and sophisticated approach. Like biting into a chocolate cherry cordial, this variation is lush and nuanced, with subtle vanilla and chocolate notes from crème de cacao meeting the sweet corn and barley flavors of Nikka Coffey vodka, which is softened by the fruity personality of Pineau des Charentes while Cocchi Americano Rosa adds floral rose and raspberry tones. Barley shōchū is another option for the base spirit if you do not have Nikka Coffey vodka or want to explore a variation. *Serves one*

1¼ ounces Nikka Coffey vodka or Mizu Saga Barley shōchū

½ ounce Pineau des Charentes

¼ ounce Tempus Fugit Spirits crème de cacao

¼ ounce Cocchi Americano Rosa

GARNISH Sprig of chocolate mint

In a mixing glass, combine the vodka or shōchū, Pineau des Charentes, crème de cacao, and Cocchi Rosa. Add ice and stir to chill. Strain into a chilled cocktail glass. Garnish with a sprig of chocolate mint.

VALENTINE'S DAY IN JAPAN

Valentine's Day is one of the many Western holidays adopted by Japan, but in true Japanese form our customs surrounding the event differ slightly. On February 14, it is considered customary for women to give a chocolate, not just to a person of romantic interest, but to schoolmates, co-workers, or other colleagues as an expression of gratitude and politeness. A month later, White Day calls for the people who received chocolate on Valentine's Day to reciprocate with flowers or white chocolate.

SNOWFALL TURNS TO RAIN

rain moistens the soil, mist starts to linger,
grass sprouts and trees bud

Saké production traditionally takes place from late fall through the winter, with the first release of shinshu, or new saké, coinciding with the emergence of budding umé trees across the country. It is the freshest you will ever taste—like standing in the kura (saké brewery) and pulling a dram straight from the tank—because the young liquid is also nama (unpasteurized). To mark the occasion, izakaya and bars decorate their doorsteps with a manicured orb of Japanese cedar branches called sugidama. As time goes by the branches fade from an incandescent emerald green to a muted bronze—a visual representation of the life cycle of saké production. In bars, we drink shinshu by the bottle and carafe, often alongside grilled fish or hōrensō no goma miso aé, a lightly blanched spinach dish laced with sesame miso dressing. In more contemporary bars, you might find cocktails mixed to highlight the colors of the season, like the layered pink and green Hishimochi Bitters and Soda (opposite).

HISHIMOCHI BITTERS AND SODA

As the country waits for sakura trees to bloom, a holiday known as Hinamatsuri (which translates to Doll Festival or Girl's Day) offers the first taste of the season's colors. The old tradition is still practiced in some rural areas, marked by floating paper or straw dolls downriver as a way of casting out the evil, sickness, and depression that comes with winter. It is also considered a moment to celebrate girls and hope for their health and happiness for the year (don't worry, boys get a special day, too).

Hishimochi is a rhombus-shaped ceremonial dessert eaten on this day. The wagashi has three layers from top to bottom: pink, white, and green, which represent security, purity, and health or long life, respectively. Inspired by the colorful layers and the intention behind Hinamatsuri, I came up with this bitters and soda variation that is served layered with matcha syrup on the bottom, followed by club soda and a generous dashing of Peychaud's bitters on top. The matcha brings a semisweet, vegetal quality to the drink, which opens up when paired with the club soda, while the layer of bitters on top brings notes of aniseed and baking spices. Whether sipped top-down or mixed up and imbibed as such, the colors are striking to behold and delicious, too! *Serves one; photo on page 121*

¼ teaspoon matcha powder

1 ounce hot water (about 130°F)

¾ ounces Simple Syrup (page 318)

3 to 4 ounces club soda

GARNISH 5 to 7 dashes Peychaud's bitters

Fill a collins glass with ice to chill. Sift the matcha through a tea strainer into a chawan or shallow bowl. Add the hot water and whisk until it becomes a paste. Add the simple syrup and whisk to incorporate. Pour off the chilling ice from the glass. Pour in the matcha syrup mixture and fill the collins glass with crushed ice. Slowly pour the club soda into the glass, without agitating the layers. Garnish with the Peychaud's bitters and serve with a Japanese-style stir stick (madorā) or reusable straw.

MATCHA

Matcha originated in China and was brought over to Japan through cultural liaisons and Buddhist monks. Made from shade-grown tea leaves, they go through a special process of steaming, cooling, and drying. Before the leaves are ground into a fine powder using a stone mill, the tea is called tencha.

In Japan, matcha isn't graded in the same way it is in America. In America, sometimes arbitrary titles are attributed to the tea, though "culinary" grade and "ceremonial" grade are the most common. In Japan, the cost of the matcha is determined by several factors: cultivation, processing, and freshness. First-harvest leaves grown under tented coverings and sold mere weeks after packaging are the most expensive and used for tea ceremonies. That same tea packaged a year later will be sold at a lower price because the tea is not as fresh anymore. Matcha produced from late-harvest and machine-harvested plants is usually immediately labeled for culinary use. The flavor is still nice, but it is more bitter and astringent, and has less of a vibrant emerald hue.

To make a cup of usucha (thin tea), warm water to 150°F. (To make koicha—rich or thick tea, more typical for tea ceremony—the water is to be more hot as less is used and the temperature drops immediately upon contact with the tea. That said, I will be focusing on usucha in this book.) Set out your chashaku (tea scoop) and chakoshi (tea strainer), and warm your chawan (tea bowl) and wipe dry with a clean towel. Sift 2 to 3 chashaku (about ½ teaspoon) of matcha into the chawan. Measure around 2½ ounces of prepared water over the tea and whisk briskly using your wrist, causing the tines of the whisk to dance just below the surface of the water, not necessarily scraping the bottom of the chawan. Whisk for around 30 to 45 seconds, until a rich layer of froth rests over the surface.

When working with matcha in cocktails, I work with it à la minute (batching matcha ahead of time will "cook" it in alcohol and the matcha will oxidize, changing not only its color but its flavor as well). I always use a chakoshi and chashaku to ensure that the matcha is loose and less prone to clumping. It is the last thing I add to the tin before shaking, even after ice, in order to keep it as fresh and lively as possible. Matcha imparts a glorious emerald green shade to a cocktail along with umami notes of the sea and sometimes hints of young mushrooms or even strawberries and cream.

HISHIMOCHI
BITTERS
AND SODA

(page 119)

SAKÉ AND SONIC

Taking inspiration from the aperitivo template of the Americano cocktail (sweet vermouth, Campari, and soda water), a soft rice-based shōchū comes together with Japanese saké to strike a similar low-proof balance in this simple highball. Like the Italian cocktail, this one also drinks like an apéritif, but is fashioned for leisurely sipping over a table of otsumami as the sweet tone of rice is juxtaposed with bitter tonic water. Try a couple of Saké and Sonics alongside dashimaki tamago, spinach with sesame miso dressing, or crisp, young greens to fully welcome spring. *Serves one*

1 ounce Hakutake Ginrei Shiro
  rice shōchū

1 ounce Chiyonosono Shared Promise
  junmai

2 ounces club soda

1 ounce tonic water

In a highball glass, add two large pieces of ice, then pour the shōchū and saké into the glass. Stir gently to chill. Add two parts club soda to one part tonic water. Give the drink a gentle nuzzle by scooping the barspoon under the bottom piece of ice. Keep the ice lifted for a few moments, then lower it gently and serve.

ROSE MANHATTAN

Japanese bartenders do not shy away from using commercial syrups or liqueurs in their cocktails, so in that spirit, this Manhattan variation celebrates spring via a floral liqueur and a grassy cane syrup from Martinique. The qualities of Hibiki Japanese Harmony whisky—a banana-like lightness along with sherry and smoke notes—pair sublimely with the Cocchi Rosa and oloroso sherry. A good fit for fans of the Reverse Manhattan or Adonis cocktail, the bright floral characteristics of the drink swim with flavors of dried roses and wrinkled stone fruit. *Serves one*

1½ ounces Hibiki Japanese Harmony whisky

½ ounce Cocchi Americano Rosa

¾ ounce Valdespino Don Gonzalo oloroso VOS sherry

1 barspoon Petite Canne sugarcane syrup (or Rich Cane Syrup, page 318)

1 barspoon Combier Liqueur de Rose

GARNISH Lime peel

In a mixing glass, combine the whisky, Cocchi Americano Rosa, oloroso sherry, cane syrup, and rose liqueur. Add ice and stir to chill. Strain into a chilled coupe or cocktail glass and gently twist a lime peel over the cocktail, just enough to wake up the oils, and garnish.

keichitsu

INSECTS AWAKEN

hibernating insects surface, first peach blossoms,
caterpillars become butterflies

The soil thaws and with it the insects, amphibians, and other creatures
start to stir. Caterpillars come out of cocoons and morph into
beautiful butterflies—we used to chase them with big, billowing nets in
the fields across from our house. Taking note from the emerging flora
and fauna, humans also start venturing outside after many months of
hibernation, sometimes to pick fresh fruits like strawberries. There
is nothing like the flavor of biting into a berry at peak ripeness, so in
strawberry season people flock to the stores to purchase the sweetest
varieties. If you time your visits just right, you may receive a single
amaou, benihoppé, or other special variety of strawberry as your
otōshi at a cocktail bar.

ICHIGO SOUR

Strawberries find a home in all kinds of delightful confections, on snack trays, and in cocktails this time of the year. Ichigo daifuku (strawberry-stuffed omochi) are a classic Japanese confectionery, typically a shell of chewy rice-based mochi wrapped around a strawberry and sweet red bean paste. To capture this essence in a cocktail, sweet potato shōchū and rice vodka form an earthy but agreeably sweet base. Airy egg whites represent the soft caress of the omochi shell, while herbaceous dry vermouth brings a solid balance to the strawberry syrup. This cocktail is perfect for the Clover Club drinker, or for someone who simply loves egg white cocktails. *Serves one; photo on page 128*

1½ ounces Nishi Shuzō Satsuma Hozan sweet potato shōchū

½ ounce Suntory Haku vodka

½ ounce Strawberry Syrup (page 319)

½ ounce Noilly Prat Original Dry vermouth

½ ounce fresh lemon juice

1 egg white

GARNISH 2 or 3 dashes Peychaud's bitters

In a shaker tin, combine the sweet potato shōchū, vodka, strawberry syrup, dry vermouth, and lemon juice. Add the egg white and shake without ice to emulsify. Add ice and shake briskly to aerate and chill the cocktail. Strain into a chilled cocktail glass. Garnish with artful dashes of Peychaud's bitters.

ICHIGO SOUR

(page 127)

USING EGGS IN COCKTAILS

Whole eggs, egg yolks, and egg whites have always had a home in cocktails, favored for the unique textural qualities they bring to a drink. There are a few things you need to know about working with eggs, though. First, when selecting the right egg for your cocktail, make sure it is as fresh as possible. Salmonella can sometimes live on the shell of the egg, and over time it will move inward through the membrane, so only work with eggs that are fully intact (cracks mean there is a greater risk of the egg being contaminated). Make sure the eggs are refrigerated at a temperature below 40°F, as recommended by the USDA.

CRACKING THE EGG

If a cocktail calls for a whole egg: Tap the egg on a flat surface to make an initial indent in the shell, then pull the shell open with your fingers to allow the egg yolk and egg white to fall out cleanly together. I recommend cracking the egg into an empty glass first, not with the rest of your ingredients in a mixing tin, as this ensures a bad egg may be easily identified and disposed of. It also prevents the egg from "cooking" in the alcohol and citrus. If a cocktail calls for just egg whites: Tap the egg on a flat surface and separate the halves using your thumb, pointer finger, and middle finger. The motion is almost like turning a door handle. Over the shaker tin, roll the egg back and forth with a few twists of your wrist to encourage the egg white to fall from the crack in the shell into the tin, leaving the whole yolk behind. Of course, it is perfectly fine to use an egg separator as well.

SHAKING WITH EGGS

Distinct steps are necessary to bring egg-based cocktails together in harmony. For this reason, dry shake (shake without ice) first to emulsify. It doesn't have to be a prolonged activity—I use a brisk and strong whip shake to get the right integration and fluffy texture. Then add ice and shake again to chill. This is when the drink starts to chill and aerate further. When the cocktail seems to thicken and you can feel the cubes shrinking and moving slower in the tin, the drink is ready to strain.

CLEANLINESS AND EGGS

Finally, I recommend designating a specific shaker tin and strainer for egg-based cocktails because you do not want the remnants of egg whites to interrupt the flavors of other cocktails. Remember to thoroughly clean your tools after use.

KISS OF FIRE

Named after the Louis Armstrong song, the Kiss of Fire cocktail was created by bartender Kenji Ishioka and won first place in the All-Japan Drinks competition of 1953. While the drink never gained notoriety overseas, it quickly rose to the status of modern classic in Japan, especially in Ōsaka, where Ishioka-san's grandson Yūji Uyama features the cocktail on the menu at his bar, Trickies. It is a somewhat unexpected combination of flavors as the rich red fruit from the sloe gin balances the sharpness of the vodka and the dry vermouth. The drink has an acidity that makes my mouth water and yet somehow it still strikes balance with just the sugar rim for sweetness. *Serves one*

¾ ounce Suntory Haku vodka

¾ ounce Sipsmith sloe gin

¾ ounce Noilly Prat Original Dry vermouth

1 barspoon fresh lemon juice

Sugar and a lemon wheel, to rim the glass

Combine the vodka, sloe gin, dry vermouth, and lemon juice in a shaker tin with ice. Shake briskly, but not for long. Too much dilution and the drink will feel thin on the palate. Use more of a rolling canter of a shake, mostly to chill. Prepare a "snow style" sugar-rimmed cocktail glass by wetting the rim of the glass with the freshly cut edge of a lemon wheel and then dipping the wet rim into a dish of sugar. Strain the cocktail into the rimmed glass. With each sip, a little bit of sugar falls from the rim like snow, sweetening your lips and acting as a reminder of the fleeting nature of the seasons.

WASHITSU

The islands of Okinawa are the heart of awamori country. When I think of the lively, funky island spirit, my mind usually meanders toward the realm of tropical drinks—awamori is savory and slightly fruity, a fitting partner for sultry flavors. In this cocktail, I wanted the drink's escapist nature to be rooted in Japanese sentiment, so matcha adds a vigorous green tannin element to the combination of awamori and white rum, while the crème de cacao brings a dark sweetness to the mix. I particularly love the Château d'Arlay Macvin du Jura blanc, a French mistelle, because it reminds me of the smell of fresh bamboo and tatami floors. *Serves one*

¾ ounce Masahiro Shuzō Shimauta awamori

¾ ounce Banks 5 Island Blend white rum

¾ ounce fresh lime juice

½ ounce Tempus Fugit Spirits crème de cacao

½ ounce Château d'Arlay Macvin du Jura blanc mistelle

½ ounce Rich Cane Syrup (page 318)

1 chashaku (traditional utensil used for measuring matcha) matcha powder (about ¼ teaspoon)

GARNISH Grated dark chocolate and grated cinnamon

In a shaker tin, combine the awamori, rum, lime juice, crème de cacao, mistelle, and cane syrup. Sift the matcha into the tin. Add one large ice cube and whip shake (short and rapid) to aerate and fold the powdery matcha into the other ingredients without creating clumps. Strain into a large tulip glass over crushed ice. Garnish with grated dark chocolate and cinnamon.

shunbun

SPRING EQUINOX

sparrows start to nest, first cherry blossoms, distant thunder

If spring had a color in Japan, it would be pink. Not bubblegum pink or baby pink, but an alluring mix of flamingo and powder pinks suspended in the air. Like a cascading ripple from Kyūshū to Hokkaidō, the exquisite cherry blossoms unfold, drawing crowds from around the world to witness their striking beauty. The weather can be mixed, with bright blue skies gracing some parts of the country and rolling thunder signaling storms in others. When the seasonal rains wash away the cherry blossoms it creates a moment of bittersweet pause; as melancholy as it feels to watch the flowers flutter to sidewalks and rivers, we know the leaves of the trees will soon sprout lush, green, and full of life. On our tables, we find solace in sakura-inspired cocktails and drinks made with Shiozakura (page 141), a salty-sweet preserve of the ephemeral blossoms.

SPIRITFREE

SHIOZAKURA HIGHBALL

Everyone should be able to have a taste of sakura season, so I created a spiritfree imbued with the graceful beauty of the sakura blossom. The shiozakura saline shines when paired with lemon, while sweet potato vinegar brings a weightiness to the combination. For fans of drinks like kombucha or salted lemonade, this is an ethereal sipper with decided balance. *Serves one*

¼ ounce Shiozakura Saline Solution (page 316)

¾ ounce Purple Sweet Potato Vinegar Syrup (recipe follows)

½ ounce fresh lemon juice

Club soda, to top

GARNISH Fresh mint sprig and rinsed shiozakura blossom (see page 141)

In a mixing glass, combine the shiozakura saline solution, purple sweet potato vinegar syrup, and lemon juice with ice, and stir to chill. Strain into a collins glass over fresh ice. Top with club soda. Garnish with a sprig of fresh mint and a rinsed shiozakura blossom.

PURPLE SWEET POTATO VINEGAR SYRUP

In a large bowl, combine ½ cup beniimosu (purple sweet potato vinegar), 2 cups granulated sugar, and 1 cup room-temperature filtered water and whisk until the sugar is fully dissolved. Store refrigerated for up to 3 weeks. *Yields 16 ounces*

SAKURA COLLINS

SHIOZAKURA HIGHBALL

(page 135)

SAKURA COLLINS

The classic Tom Collins is fresh, bright, and easygoing—a lovely option for spring sipping. To make a version for sakura season, I built upon the standard combination of gin, lemon juice, and soda by adding a few special touches of cherry blossoms. Between the Roku gin, sakura vermouth, and saline solution, the bubbly cocktail has a floral quality that tiptoes between roses and honeysuckle, bolstered by a ribbon of cinnamon and salt, and finishes in a fruity way that makes me think of sour cherries, aloe, and peaches. The drink transforms into a work of art as the flower garnish becomes suspended in the glass. *Serves one*

1½ ounces Suntory Roku gin

¼ ounce Mancino Sakura vermouth

¼ ounce Shiozakura Saline Solution (page 316)

½ ounce fresh lemon juice

½ ounce Simple Syrup (page 318)

Club soda, to top

GARNISH Rinsed shiozakura blossoms (see Note)

In a collins glass, combine the gin, sakura vermouth, shiozakura saline solution, lemon juice, and simple syrup. Add some ice and give it a quick stir to incorporate the ingredients. Top it off with more ice to fill the glass and then finish with a splash of club soda. Garnish with a few shiozakura blossoms—use tweezers or the trident end of a barspoon to arrange them in the glass, so they dance around the cocktail as it is sipped.

NOTE | For information on shiozakura blossoms, see page 141. For this cocktail, I use rinsed shiozakura blossoms left over from making the saline solution.

CHERRY BLOSSOM COCKTAIL

Many bartenders across the globe have created cocktails in homage to sakura season, but the very first was likely created by Tasaburō Tao, who opened the prestigious Café de Paris in Yokohama in 1923. His cocktail of Cognac, Cherry Heering, grenadine, lemon juice, and Curaçao has since secured its place as the standard cocktail bearing the coveted name Cherry Blossom. The drink is a bold red, like American cherries rather than the pale pink and white cherry blossoms of Japan. For this reason, there is a notion that Tao created the drink for Western tourists and businesspeople who were visiting Yokohama, to give them a taste of home. This may or may not be true, but I appreciate the sentiment behind the tale.

As with many drinks invented over a hundred years ago, Tao's original cocktail leans much sweeter than what modern palates tend to appreciate, so for my iteration of the drink I removed the grenadine and brought up the citrus elements, reaching for Royal Combier Grande Liqueur for its profile of orange, vanilla, and spices. The heart of the cocktail remains intact, with the vivacious cherry liqueur shining through, supported by notes of vanilla and oak. It maintains a satisfying amount of sweetness, which I find best suited for a dessert cocktail, perhaps alongside super-dark bitter chocolate or a hearty cheese board. For the same reason, I also serve such cocktails in smaller doses, to be sipped as a petite nightcap instead of a regular-size quaff. To make a full-size version, just double the recipe. *Serves one*

½ ounce H by Hine VSOP Cognac

½ ounce Cherry Heering

1 barspoon fresh lemon juice

1 barspoon Royal Combier Grande orange liqueur

In a shaker tin, combine the Cognac, Cherry Heering, lemon juice, and orange liqueur with ice. Shake to chill, then strain into a well-chilled cocktail glass.

SAKURAZUKÉ MARTINI

When sakura season arrives we make pink snacks to celebrate, including sakura-mochi—a sakura-hued mochi filled with koshian (sweet red bean paste) and wrapped in pickled sakura leaves. The koshian tastes sweet and earthy, almost like black pepper when put next to the salty sakura rice, and the pickled sakura leaf wrapping tastes of sweet cinnamon and fresh tobacco leaves. In this cocktail, I pay homage to the snack. The saké, which represents the rice, brings a supple base to the drink, while sakura vermouth contributes a lightly sweet and floral bouquet. Campari saunters in with its bold grapefruit and clove-studded orange qualities, dyeing the contents of the glass a gorgeous crimson hue. Like a big bold slice of grapefruit dipped in salt, it is a cocktail for those who like their drinks with an audacious streak. *Serves one*

1½ ounces Amabuki Gin no Kurenai junmai

½ ounce Mancino Sakura vermouth

¾ ounce Campari

1 barspoon Shiozakura Saline Solution (page 316)

GARNISH 1 shiozakura blossom and lemon peel

In a mixing glass, combine the saké, sakura vermouth, Campari, and shiozakura saline solution. Add ice and stir to chill. Place the sakura blossom in the bottom of a chilled cocktail glass. Strain the cocktail over the sakura blossom, unfurling the petals in a lively display of springtime delight. Express the oils of the lemon peel over the top of the drink (discard the peel).

SHIOZAKURA

Within the hundreds of varieties of sakura, the yaezakura, a double-petaled variety with a multitude of pale pink petals like the frills of a ballerina's tutu is the flower of choice for salt-pickling. They are often used to make wagashi, or are incorporated into onigiri as sakura viewing snacks. I use shiozakura in cocktails for salinity, hints of baking spice, and an incomparable bouquet. When you rinse the salt from the flowers you end up with both an edible garnish and a floral saline solution, which may be used in cocktails and spiritfrees alike.

DELICATE REFUSAL

While running the bar program at GreenRiver in downtown Chicago, I created this drink to overturn preconceived notions about sakura cocktails. To achieve this, I incorporated ingredients that represent the cherry tree as a whole. The green notes of blanco tequila and sotol represent the earth, like the lichen-cloaked bark at the base of the tree. Verjus blanc, apricot eau-de-vie, grapefruit liqueur, and fino sherry meld together to represent the blossoms themselves, and the final touch of bitters represents the spring rains that eventually come to wash the flowers away. It is a springtime cocktail for the martini drinker.

As the cocktail is poured, the flower blooms before your eyes as it flutters open in the liquid representing the coming of spring, and then witness the layer of pink cast over the surface with the garnishing of bitters, like the spring showers that carry the blossoms. *Serves one*

1 shiozakura, rinsed (see page 141)

1 ounce Tequila Fortaleza Blanco

1 barspoon Sotol Por Siempre

¼ ounce verjus blanc

¼ ounce Blume Marillen apricot eau-de-vie

¼ ounce Combier Crème de Pamplemousse Rose pink grapefruit liqueur

¾ ounce Valdespino Inocente fino sherry

GARNISH 5 sprays Peychaud's bitters

Place the rinsed shiozakura in a chilled cocktail glass and set aside. In a mixing glass, combine the blanco tequila, sotol, verjus blanc, apricot eau-de-vie, pink grapefruit liqueur, and fino sherry. Add ice and stir to chill. Strain into the prepared cocktail glass. Finish with a spritz of Peychaud's bitters over the top of the cocktail, enough to cast a layer of dark pink over the surface (about 5 sprays).

NOTE | Sometimes a cocktail benefits from a spray of bitters instead of using dashes or drops, because this method coats the surface of the drink in a light and even layer. In this case, I like to use little glass misters or atomizers, which can be bought online in various sizes. When spraying bitters over a cocktail, do a test to the side first to get a feel for how wide and intense the spray will be. Keep your mister far enough from the glass so it doesn't overflow the liquid, but not so far that the droplets spill all over the bar surrounding the glass.

seimei

PURE SUNLIGHT

swallows return, wild geese
fly north, first rainbows

The first spring rains have come and gone, and with them the pink clouds of sakura blossoms. If we are lucky, the trees may still be blooming for the first day of school, typically April 7 or 8. The air is growing warmer and sometimes you can catch a cloud bursting before the sun, casting a rainbow in its wake. There is a sense of invigoration that is channeled into new beginnings, whether it be school, work, or a night out on the town. This time of year we are also excited for fresh greens that are emerging anew. Specifically, kinomé, the tiny leaf clusters of the sanshō tree. With a citronesque verve laced with florality, kinomé is one of my favorite garnishes for cocktails (like the Kinomé Martini, page 149), and is increasingly used as a botanical to infuse Japanese-made gins.

MOMOSÉ MARTINI

Seimei means clear, bright, and pure, and to me that is exactly how a great martini should look and taste—clean, crisp, and revitalizing. Dry gin martinis are plentiful in Japanese cocktail bars and every masutā (master bartender) has their exact preferences for how the drink should be made. More often than not, the martinis you find in Japan are dry—usually 5:1 gin to vermouth—made with chilled Gordon's, Bombay Sapphire, or Beefeater and paired with Noilly Prat Original Dry vermouth. I also prefer the 5:1 ratio at Kumiko, reaching for the bottle of Suntory Roku gin from the freezer for our house martini, or the Ki No Bi dry gin from The Kyōto Distillery for a martini with a more voluptuous body.

For times that call for something even more extravagant, I have an extra-special build that speaks to my personal tastes, made with Noilly Prat Original Dry vermouth, equal parts Ki No Tea gin and Monkey 47 gin, and yuzu bitters from the aptly named brand, The Japanese Bitters (see page 146). I chill the cocktail glass with a full pour of dry vermouth over crushed ice first. When the glass is chilled, the vermouth and crushed ice are poured into a rocks glass, layered with absinthe, and served as an apéritif. For the martini itself, a medley of Japanese and German gin botanicals unite, and the yuzu bitters add luminosity. What may feel like an excess of steps to some, to me is a satisfying ritual and a stylish cocktail experience. *Serves one; photo on page 147*

2 to 3 ounces Noilly Prat Original Dry vermouth

1¼ ounces The Kyōto Distillery Ki No Tea Kyōto dry gin

1¼ ounces Monkey 47 Schwarzwald dry gin

21 drops The Japanese Bitters yuzu bitters (about a dash and a half)

½ ounce absinthe

GARNISH Lemon peel, lemon twist, and olives

Fill a small cocktail glass with crushed ice and add the Noilly Prat Original Dry. In a mixing glass, combine both gins and the bitters. Add ice and stir to chill. Returning to the prepared cocktail glass, transfer the crushed ice and vermouth to a tumbler, layer the absinthe on top, and serve. Strain the martini into the seasoned cocktail glass, reserving a portion in a sidecar in a bed of crushed ice. Express the lemon peel oils over the cocktail (discard the peel), and arrange the lemon twist and olives carefully atop the ice in the sidecar so they remain cold (see Note, page 146).

THE JAPANESE BITTERS

Many bartenders in Japan tend to lean into well-known brands of spirits and bitters for their libations, but Yuki Yamazaki decided to try a local approach by creating his own line of bitters that are distinctly Japanese. The Japanese Bitters debuted in Japan in 2018 and came to America in 2019. The first flavor, shiso bitters, is pungent, spiced, and herbaceous, with a depth that resonates like an amaro yet stays fresh at the same time. The second expression, umami bitters, is the most savory of the trio, reminiscent of dashi, made with kombu, bonito, and shiitake, with just a hint of yuzu. And the third, the yuzu bitters, is an instant classic. Floral and citrusy, it makes an ideal match for a luscious sherry and soda, a sprightly gin and tonic, soothing shōchū on the rocks, or the Momosé Martini (page 145 and opposite).

NOTE | For drinks like the martini, which is best served ice cold, sometimes a bartender will serve the cocktail in a glass that is smaller than usual with the remaining portion set aside in a carafe-like glass called a sidecar. I always keep the sidecar nestled in crushed ice so the liquid stays cold from start to finish—as a guest empties the first part of their cocktail, the glass they drink from can be topped off with ice-cold liquid from the sidecar so they may enjoy a perfectly chilled drink from start to finish.

MOMOSÉ MARTINI

(page 145)

KINOMÉ MARTINI

To celebrate the personality of seasonal kinomé (sanshō leaves), I created a martini variation using Nikka Coffey gin, which vibrates with the tingling sensation of sanshō. Japanese Bermutto, a vermouth-adjacent ingredient made with yuzu, kabosu (citrus that grows in Ōita and Kyūshū), mugwort, and sanshō, softens the sharp edges of the gin, while building on the sanshō flavor exponentially. (Noilly Prat Original Dry vermouth is a suitable substitution for the Bermutto, but lacks the robust quality the rice-based spirit provides.) When freshly poured, this martini bursts with piny citrus with an invigorating sanshō finish. It reminds me of the aromas of walking through a Japanese forest on a chilly spring morning just as the sun hits the leaves. *Serves one*

1½ ounces Nikka Coffey gin

1½ ounces Japanese Bermutto
  or dry vermouth

GARNISH Kinomé sprig

In a mixing glass, combine the gin and Japanese Bermutto. Add ice and stir to chill. Strain into a chilled cocktail glass. I recommend preparing a sidecar on ice (see Note, page 146) so the martini is as cold as possible as you sip and savor. To garnish, press the kinomé leaves briefly with tongs to awaken the oils—the leaves are hearty (more so than mint) and withstand some agitation. Then place them on top of the drink as garnish. The leaves are edible, though I suggest tasting one at a time to get a sense of the potency.

JAPANESE BERMUTTO

One of the most exciting ingredients to come from Japan in recent years is the Oka brand Japanese Bermutto, a nihonshu-based "vermouth" made in conjunction with the Tsutsumi Distillery, which has been producing traditional shōchū for over 140 years. Using saké and rice shōchū as the base (which is why it cannot be called a vermouth), the citrus-forward modifier melds four distinctly Japanese ingredients in the maceration: sanshō, kabosu (a citrus), yomogi (mugwort), and yuzu. At 18% ABV, it is a pleasing amalgamation that sets the course for a new style of aromatized modifiers. Used in shaken cocktails, the tart elements meld effortlessly with citrus juice while holding true to the distinctly herbaceous, peppery, and bitter notes.

KUMIKO BLOODY MARY

I think of the Bloody Mary mostly in the springtime when I wake up a little bit earlier in the day to catch the sun. In Japan, the brunch drink is usually prepared with only vodka, tomato juice, and lemon. Garnishes are similarly minimal—sometimes a celery stick, or a few dashes of salt or cracked black pepper. I offer a Bloody Mary at Kumiko that is almost identical to the ones served in Japan—it just isn't on our menu. To please all types of drinkers, I offer both gin and a house-infused vodka as options for the base spirit—specifically, Nikka Coffey gin for its sanshō profile, or elegant Suntory Haku vodka infused with pink peppercorns, hibiscus, salt, and wasabi. *Serves one*

1¼ ounces Nikka Coffey gin or Spice-Infused Vodka (page 320)

4 ounces V8 Original vegetable juice

1 barspoon fresh lemon juice

GARNISH 1 lemon wedge

Fill a rocks glass with ice. Measure the spirit of your choice, tomato juice, and lemon juice over the ice and stir gently, just to incorporate. Serve on a saucer with a Japanese-style stir stick (madorā) and a lemon wedge on the side.

WASABI

In America, most people probably think of wasabi as that little green volcano of spice that lives on the side of a sushi platter, or the green plastic tube found in grocery stores. However, these are usually Western horseradish-based imitations of genuine wasabi. In Japan, true Japanese wasabi is called *hon*, the same word used to indicate true shōchū (honkaku). When we speak of hon-wasabi, we are referring to the underground stem of the plant, under whose brown and dimpled skin lies a pastel green flesh with a grassy, woodsy, and floral aroma.

Grated wasabi releases a pungent compound called allyl isothiocyanate, which is also found in mustard seed oil, radishes, and horseradish. This compound is what makes your nose crinkle when you eat it. The spicy sensation of hon-wasabi doesn't last as long as the imitation varieties, which actually have mustard and horseradish in them. Instead, it cleanses the palate just enough to allow the flavor of the dish to shine through.

Hon-wasabi is a classic example of yakumi, a garnish meant to enhance the flavor of a dish while increasing appetite and aiding in digestion. When using wasabi in Japanese dishes (or cocktails like this Bloody Mary), I encourage you to find the real thing.

kokuu

NURTURING RAINS

first reeds sprout, last frost and rice
seedlings grow, peonies bloom

The last frosts are melting, making way for new growth. Farmers in
Southern Japan hunch over in the fields, planting rice seedlings to the
slow methodical beat of seed by seed by seed, setting the stage for a
bountiful season to come. As bamboo starts to wiggle up through the
soil, we nibble on takenoko gohan, or rice steamed with tender shoots.
To complement this dish, we sip on nourishing green teas when the
first flush of the year arrives. The most prized and expensive teas,
which feature the very first leaves of the plant, are called shincha (new
tea). These leaves exude layers of flavor that have built up over the
long winter months. Harvesters traditionally pick them by hand, to
avoid damage to the leaves.

GIMLET

The classic 1920s-era gin gimlet, as printed in Harry MacElhone's *Harry's ABC of Mixing Cocktails*, is equal parts gin and lime cordial. With a clean, brisk nature, the drink is famously embraced by Japanese bartenders. Lime cordial is what makes the gimlet come alive—the undertone of bitterness complements the gin in a manner that fresh lime juice cannot match. Rose's Lime Cordial and Cocktail Lime specifically are still commonly used in Japanese cocktail bars, though increasingly I am seeing bartenders turn to fresh lime juice and sugar syrup instead. In America, the overly sugary nature of the ingredient has persuaded many bartenders to make their own versions, myself included. As a two-ingredient cocktail, the quality of the gin or vodka you choose can mean the difference between a good gimlet and a fantastic one, so I recommend something from Japan for the base. *Serves one*

2 ounces Suntory Haku vodka
  or Nikka Coffey gin

¾ ounce Lime Cordial (page 318)

In a shaker tin, combine the preferred spirit and lime cordial with ice. Shake and strain into a coupe. I prefer my gimlet served up with ice shards floating on the top, but the drink is also delightful when poured over a few cubes of ice. In that case, shake for a shorter period of time to leave room for continued dilution once strained.

RYŪKYŪ GIMLET

For this variation on the classic gimlet, the complex qualities of awamori and shōchū contrast with the brightness of fresh lime juice. The drink sings of spring—pale green and alive, evocative of rain-kissed bamboo, savory shiitake, and zesty lime. If you enjoy a daiquiri made with rhum agricole, or a margarita made with mezcal, give this one a whirl; you may be pleasantly surprised. *Serves one*

1 ounce Masahiro Shuzō Shimauta awamori

½ ounce Mizu Saga barley shōchū

¾ ounce Mizu green tea shōchū

¾ ounce fresh lime juice

½ ounce Simple Syrup (page 318)

GARNISH Lime peel

In a shaker tin, combine the awamori, barley shōchū, green tea shōchū, lime juice, and simple syrup with ice. Shake it hard to chill and aerate. Strain into a chilled cocktail glass, allowing some ice chips to come through into the drink. Garnish with a lime peel.

RYOKUCHA-HI

Ryokucha translates directly to "green tea"—a broad category with many sub-styles. Tea doesn't always have a home in cocktails in Japan, but it is common to find the ingredient in izakaya via a drink called ryokucha-hi, a simple highball of shōchū and green tea. This version was inspired by genmaicha, a traditional blend of toasted rice and green tea. In the glass, the rice is represented by a soothing shōchū and the tea is a cold-brewed sencha, which I often prefer in the warmer months for its restorative balance of tropical fruit and umami characteristics. *Serves one*

1½ ounces rice shōchū

3 to 4 ounces Cold-Brew Sencha
  (page 320)

GARNISH Edible flowers or fresh herbs

Fill a collins glass with ice. Measure the rice shōchū and the chilled sencha over the ice and stir to chill. Top off with fresh ice as needed. Garnish with aromatic edible flowers or herbs. I use stock flowers at Kumiko for the vanilla aroma and contrast of purple against pastel green.

WISTERIA COCKTAIL

Wisteria blooms don't get as much attention as the sakura do, but for many Japanese people their rebirth in late spring is a special moment. Fat bumblebees dance around the purple flowers, drooping heavy like succulent grapes from the willowy branches. Their perfume—like a bundle of fresh lilac, violet, and honey—floats through the air like a sheet of cashmere. In honor of these intoxicating blooms, I invented this cocktail using crème de violette for its floral qualities and amethyst hue. The juicy botanicals of gin surface when paired with yuzu-shu (see page 273), and white rum interjects with subtle grass and vanilla. Whenever I sip this cocktail, my attention always comes back to the gorgeous crème de violette, the way it illuminates the glass and infuses the air around it. *Serves one*

1 ounce The Kyōto Distillery Ki No Bi Kyōto dry gin

¼ ounce Banks 5 Island white rum

½ teaspoon Rothman & Winter crème de violette

¾ ounce Tsukasa botan Yama yuzu-shu

½ ounce Simple Syrup (page 318)

¾ ounce fresh lemon juice

3 dashes absinthe

GARNISH Lemon peel

In a shaker tin, combine the gin, rum, crème de violette, yuzu-shu, simple syrup, lemon juice, and absinthe with ice. Shake to chill and strain into a chilled coupe. Express the oils of the lemon peel over the top of the drink and garnish with a manicured peel.

SUMMER

Japan endures a fever of sticky heat in the summertime. I remember waking up to the sound of cicadas, their humming song building like the crescendo of a thousand fans trying to wash away the heat. The sun seemed to climb slowly through the sky, swimming through the misty haze of humid air, which hung heavy, like a blanket still wet from the wash. Our house in Tomio did not have air conditioning in most of the rooms—there was a unit in the dining area and one in my father's office—so my brothers and I would plant ourselves firmly in front of an oscillating fan when temperatures would start to climb. We weren't allowed to fix the fan in place because that would be selfish, but if you were to lean at a certain angle you were guaranteed two passes of cool air for everyone else's one.

We found further relief in the form of oyatsu, or the little snacks mom would prepare. She always seemed to know just what we needed. Whether it was salt to replenish what we lost to the rivers of sweat dripping down our faces or something sweet to counterbalance a bitter tea, it always felt right. I remember small plates with osenbei (rice crackers) fanned out on display with slices of fruit on the side. Sometimes they would be accompanied by a glass of cold mugi-cha, or iced ryokucha. An extra special drink would be a homemade treat like a satisfying glass of umé-su and soda. The sweet-tart acidity of the umé is one of my favorite flavors this time of year.

During Japanese summers, visiting an izakaya often means wading into a thick layer of cigarette smoke. Owners crack windows in search of some semblance of a breeze. Cocktail bars on the other hand often set an air conditioner to the optimal temperature so when you settle in for an ice-cold martini the environment also rises to the occasion. Though most bartenders focus on classic recipes year-round, more modern establishments run drink specials featuring fresh fruit typical of the season. Japanese farmers take great care in growing produce that is beautiful and also bursting with ripe flavor, and there is nothing better in the summer than ripe cherries or cucumbers muddled into a contemporary smash. Myōga, a form of Japanese ginger, inspires a mojito variation (see Kamakiri, page 179), and bubbly highballs taste even more satisfying alongside a plate of ripe tomatoes drizzled with Kewpie mayo.

THE MICROSEASONS OF SUMMER

RIKKA | *summer begins*

Midori Shōchū Sour

Spindrift

Daiquiri

GESHI | *summer solstice*

Umé Shōchū Sour

Grey Wolf

SHŌMAN | *early blooms appear*

Campari Soda

Sakuranbō Americano

Elderflower Sour

SHŌSHO | *small heat*

Murasaki Sonic

Spiritfree: Magenta Cooler

Suika Spritz

Apricots and Cream

BŌSHU | *grains flourish*

Mojito

Kamakiri

Mugi Gin and Tonic

Spiritfree: Mugi Tonic

TAISHO | *intense heat*

Sol Cubano

TSC (Tomato Sherry Cobbler)

Bell Pepper Margarita

Bamboo Cocktail

Kyūri Cocktail

rikka

SUMMER BEGINS

frogs start singing, worms surface, bamboo shoots sprout

There aren't many extended national holidays in Japan when people get significant time off work, but the beginning of May is an exception. Known as Golden Week, it is one of the most anticipated vacation times of the year. My family would take trips to the beach, or to the cerulean Lake Biwa, where we'd catch fresh bluegill and blackbass to cook and eat in a cabin made of cedar. Many bars close for the holiday, so grocery shops get busy as people stock up on ingredients for picnic snacks like onigiri (rice balls) and tamago-sando (egg salad sandwiches)—beloved for their simplicity. We drink lots of chilled mugi-cha and cold-brew ryokucha at home, and in the cocktail bars that are open, fruits like juicy melons steal the show.

MIDORI SHŌCHŪ SOUR

When I was a kid we would drink *kurīmu-sōda* or "cream soda" at family restaurants with all-you-could-drink soda fountains. Unlike American cream soda, kurīmu-sōda is a melon soda float with vanilla ice cream and a maraschino cherry on top. Every time I smell Midori I think about inventing elaborate concoctions with my brothers, as we would layer ingredients onto the basic formula of the kurīmu-sōda for a sugar-rich accent to our meal.

In the cocktail world, Midori is perhaps best known for its namesake role in the Midori Sour. The cocktail—made with the liqueur, sour mix (or sometimes lemonade), and a maraschino cherry garnish—was invented at Studio 54 in New York City and remained quite popular in America through the 1970s and '80s. In my modern version, bright notes of melon contrast with the herbaceous undertones of green tea shōchū, which brings structure and complexity to the drink. The green tea flavors, with subtle notes of passion fruit and unripe banana, enhance the Midori. With each sip, there's a layer of bright fruit and a flavor similar to lemon curd that gives way to the earthy tea and barley. Playful and fun, and yet still decidedly adult, it is an elevated version of the disco classic. *Serves one; photo on page 165*

1½ ounces Mizu green tea shōchū (see Note)

1 ounce Midori melon liqueur

½ ounce fresh lemon juice

½ ounce fresh lime juice

½ ounce Simple Syrup (page 318)

Splash of club soda, to top

GARNISH Melon ball

In a shaker tin, combine the green tea shōchū, Midori, lemon juice, lime juice, and simple syrup. Dry shake to aerate and pour the mixture over fresh ice in a highball glass. Top off with club soda. Carefully slide a spoon down the side of the inside of the glass and scoop upward to nuzzle the ice up, allowing the ingredients to come together. Top off with ice as needed. Garnish with a melon ball and serve.

NOTE | If you can't find green tea shōchū, I suggest using another rice-based shōchū. Something sleek, like the Hakutake Shiro shōchū or Chiyonosono 8,000 Generations.

MIDORI

Midori means "green," in Japanese, an accurate description of the neon-colored melon liqueur invented by the Suntory company in 1964. Originally called Hermes Melon, after the name of the company's 1950s-era line of liqueurs, the melon-flavored ingredient comes packaged in a frosted and dimpled glass bottle. By 1971, Midori found a place in cocktails at the International Bartender's Association (IBA) Cocktail Championship in Tōkyō, where it also caught the attention of bartenders from overseas. Seeing their reactions, Suntory rebranded the product as Midori Melon Liqueur.

Midori arrived in America in 1978 via New York City, where it launched at Studio 54. During its heyday over the next few decades, bartenders around the world invented emerald green cocktails like the Melonball (Midori, vodka, orange juice, and melon balls garnish), Midori Sour (Midori, sour mix, and lemon wedge garnish), and the Japanese Slipper (Midori, triple sec, lemon juice, and maraschino cherry), but when the cocktail renaissance of the early aughts placed a renewed focus on natural ingredients instead of artificial ones, many bartenders left bottles like Midori to gather dust on the shelf.

This prompted Suntory to tweak the recipe to keep up with the times. For the relaunch in 2013, the new recipe featured two types of melon: Yubari melons, a cantaloupe cultivar prized for its orange flesh and natural honeyed sweetness, grow in volcanic soil near Sapporo. Muskmelons, from the prefectures of Aichi and Shizuoka just southwest of Tōkyō, are harvested through June and July and made into a pulp, which is then flash-frozen until Suntory is ready to make a batch of liqueur. Production begins in low-pressure stills with separate distillations of yubari and muskmelon. These distillates are then blended together with young Cognac, sweetened with cane sugar, and diluted with water to 20% alcohol by volume before food coloring is added. Thanks to the revitalized recipe, and the growing global bartenders' interest in Japanese cocktail culture, the liqueur has come back into favor with cocktail bartenders everywhere.

MIDORI SHŌCHŪ SOUR

(page 163)

SPINDRIFT

As radiant summer unfurls her wings, melons come into season. Cantaloupe and watermelon are cut into slices and eaten as a midday snack or at the end of a meal, and muskmelons—the epitome of luxury in Japan—dazzle with their wrinkly skin and sweet green flesh. For this cocktail inspired by the fresh seasonal fruits, a lightly cloudy saké called sasanigori sets a fruity foundation for the drink, while cachaça, a fresh-pressed sugarcane rum from Brazil, adds a savory green olive undercurrent. The melon juice, the star of the show, ties all the disparate flavors together and the drink is garnished with a salty olive and a crack of black pepper.

Depending on the sweetness of the melon, I suggest adjusting the lime juice or simple syrup to taste. This might take some experimentation before landing on the right balance, but the general key is that if the drink tastes too sweet, you can increase the amount of lime juice. If it's not sweet enough because you have a melon that doesn't have a lot of natural sugar, increase the volume of simple syrup. *Serves one*

1 ounce Shirakawago sasanigori junmai ginjō

½ ounce Novo Fogo cachaça

1½ ounces honeydew melon juice (recipe follows)

½ ounce fresh lime juice

½ ounce Simple Syrup (page 318)

GARNISH Olive and freshly cracked black pepper

In a shaker tin, combine the sasanigori, cachaça, melon juice, lime juice, and simple syrup with ice. Shake briskly to chill, then strain into a rocks glass over a few pieces of large cracked ice. Garnish with a high-quality fruity olive (such as Filthy Foods coastal Greek or Sicilian Castelvetrano) and freshly cracked black pepper.

HONEYDEW MELON JUICE

Cut a ripe melon in half, scooping out the seeds with a large spoon. Juice with a masticating juicer. If you don't have a juicer, place melon chunks in a blender and blend until smooth. Using a spoon, push the blended liquid through a fine-mesh sieve.

DAIQUIRI

With three simple ingredients—rum, lime juice, and sugar—the classic daiquiri originated in Cuba in the late 1800s. It came to the States shortly thereafter, and the drink subsequently found a home within the canon of cocktails beloved by Japanese bartenders. In the 1970s and '80s, the original recipe took a detour in Japan when an oil crisis impacted the import of many goods, including limes. Lemons were the replacement. They were easier to find, and as bartenders realized how the citrus made for a less bitter version of its lime-based counterpart, many adopted the switch permanently. You will still see certain bars using lemon juice today.

The following recipe is one I created for the menu at GreenRiver in Chicago. I use a split base of Plantation Barbados 5-Year rum and Rhum Clément Select Barrel agricole, with lime juice. I like the contrast between the lively, grassy notes of agricole and the opulence of the aged rum—together they lead to a daiquiri with a rich flavor profile, round mouthfeel, and snappy finish. *Serves one*

1½ ounces Plantation Barbados
  5-Year rum

½ ounce Rhum Clément Select
  Barrel agricole

¾ ounce fresh lime juice

½ ounce Rich Demerara Syrup
  (page 318)

Combine the rum, rhum agricole, lime juice, and demerara syrup in a shaker tin and shake briskly with ice. Strain into a chilled cocktail glass. No garnish.

shōman

EARLY BLOOMS
APPEAR

the silkworm awakens and eats the mulberry,
the safflower blooms, the time for wheat

As early summer temperatures rise, the desire to eat often dwindles. In times like these, crunchy snacks like tataki kyūri—pounded cucumber with soy sauce and sesame oil—pair well with late-night beers and highballs at the local izakaya. When I was young, dinners were often followed by the joys of multicolored kakigōri, or Japanese shaved ice. Served in an array of fruity flavors, we'd buy them from trucks that roamed the neighborhoods, inching along narrow streets, broadcasting a catchy tune—one of the many sounds of summer.

CAMPARI SODA

Originally invented in Italy, the Campari Soda has earned favor around the world for its balance of bracingly bitter Campari and the kiss of fizzy bubbles. Japanese cocktail bars are not immune to the allure of the highball—at places like Bar Shake in Ginza, master bartender Masayuki Kodato takes every aspect of the cocktail into consideration to make his most perfect version. Made with one piece of cracked ice, a bottle of Wilkinson club soda, chilled Campari, and lemon juice, it is a drink for which people travel from far and wide to get a taste. My recipe pairs respect for the one made by Kodato-san with my admiration for the version served over crushed ice at the Camparino in Galleria bar in Milan. Chilling the Campari in the freezer numbs some of its bitterness, and as it melts, the orange notes of the elixir bloom. I don't use an entire bottle of club soda in my version so the Campari can shine, but I do include Bar Shake's citrus, as it sets the drink in an eternally summery profile. *Serves one; photo on page 173*

1½ ounces Campari, chilled in the freezer

1 lemon wedge (about ⅛ of a lemon)

4 ounces club soda, to top

Fill a chilled collins glass one-third of the way with pebble ice. Add the chilled Campari, then squeeze the lemon wedge over the top to impart both juice and aromatic oils to the drink (discard the spent wedge). Top off with the club soda and give the drink a slight nuzzle with a barspoon or stir stick to integrate the ingredients

SAKURANBŌ AMERICANO

One of my favorite summertime treats growing up was kakigōri, or shaved ice. Unlike American sno-cones, kakigōri is sheared into super fine sheets that melt like snowflakes on the tongue. Piled high into small bowls, they are drizzled with flavored syrups like strawberry with condensed milk or matcha; and in specialty cafés they sometimes come decorated with adzuki beans and omochi (rice cake). In this Americano-inspired cocktail, cherry liqueur pays homage to one of the best kakigōri flavors and most prized ripe fruits of the season: cherries! Called sakuranbō, sweet cherries are a delicacy in Japan, as most sakura trees do not bear edible fruit. The ones that do have cherries lighter in color and tarter than their rich, inky American counterparts known as Bing cherries. This cocktail won't give you the same brain-freeze and sticky fingers as a good summertime kakigōri might, but the flavors may evoke nostalgia for those moments. *Serves one*

1 ounce Campari

½ ounce Cappellano Barolo Chinato

½ ounce Cherry Heering

Splash of club soda

GARNISH Fresh cherry

Fill a highball glass with crushed or shaved ice. Pour in the Campari, Barolo Chinato, Cherry Heering, and a very small splash of club soda. Top with more fresh ice (as the first batch will have settled with the addition of the cocktail, leaving room at the top for more). Garnish with a cherry.

CAMPARI SODA

(page 171)

SAKURANBŌ
AMERICANO

ELDERFLOWER SOUR

Japan loves Scotch, not only for its historic connection to Japanese whisky, but because of its strong tradition and sense of place. Inspired by how the darker grain and chocolate notes of a blended scotch pair with nihonshu, I created this cocktail in homage to those noble ingredients and how well they work in tandem with one another. The drink starts with the perfume of elderflower liqueur, bolstered with lightly peated whisky, layered under a fluffy blanket of egg white. For the nihonshu, something floral and fruity like Fukucho Moon on the Water junmai ginjō pairs best with the bright citrus, frothy egg whites, and smoky whisky. *Serves one*

1½ ounces Chivas Regal 12-Year Blended Scotch whisky

½ ounce Fukucho Moon on the Water junmai ginjō saké

¾ ounce fresh lemon juice

½ ounce Simple Syrup (page 318)

¼ ounce Pür Likör Blossom elderflower liqueur

1 egg white

GARNISH Angostura bitters

In a shaker tin, combine the Scotch, saké, lemon juice, simple syrup, elderflower liqueur, and egg white. Dry shake to aerate and combine the ingredients. Add ice and shake again to chill. Strain into a chilled coupe. Garnish with a flourish of Angostura bitters.

bōshu

GRAINS FLOURISH

praying mantises hatch, rotten grass becomes fireflies, umé turn yellow

Grain seedlings like barley and rice are planted in the northern parts of Japan, and rainy season comes to welcome billowing ajisai (hydrangeas). Fireflies rise to float above the fields. The heat and humidity demands something brisk to sip on to help make it all a bit more bearable, and a restorative Mugi Gin and Tonic (page 180) is just the thing. Hiyayakko, or chilled tofu, brings relief in its simplicity at the dinner table, and bitter herbs and summery rhizomes like ginger also come into season. The delicate shoots of myōga, the cousin of ginger, taste spicy and refreshing all at once—the perfect antidote to summer swelter.

MOJITO

This muddled mint cocktail rose to popularity in America in the 1990s, sparking a wave of mojito-inspired concoctions, desserts, and other gimmicky iterations. If you order a mojito in the US today you may get a slight groan or a raised eyebrow from the bartender, but in Japan it has always been a much-loved cocktail. Historically, the mint is muddled to bring the oils of the herb directly into the liquid, but I prefer to shake the mint with the cocktail then fine-strain it to capture the essence of the mint without small bits of greenery floating in the glass. It is a true delight, served over crushed ice or cubed ice, depending on how hot the day feels and how quickly you wish to sip. *Serves one*

7 fresh mint leaves

1 ounce Grace Rum Cor Cor Green

1 ounce fresh lime juice

1 ounce Simple Syrup (page 318)

Club soda, to top

GARNISH 2 to 3 sprigs of mint

In a shaker tin, combine the 7 mint leaves, rum, lime juice, and simple syrup with ice. Shake briskly to chill, then fine-strain into a chilled collins glass over fresh ice. Top off with club soda. Garnish with a healthy bunch of mint sprigs.

KAMAKIRI

One of my favorite early summer flavors is myōga, a type of Japanese ginger prized for its flowers, buds, and shoots—each part of the plant has a zingy quality more youthful in nature than ginger root. At the Japanese table, myōga is often thinly sliced and served with sashimi or floating in a delicate clear broth. Finding myōga in America can be difficult, but I still wanted to pay homage to its flavors, so with the Kamakiri, named after the praying mantis, I have taken a classic ginger cocktail, the Moscow Mule, and intertwined its ginger spice with the fresh mint of a mojito. The spirits that make up this cocktail showcase a sense of terroir: Cor Cor Red, coming from the island village of Minamidaitōjima, brings dueling qualities of rich molasses and high tones of peppery papaya to the mix, while Ochiai's Rihei Ginger shōchū offers a cleansing ginger spice that brings harmony to the rum, citrus, and mint. *Serves one*

7 to 10 fresh mint leaves

½ ounce Grace Rum Cor Cor Red white rum

1 ounce Ochiai Distillery Rihei Ginger shōchū

¼ ounce kabosu juice (see Note)

½ ounce fresh lime juice

¾ ounces Simple Syrup (page 318)

Splash of Fever-Tree ginger beer

Splash of Q club soda

GARNISH 3 mint sprigs

In a shaker tin, combine the mint leaves, white rum, ginger shōchū, kabosu juice, lime juice, and simple syrup with ice. Shake briskly, then fine-strain into a chilled collins glass over fresh ice. Top with a splash each of ginger beer and club soda. Garnish with a healthy bouquet of mint sprigs.

NOTE | Kabosu is a citrus native to southern Japan. In America, we can buy the pasteurized juice, in which I taste a hint of green melon within the bitter and green citrus juice. This element complements the ginger in a delightful manner. If you can't find any, use yuzu juice with a splash of lime.

MUGI GIN AND TONIC

The gin and tonic grew to such popularity in Japan that many people say the reason why Japanese barspoons have a trident on the end is to push a lime slice deep down into the drink. I invented this variation for summers so hot the thought of eating barely crosses the mind. For the gin, I chose Ki No Tou Old Tom gin from The Kyōto Distillery, which is sweetened with kokutō (black sugar) from the Okinawan island of Yonaguni. This brings an underlying caramel kiss to the drink. As you sip, notice how the toastiness of the barley tea arrives first, almost like the gin is waiting to get noticed in the background. Once the gin comes into play you get a wash of fresh lemon aroma, followed by flavors of peppercorn, juniper, coriander, and orange. A complex highball that is just sweet enough to comfort, but not to cloy. *Serves one*

1½ ounces The Kyōto Distillery Ki No Tou Old Tom gin

2 ounces Chilled Mugi-cha (page 320)

Indian tonic water, to top

GARNISH Lemon twist

Fill a highball glass with ice. Stir the ice slowly, then add more ice to almost fill the glass and stir again until ice fills only about three-quarters of the glass. Strain the residual water out of the highball glass using a julep strainer. Measure the gin into the glass and stir softly, around 7 rotations. Add the mugi-cha, stir once more to incorporate, and top with tonic water. Carefully slide a spoon down the inside of the glass, scoop the ice upward to allow the ingredients to meld together, then lower the ice gently. Top with ice as needed and garnish with a lemon twist.

SPIRITFREE
MUGI TONIC

In the Mugi Gin and Tonic (page 180), mugi-cha creates a medley of burnt sugar, soy, and spice flavors when paired with rich Old Tom gin, which got me wondering how to re-create the drink as a spiritfree. I started with Okinawa kokutō (black sugar) and incorporated some of the same botanicals found in a classic gin, like coriander and anise. The spices are cooked into a syrup with the kokutō to incorporate the savory and herbaceous qualities. The highball has the same stimulating personality as the spirited version, with depth and sweetness. I like to make this drink in individual portions at the bar, but at home, I will make a carafe and sip leisurely throughout the course of the day. Keep the tonic chilled on the side to retain the effervescence. *Serves one*

2 to 3 ounces Chilled Mugi-cha
 (page 320)

½ ounce Spiced Kuromitsu (page 253)

Indian tonic water, to top

GARNISH Lemon twist

In a chilled highball glass, combine the mugi-cha and spiced kuromitsu and stir (without ice) to incorporate. Add ice and stir to chill. Top with tonic water. Carefully slide a spoon down the inside of the glass and nuzzle the ice upward, allowing the ingredients to come together. Top with ice as needed and garnish with a lemon twist.

KOKUTŌ

One of the most delightful ingredients in the Japanese pantry
is kokutō, a type of black sugar from the islands of Okinawa and
Kagoshima where sugarcane grows plentifully. For kokutō, the
sugarcane is pressed the day it is cut to extract the fresh juices from
the woody stalks. After allowing the juice to settle, producers decant
it, separating any fibers and impurities, and then bring the sugarcane
juice to a boil. When it has reduced, the molten syrup is poured
into small batches and stirred as it cools into dark bricks, which
are subsequently cut into smaller cubes. Certified Okinawa kokutō
producers take great care to not only ensure they have the best quality
product, but that they tend to the needs of the earth around them as
well—the leftover sugarcane scraps are used to feed the fires that are
used to boil the juice, and all of the oddments that get strained out are
used as compost for the fields.

True kokutō is subtly sweet with a touch of saltiness, bitterness,
and slight acidity. It is truly complex and straddles the line between
savory and sweet, much like a fine rum or sweet potato shōchū. In
Japanese cuisine, it plays a prominent role in soups, marinades, and
desserts. The special sugar is also used to make rum and shōchū in
the Amami Islands, and is also sometimes turned into a syrup called
kuromitsu (page 253)—the dark brooding flavor is quite pleasing in
cocktails as an alternative to demerara or other brown sugar syrups.

You can easily find kokutō in brick or powdered form (sometimes
called kurozatō) at many Asian markets and online, and some of these
also sell ready-made kuromitsu, which will also do the trick. Look out
for the name Okinawa on the label to signify the best quality.

geshi

SUMMER SOLSTICE

self-heal leaves wither, the iris blooms,
the crow-dipper sprouts

The nights fly by quickly and the days stretch endlessly as summer solstice arrives. We linger indoors and out of the sun, busying ourselves with intricate cooking tasks that don't involve much heat, like making umé-su or umé-shu—a great way to pass the time when venturing outdoors is not as appealing. Similarly, my mom would make chilled dishes like sōmen (thin noodles made from wheat flour) and light salads to help us cool off and stay nourished during the hot days. Umé-su from years prior comes out of the cupboards during these days, a welcome reminder of what is to come from the labor of love set before us as we pluck, rinse, and steep the green fruit to the tune of the singing wind-chimes.

UMÉ SHŌCHŪ SOUR

The inspiration for this drink came from a pairing I did at Kumiko for the first cocktail omakasé we offered. The dish was A5 Miyazaki Wagyu served with compressed plums, shiso, and an uméboshi vinaigrette. For the cocktail, I made a shōchū drink with umé-shu from Meiri Shurui, which is sweetened with honey, fortified with brandy, and aged for five years, making for a complex ingredient all on its own. In the drink, the tart stone fruit notes of umé-shu sing high above a layer of golden honey and lemongrass shōchū. Pineau des Charentes, a French apéritif made from the juice of Cognac grapes and fortified with young Cognac, supports the fruity qualities of the cocktail. Everything comes together when shaken with fresh lemon juice to create a citrus-forward sour with expansive layers of flavor. *Serves one; photo on page 186*

1½ ounces Mizu lemongrass shōchū or homemade lemongrass-infused shōchū (page 221)

1 ounce Pineau des Charentes

¾ ounce fresh lemon juice

½ ounce Rich Honey Syrup (page 317)

½ ounce Umé-shu (page 317)

GARNISH Lemon peel

In a shaker tin, combine the shōchū, Pineau des Charentes, lemon juice, honey syrup, and umé-shu with ice. Shake until the shaker feels cold to the touch. Strain the cocktail into a chilled cocktail glass or coupe. Express the oils of a lemon peel over the top of the drink and garnish with a manicured lemon peel.

UMÉ SHŌCHŪ SOUR

(page 185)

HONKAKU SHŌCHŪ, THE PROCESS

On the label of most honkaku shōchū bottles, you will see the term in Japanese written 本格焼酎. Honkaku means "authentic," or "genuine"; this is a sign of quality and purity, thanks to its process of distillation. So, what is that process exactly? Once the raw materials have been harvested for production, honkaku shōchū begins in a way that is similar to saké: with kōji fermentation. There are three types of kōjikin that are used to make shōchū: black, yellow, and white. White kōji yields a sweet and round texture in shōchū; yellow kōji, the same used in saké production, can create floral aromatics; and black kōji is wild and savory, creating deep and earthy qualities. Kōji is always grown on rice for saké production, but in the case of shōchū, producers may use other grains, tubers, and roots.

The kōji-inoculated starter is combined with water and yeast for the first round of fermentation, called ichijishikomi, which takes about a week. Then the base ingredient—the rice, buckwheat, sweet potato, and so forth—is introduced to the mash, more water is added, and a second fermentation continues for another eight to fourteen days, depending on the producer. The mash then goes through a pot still (traditionally, though this also varies) only once. Producers may use atmospheric distillation for full-bodied shōchū, or vacuum distillation for a lighter style. At times they will even blend distillates from two different types of stills to incorporate an even more broad range of flavor in their shōchū.

Just like undiluted saké, the shōchū distillate created at this point is called genshu. At this stage the only thing that can be added to honkaku shōchū is water. Most producers allow the genshu to rest for a period to soften the edges—this usually takes less than a year, but there are some types left to age for ten or more years to allow the flavors to settle and mellow. Some producers use unglazed clay pots to rest the shōchū, and others use wood casks for a layered finish. When the distiller deems it ready, the shōchū is diluted with water so that the ABV is below 45 percent, and it is bottled.

Sometimes there are exceptions to the rules. A key example is Munemasa Distillery of Arita city in Saga prefecture. Their distillation methods are in line with honkaku shōchū production, but they use locally grown lemongrass which, technically, is not an approved ingredient for honkaku shōchū. One of the most beautiful things about shōchū is how deeply connected it is to local agriculture, making it a hyper-regional spirit. Japan's geography is diverse, and local shōchū cultures are very much about what grows best in that region. More often than not, the same water that fed the grains or produce is also the water used to make the shōchū, resulting in an extremely terroir-centric spirit. I think it is exciting to see producers like Munemasa Shuzō highlighting quality ingredients such as lemongrass that are local to them, while following the process of distilling honkaku shōchū.

geshi

GREY WOLF

In Japan, the old fashioned never quite reached the level of ubiquity it did in the United States, but for me, it is a tried-and-true classic. Inspired by the flavors derived from the old fashioned technique that incorporates a muddled sugar cube, maraschino cherry, and orange wedge, I developed a new template by incorporating drinking vinegar in lieu of muddled fruit. The umé-su imbues a fruity note to the cocktail that echoes the richness you'd find in a good sherry—round and textured but with a bright acidity for balance. Together with the bitters and Bénédictine, the results are a bouquet of honeyed spice and oak. *Serves one*

2 ounces Mars Iwai 45 Japanese whisky

1 barspoon Bénédictine

1 barspoon Umé-su (page 316)

2 dashes Angostura bitters

¼ ounce Rich Demerara Syrup (page 318)

GARNISH Grapefruit peel and (optional) umé macerated in syrup

In a mixing glass, combine the whisky, Bénédictine, umé-su, and Angostura bitters. Add ice and stir. Strain into an old fashioned glass over a single sphere of clear ice. Express the oils of a grapefruit peel over the top of the drink (discard the peel). If available, an uméboshi macerated in syrup makes an excellent secondary garnish.

shōsho

SMALL HEAT

warm winds blow, first lotus blossoms,
hawks learn to fly

Though this season is called "small heat," as we move into the heart of July, the burden of the weather becomes even more cumbersome. This is when the true essence of summer arrives, bringing with it the reward of fresh produce. Juicy watermelons and spicy shiso leaves illuminate food and drinks alike, and tomatoes drip with sweet acidity. Thirsty people everywhere turn to iced coffee for refreshment (page 198), at home or in a nook of their favorite local café. As the world grows more colorful this time of year, I find pleasure in pouring the vibrancy into delicate tumblers and stemware, a way to cup summer and drink in every drop.

MURASAKI SONIC

Shiso is one of summer's finest herbs, and one that always reminds me of home as my mom has cultivated a rather impressive crop in her garden over the years. The paper-thin leaves come into full bloom in late July, when she makes a special summertime drink called shiso no jyūsu (shiso juice). It tastes delicious on its own, over ice, or topped off with a splash of club soda or chilled green tea. After a trip home a couple of years ago, I was inspired to use shiso no jyūsu in cocktails. This particular highball harnesses the inherent duality of the herb by opening up its flavors of mint and baking spices with club soda. The vacuum-distilled barley shōchū creates supple structure for the drink and the bitter citrus notes of the tonic make for a great accent to the shiso and delicate barley shōchū blend. *Serves one; photo on page 192*

1½ ounces The Yanagita Koma Honkaku barley shōchū

½ ounce Shiso no Jyūsu (page 316)

Splash of club soda

Splash of Fever-Tree Mediterranean tonic water

GARNISH Lemon peel and shiso leaf

Fill a tumbler with ice and stir to chill. Strain off the melted water and measure in the shōchū and shiso no jyūsu. Stir gently to chill. Top with club soda and tonic water. Add more ice if needed. Express the oils of a lemon peel over the drink (discard the peel) and garnish with a shiso leaf and a manicured lemon peel.

MAGENTA COOLER

MURASAKI SONIC

(page 191)

SPIRITFREE

MAGENTA COOLER

This mixture of shiso no jyūsu (shiso juice) with lemon juice and cold-brew sencha cools the palate with an energizing contrast of minty spice and bright citrus—a favorite for cooling off on a relaxing summer afternoon. *Serves one*

1½ ounces Shiso no Jyūsu (page 316)

¼ ounce fresh lemon juice

2 ounces Cold-Brew Sencha (page 320)

Club soda, to top

GARNISH Lemon wheel and shiso leaf

Add cubed ice to a chilled tumbler. Layer the shiso no jyūsu, lemon juice, and cold-brew sencha over the ice. Add a splash of club soda. Garnish with a thinly sliced lemon wheel and a manicured shiso leaf.

SHISO

Part of the mint family, shiso is a large, thin, pungent herb that grows wild and requires very little attention to flourish. Its flavors remind me of a complex chai blend: heady and spicy with notes of clove, anise, sweet cardamom, and citrus. Two main varieties grow abundantly in Japan—the blueish-green aojiso is commonly used as a garnish because it can be enjoyed raw, often alongside sushi. Akajiso, or "red shiso" (which is actually closer in color to magenta or purple), can taste a touch more intense in flavor than the tranquil spiced-orange notes of the blue-green variety, so it is more appropriate for adding a pop of color and flavor to uméboshi (salt-cured umé).

Shiso leaves of both varieties have also found a home in contemporary cocktails in the form of a select gin botanical, as well as a stunning garnish. Shiso adorns the glass like an unfurled fan wafting aromas of cooling mint and pungent cardamom. They serve well when placed at the lip of the glass, tucked next to the ice, or julienned atop a sour.

SUIKA SPRITZ

When we'd go to the beach in the summer, my brothers and I would play a game called suikawari, where you blindfold someone and guide them with your voice to break a watermelon open with a stick. Everyone would eat the juicy fruit with salty fingers after swimming in the ocean, and even though the whole melon would be well covered in sand by then, everything in that instant made the melon taste even more delicious. The Suika Spritz is a gleeful wave back to those summers and is loosely modeled after the Aperol Spritz. Awamori brings a floral and grassy quality to the pairing of watermelon and sparkling wine and adds a slight peppery undercurrent to the drink that keeps everything in balance. In the spirit of the classic, the lower-proof awamori base keeps the drink at a sessionable strength.
Serves one

Lemon or lime wedge, to rim the glass

Salt and Pepper Mix (recipe follows), to rim the glass

2 ounces watermelon juice

1 ounce Masahiro Shuzō Shimauta awamori

1 ounce Aperol

Splash of club soda, to top

Splash of dry sparkling wine, to top

Prepare a spritz glass by running a lemon or lime wedge along the outer edge of the rim. Pour a line of salt and pepper mix on a plate and gently tap the prepared glass along the spice blend to create a light dusting halfway around the rim. Fill the spritz glass three-quarters of the way with ice. Add the watermelon juice, awamori, and Aperol and stir briefly to combine and chill. Add more ice if needed, then top with club soda and sparkling wine. Finish with a gentle nuzzle.

SALT AND PEPPER MIX

Press 1 tablespoon of whole pink peppercorns through a fine sieve to separate the pink shell from the pepper-core. Combine the sifted pink shells with ¼ cup granulated sugar and 1 tablespoon sea salt.

APRICOTS AND CREAM

When the mornings become just as sticky as midday, it is hard to imagine sipping a hot cup of coffee with such heat bearing down on the body. For this reason, iced coffee is exceptionally popular in Japan. In bars, coffee-infused shōchū and the espresso martini are common coffee-based drinks, and growing up, one of my favorite summertime treats was a parfait made with coffee jelly and a drizzle of cream, a sign of the coffee lover I was to eventually become. To bring coffee into a cocktail, I found inspiration in the balance of the stone fruit and nuttiness of Kumiko's first signature coffee. Roasted by Sparrow Coffee Roastery in Chicago, the first coffee we served was a nuanced single origin from the Guji Tero Farm in Ethiopia. Apricot liqueur highlights those lavish qualities and The Yanagita Koma barley shōchū complements with its floral grain structure. This cocktail is a fun way to put a little pep in your step, whether it is a midday treat or a late-night luxury. *Serves one*

2 ounces cold-brew coffee concentrate (see page 199)

½ ounce The Yanagita Koma Honkaku barley shōchū

¼ ounce apricot liqueur

Honey Cream (recipe follows), to top

In a small cordial glass, combine the cold-brew coffee concentrate, shōchū, and apricot liqueur and stir to combine. Layer with honey cream.

HONEY CREAM

Combine 1 part wildflower honey to 4 parts heavy whipping cream. Whip lightly, until the mixture thickens but still has enough viscosity to pour smoothly. Use immediately.

AISU KŌHĪ | COLD COFFEE

Just as Japanese cocktail bartenders work for decades to perfect their craft, so do Japan's coffee makers. With a carefully considered, precise approach, these baristas have created a name for themselves in the coffee world. Here are two of my favorite brew methods for summertime coffee making.

JAPANESE ICED DRIP COFFEE

This is a pour-over brewing method in which hot coffee is brewed directly onto ice, which counts for a portion of the water ratio of the coffee. This method chills the coffee instantaneously, and is one of the most vibrant cold coffees I have experienced. It is also one of the fastest ways to create a cold coffee, and not at the expense of flavor. The thing to keep in mind with this method is that you have to be precise for it to be effective, so be sure to use a scale and pay attention to the coarseness of your grind. *Serves two*

30 grams ground coffee (medium-fine grind)
135 grams ice (from filtered water)
225 grams hot water (about 207°F)

Boil a kettle of water. Line a V60 pour-over brewer with a paper filter. Rinse the filter and then add the ground coffee. Place the ice into a carafe and set the brewer on top. Bloom the coffee with 30 to 45 grams hot water, pouring slowly over the grounds from the center outward. Let the coffee bloom for 30 seconds. Then, pour again, starting at the center of the grounds, pausing every now and then as you increase the size of the circular pour so as to evenly wet all of the grounds. For each pour, keep the circular movements within the outer ring, bringing the level of the water up less and less with each pour until the full 225 grams of water has been dispersed over 3 to 6 pours (this depends on your style and preference). As the coffee drips over the ice it will chill instantly, capturing the essence of the brew.

COLD-BREW COFFEE CONCENTRATE

This popular method of making cold coffee infuses coffee grounds into cold water over the course of 12 to 24 hours, which results in a concentrate that may be cut with water, enjoyed in cocktails, or served over ice. I like to do a hot-bloom-cold-brew, which involves blooming the coffee grounds with hot water first, then filling with cold water for a cold brew. This method brings forth just a hint of the bright acidity of a hot brewed coffee to match the deeper notes achieved from a long and slow cold-brew. *Serves six to eight*

112½ grams coffee (medium-coarse grind)
750 grams water, 250 grams heated to 207°F and 500 grams at room
  temperature

Measure the ground coffee into a glass brewing vessel. Slowly pour the 250 grams of just-boiled water in small circular motions over the center of the coffee to bloom the grounds. After 30 seconds, pour the room temperature water softly over the grounds. Cover loosely and allow to sit refrigerated for at least 12 hours (and up to 24 hours, depending on how strong you want the coffee to taste). Strain through a damp coffee filter (if you are making a larger batch, a cloth filter or a filter bag may be more efficient) and store in the refrigerator. Mix with equal parts water or pour straight over ice.

taisho

INTENSE HEAT

paulownia trees produce seeds, earth is damp, air humid, great rains sometimes fall

There would come a point each summer when it felt that if the heat were to swell any further the sky itself would burst. This is taisho, the great wave of humidity that arrives at the end of July. Random bursts of heavy rain charge through, wrapping the earth in sheets of water. Bell peppers, tomatoes, and cucumbers are outstanding this time of year, eaten raw with salt or a drizzle of Kewpie mayonnaise. But they also bring incredible flavor to the cocktail glass in drinks like the Bell Pepper Margarita (page 205). At the table, we fight fire with the spicy fury of karēraisu, or Japanese curry rice. Beads of sweat glisten on our foreheads as we happily dig through bowls and bowls of rice nestled with a rich curry sauce of sanshō, fennel, turmeric, ginger, and cloves to both welcome and ward off the heat with each bite.

SOL CUBANO

Not all cocktails that win competitions become standard cocktails (the equivalent of a classic or a modern classic in America). I have tested and tasted many of these competition-winning cocktails, and when I came across the Sol Cubano, I was delighted by the appealing balance of moderate sweetness from the rum and the grapefruit, balanced with the refreshing acidity of the citrus and bitterness of the tonic water. It is the perfect summertime (or wintertime, if you need an escape) cocktail. Yoshihisa Kimura created this award-winning cocktail for Suntory's first Tropical Cocktail Competition in 1980. He named it after Cuba's sun, and you can visit the master himself at his bar, Savoy Kitanozaka, in Kobé. *Serves one*

1½ ounces white rum (Kimura-san uses Bacardi Superior)

1½ ounces fresh grapefruit juice

Indian tonic water, to top

GARNISH grapefruit wheel, mint sprig, and a reusable straw

Fill a footed tulip glass with ice. Stir to chill and pour off the melted water. Combine the rum and grapefruit juice in the glass. Give a gentle stir to chill, and top with tonic water. Take care to pour the tonic directly into the chilled liquid to retain carbonation. Nuzzle a barspoon into the glass and lift the ice gently to mix the ingredients. To garnish, place a grapefruit wheel atop the glass and finish with a straw and mint sprig through the center.

NOTE | The garnish is a key element in Japanese cocktail competitions. Kimura was very specific with his garnish: a full grapefruit wheel rested on top of the glass with a delicate sprig of mint and a straw placed through the center. He said it was inspired by the glamorous hats worn in Cuba. I typically don't serve my cocktails with straws unless the drink is served over crushed ice. But I do keep reusable glass straws at Kumiko and would urge you to find environmentally friendly straws to use for sipping your drinks as well.

TSC
(TOMATO SHERRY COBBLER)

Fresh fruit cocktails are a staple in most authentic Japanese cocktail bars, so it's no surprise the sherry cobbler is a recipe many bartenders have embraced. The classic version features sherry as the base with a crown of berries, mint, and other fresh fruit. The TSC incorporates tomato water and takes the drink in an unexpected but still very summery direction. The rosy hue and slight acidity of tomato water interweaves with fino sherry, which is dry, salty, and tastes like Marcona almonds. I suggest sipping the TSC alongside a cheese and charcuterie board, or one of my favorite izakaya dishes: tomato wedges with Kewpie mayo and salt. *Serves one*

2 ounces Valdespino Inocente fino sherry

1 ounce Tomato Water Syrup (recipe follows)

¼ ounce fresh lemon juice

GARNISH Shiso leaf, cherry tomato, and powdered sugar

In a shaker tin, combine the sherry, tomato water syrup, and lemon juice with ice. Shake just long enough to chill, then strain into a cocktail glass with crushed ice. Garnish with a green shiso leaf and a cherry tomato. Dust with powdered sugar.

TOMATO WATER SYRUP

Stem, core, and coarsely chop 1 pound vine-ripened tomatoes. Place in a blender and blend on high until smooth. Line a sieve with a dampened kitchen towel or thick paper towels and set over a bowl. Pour the tomato puree into the lined sieve and let sit. It will take about 1 hour to yield about 10 ounces of tomato water. Weigh the tomato water and mix it with half of its weight of granulated sugar and a pinch of salt, to taste. Mix until fully homogenized. Store refrigerated for up to 1 week, or portion into ice cube trays and store in your freezer until it is time for a cocktail. *Makes about 12 ounces*

BELL PEPPER MARGARITA

The margarita is a sensational summertime sipper. In Japan, it is most common to find it made with just three ingredients (tequila, lime juice, and triple sec). This framework is often adjusted in America with the inclusion of simple syrup or agave nectar. I enjoy introducing a seasonal ingredient to the template, especially in the summertime when this cocktail is so craveable. I came up with this variation to capture the essence of fresh bell peppers, which share vegetal characteristics with awamori and tequila. You won't always find margaritas on the rocks or frozen in Japanese bars—instead, bartenders usually serve them up with a salted rim—but I think the addition of ice makes this sunny version of the classic all the more enlivening. *Serves one*

Maldon sea salt, to rim the glass

1 ounce Masahiro Shuzō Shimauta awamori

¾ ounce Tequila Fortaleza Blanco

¾ ounce fresh lime juice

¼ ounce Royal Combier Grande orange liqueur

½ ounce Bell Pepper Syrup (recipe follows)

Prepare a rocks glass by salting half the rim; set aside. In a shaker tin, combine the awamori, tequila, lime juice, orange liqueur, and bell pepper syrup with ice. Shake to chill, then strain into the salt-rimmed glass over fresh ice. No additional garnish.

BELL PEPPER SYRUP

Remove the stem, membrane, and seeds from a green bell pepper and discard. Chop the remaining green parts into smaller pieces. Put through a juicer or blend in a high-powered blender and strain into a bowl. Weigh the juice and add an equal weight of granulated sugar. Whisk in a bowl or transfer to a shaker tin and shake until the sugar is fully dissolved. Store refrigerated for up to 2 weeks.

BAMBOO COCKTAIL

Perhaps the most famous cocktail served in Japan, Louis Eppinger's Bamboo is a simple, versatile, and satisfying tipple for when you are in the mood for something dry with a whisper of umami. Many a bartender has tinkered with the ratios and there is much debate over the drink's original recipe. Some say it should be equal parts dry sherry and French vermouth with orange and aromatic bitters. Others insist the cocktail was intended to be 3:1 ratio of sherry to vermouth, partnered with a single dash of orange bitters. The result of the latter ratio is a texture that's leaner, with more subdued herbaceous tones. I enjoy my Bamboo somewhere in the middle, favoring fino as the base with a dash of orange bitters and a barspoon of rich oloroso sherry for added gravity. *Serves one*

1½ ounces Valdespino Inocente fino sherry

½ ounce Dolin Dry Vermouth de Chambéry

1 dash orange bitters

1 barspoon El Maestro Sierra 15-Year oloroso sherry

GARNISH Lemon peel, lemon twist

FOR SERVING Olives (optional)

In a mixing glass, combine the fino sherry, dry vermouth, orange bitters, and oloroso sherry. Add ice and stir. Strain into a chilled coupe. Express the oils of a lemon peel over the drink and garnish with a manicured lemon twist. Sip alongside a bowl of olives or crispy, salty otsumami, if you like.

KYŪRI COCKTAIL

While the Bamboo Cocktail (page 206) is generally enjoyed year-round, its simple framework also allows for subtle seasonal changes. For my summer-friendly take on the recipe I use manzanilla sherry from the coastal region of Sanlúcar de Barrameda in Spain, which contributes a snappy green apple flavor that melds wonderfully with kyūri (cucumber). The Japanese cucumber is as adorable as the name itself with a marvelous "green" flavor and slight bitterness from the skins. To capture that vegetal sharpness, I muddle the flesh and skins together instead of peeling away the glossy covering. Génépi, a French alpine liqueur of wormwood akin to absinthe and Chartreuse, adds a hint of bitter chamomile to the equation and bridges the flavor gaps lingering between the fruity sherry, dry vermouth, and juicy cucumber. A brisk sipper for sweltering afternoons. *Serves one*

5 cucumber slices
(a scant ⅛ inch thick)

1½ ounces La Guita manzanilla sherry

1½ ounces Noilly Prat Original Dry
vermouth

1 barspoon Guillaumette L'Authentique
génépi

GARNISH Cucumber slices

Place the cucumber slices in the bottom of a mixing glass and press with a muddler just enough to crack the skin and extract some liquid. Do not pulverize the cucumbers. Add the sherry, vermouth, and génépi to the glass. Fill with ice and stir. Fine-strain into a chilled cocktail glass so no cucumber solids or seeds end up in the drink. Garnish with cucumber slices.

AUTUMN

No matter where I am, when autumn eases in I yearn for the smell of burning rice fields, a scent that permeated my childhood. During the growing season, rice paddies are a vivid green as the tall grass shoots from the swampy earth. Then comes harvest time, typically around September and October in most of the country, when farmers drain the fields and harvest the rice. As the stalks dry, the aromas change to resemble clay baking in the sun. The final step is the burning of the stalks to clear the fields. This agricultural practice is called yakihata, or burning fields, a traditional method used to revitalize the soil for the next crop.

It is a smouldering burn as little licks of orange flames creep up above the dry, golden straw. Billowing dark smoke twists into the sky and the aroma seeps into your clothes reminiscent of a campfire. You can almost feel the temperature changing around you, and that contrast of the chilly air with the smoke—the wisps of fire and that toasty straw aroma—reminds me of my favorite Japanese whiskies. Or maybe it's the whiskies that remind me of the yakihata. Either way, when I sip on those whiskies I always feel the same glow, like I am being carried home.

Autumn in Japan is a study in contrasts. In the early months, we cling to the warmth of summer while looking ahead to the excitement of cooler weather. The honeyed flowers of the osmanthus tree bloom around the same time the rice paddies burn, a mix of smoke and pretty flowers permeates the air. We celebrate the harvest moon with round and golden foods in symbolic reference to the cousin of the sun and the momiji (Japanese maple) leaves shift from green to yellow, amber, and ruby. We relish the last days of summer with rousing drinks like the apple-forward Ringo Highball (page 216). As the season progresses, we welcome the chill with sensational stirred cocktails, like the Manhattan, Vieux Carré, and Negroni—classics that have been embraced internationally, and perfected at Japanese cocktail bars.

There's a phrase, "shokuyoku no aki," which doesn't translate easily, but generally means "fall is good for eating." With foods like kabocha squash, persimmons, and ginkgo nuts, there's a bounty of flavor at every meal, and inspiration for cocktails abounds.

THE MICROSEASONS OF FALL

RISSHŪ | *autumn begins*

Japanese Cocktail
Japanese Cocktail #2
Ringo Highball
Kyohō Sour

SHŪBUN | *autumn equinox*

Momosé Manhattan
Kinmokusei Cocktail
Spiritfree: Golden One

SHOSHO | *end of heat*

Opal Martini
Sudachi Shōchū Sour
Chawari Toddy

KANRO | *crisp morning chill*

Negroni
White Negroni
Kiku Cocktail
Spiritfree: Spiced
Chrysanthemum Latte

HAKURO | *glistening white dew*

Line Cocktail
Kaki Flip
Vector
Autumn's Jacket

SŌKŌ | *first frost*

Yaki-imo Old Fashioned
Carré Nouveau
Clarified Mezcal Milk Punch

risshū

AUTUMN BEGINS

cool winds blow, evening cicadas sing,
thick fog descends

Now we live in the space that lingers between the seasons. I find
a refreshing sense of freedom with the arrival of early fall as both
summery and autumnal moments come and go in a given day. The
weather doesn't dictate a specific mood, so you can choose autumn
with a nutty orgeat drink like the Japanese Cocktail (opposite), or
celebrate the last moments of summer sunshine with a citrusy number
like a Kyohō Sour (page 219). Apples and Concord grapes show up in
the markets and thoughts turn toward the comfort of sweet potatoes
to come. The delectable delights aren't being pulled from the earth yet,
so we reach for sweet potato shōchū and sip it on the rocks on warm
days, and as oyuwari as the nights grow more brisk, bearing witness to
the cicada's last songs of the season.

JAPANESE COCKTAIL

When I first heard about the Japanese Cocktail, the name alone made me want
to explore its origins and find something to love in its esoteric combination of
ingredients. The recipe first appears in Jerry Thomas's *How to Mix Drinks* featuring
a mix of brandy, orgeat, bitters, and lemon. In the book *Imbibe!*, cocktail historian
David Wondrich says it's one of the only recipes invented by Thomas himself,
named to commemorate the time when the first Japanese legation visited New
York in 1860. When made with top-notch ingredients, the cocktail offers a medley
of fruit, nuts, and spices that align in a way that is unexpected and exciting. For
my modern interpretation, I made a cashew orgeat spiced with toasted green
cardamom and fragrant orange flower water. Using cashews instead of almonds
lifts up the darker flavors of the Cognac and shaking instead of stirring the drink
drives the cocktail into invigorating territory. *Serves one*

2 ounces H by Hine VSOP Cognac   2 dashes Angostura bitters

½ ounce Cashew Orgeat (page 316)   GARNISH Lemon peel

In a shaker tin, combine the Cognac, cashew orgeat, and bitters with ice. Shake
to chill, then strain into a cocktail glass. I do not fine-strain this cocktail, allowing
a few ice shards to lie on the surface to enhance its refreshing qualities. If that
does not appeal to you, fine-strain into the glass before garnishing. Express the
lemon peel over the top of the drink (discard the peel).

JAPANESE COCKTAIL #2

In this version of the Japanese Cocktail, I raise the potency of the drink and amplify the connection to Japan with sweet potato shōchū. I imagine this iteration being what the original recipe would have been had a Japanese bartender collaborated with Jerry Thomas on the matter. In the drink, redolent Armagnac lends a bouquet of figs, apricots, and dark chocolate—qualities that play effortlessly with the vanilla, tobacco, and leather notes of the sweet potato shōchū. Together, the French and Japanese spirits bolster the rich cashew orgeat in a sophisticated and contemporary cocktail. *Serves one*

1 ounce Marie Duffau Bas Armagnac Napoléon

1 ounce Nishi Shuzō Tenshi no Yūwaku sweet potato shōchū

½ ounce Cashew Orgeat (page 316)

2 dashes Angostura bitters

GARNISH Lemon peel, lemon twist

In a shaker tin, combine the Armagnac, sweet potato shōchū, cashew orgeat, and Angostura bitters with ice. Shake to chill, then strain into a cocktail glass. Express the lemon peel oils over the top of the drink (discard the peel), then garnish with a manicured lemon twist.

RINGO HIGHBALL

Great highballs are those that are more than the sum of their parts. For the signature version served at Kumiko I created a template that matches a fortified wine or apéritif with Japanese whisky. When we served our first guests in January 2019, the Highball No. 1 featured a 20-year-old oloroso sherry with Mars Iwai whisky (see page 107). Distilled mostly from corn, with just a touch of barley and rye, and aged in former bourbon barrels, the whisky offers sweet grain notes alongside the rich oxidative character of the oloroso.

This second version, the Ringo Highball, is all about the apple. I wanted to celebrate one of Japan's most beloved fruits while making sure the whisky would remain the star of the drink, so I chose one of my favorite apéritifs, pommeau, as the apple element and Mars Iwai 45, a higher proof version of the standard Iwai, as the whisky. For an additional aromatic element, I drizzle Normandy apple eau de vie on the top before serving—the first sip sings with character as the salty bubbles tickle your senses. Once you get into the drink, there's a wonderful baked apple flavor underneath. The combination tastes like a whisky highball, but with a dance of apple flavors just in time for autumn. *Serves one*

1¼ ounces Mars Iwai 45 Japanese whisky, chilled in the freezer (see Note)

¾ ounce Rhine Hall La Normande pommeau

Club soda, to top

GARNISH 1 barspoon Christian Drouin "Blanche de Normandie" apple brandy

Place a highball ice prism in a highball glass. Add the whisky and pommeau, and stir to integrate. Then top with club soda, being careful to pour between the ice and the glass. Slide a spoon down the side of the glass and nuzzle the ice up, allowing the ingredients to come together. Layer the apple brandy on top of the drink.

NOTE | Storing the whisky in the freezer gives the drink a lush texture and more satisfying chill, as the ice won't melt right away when you combine the ingredients.

KYOHŌ SOUR

Japan's giant mountain grape, the Kyohō, is a bulbous, inky hybrid developed to mimic the flavors of America's popular Concord variety. The fruits have a dusty slipskin so when you squeeze them the shell comes off immediately, making for an effortless snack (most are seedless, too). In the autumn, my mom would make a grape pie that I think about to this day. In tribute to my favorite fall dessert, I concocted this youthful cocktail with an old soul. In it, Japanese vodka adds an element of pepper to Concord grape vinegar. An herbaceous note comes through from the vermouth, and Champagne delivers a dry finish and playful effervescence. *Serves one*

1½ ounces Suntory Haku vodka

¾ ounce Dolin Dry Vermouth de Chambéry

½ ounce Simple Syrup (page 318)

½ ounce fresh lemon juice

¼ ounce Concord8 wine vinegar (see Note)

Splash of dry Champagne, to top

GARNISH Mint leaf

In a shaker tin, combine the vodka, dry vermouth, simple syrup, lemon juice, and vinegar with ice. Shake to chill, then strain into a coupe. Top with a splash of Champagne. Garnish with a mint leaf.

NOTE | If you cannot find the specialty vinegar, you can make a version with grape juice. It yields a more playful mix, but the drink will have a similar temperament to the original. Combine 1½ ounces vodka, ¾ ounce vermouth, ½ ounce Concord grape juice, ½ ounce simple syrup, and ¾ ounce lemon juice. Shake with ice to chill, then strain into a coupe. Garnish with a mint leaf.

shosho

END OF THE HEAT

cotton flowers bloom,
earth begins to cool, rice ripens

A shift in the air signals cooler temperatures to follow as summer's late harvest finally wanes. Sunflowers smile and appetites return with a soft sigh of happiness. We flock to the stores and izakaya for seasonal nihonshu known as akiagari and hiyaoroshi. Both are an evolution of spring's first batches of nihonshu—the former pasteurized before resting and again when bottled, while the latter is only pasteurized once, before resting—a delicious way to welcome autumn to the table. It is a fitting time for cocktails like the Chawari Toddy or the comforting cuddle of a hot mug of bancha, demure and unpretentious.

OPAL MARTINI

Don't judge this drink solely by its charming pink hue. Underneath its flirty beauty lies a lush vivacity and sturdy balance of flavor, thanks to the union of opulent junmai-shu and fragrant lemongrass shōchū. A surprising number of green flavors come through from the fennel-like freshness of Peychaud's bitters, making it the perfect drink for clinging to the end of summer. From there, a tickle of clove and nutmeg emerges from the rum and falernum, and the saké wraps everything together in a soft blanket of sweet rice. You can use any junmai and the cocktail will taste great, but the Shared Promise from Chiyonosono is one I adore for its captivating personality. *Serves one; photo page 223*

1½ ounces Chiyonosono Shared Promise junmai

¾ ounce Mizu Lemongrass shōchū or homemade lemongrass-infused shōchū (recipe follows)

¾ ounce El Dorado 3-Year rum

1 barspoon John D. Taylor's Velvet falernum

1 dash orange bitters

3 dashes Peychaud's bitters

GARNISH Lime twist

In a mixing glass, combine the saké, shōchū, rum, falernum, and both bitters. Add ice and stir to chill. Strain into a chilled stemmed glass. Garnish with a manicured twist of lime.

LEMONGRASS-INFUSED SHŌCHŪ

Peel the outer leaves and trim the tips and tails of 2 stalks of fresh lemongrass. Rinse thoroughly and pat dry. Take the tip of a knife and slice through the lower stalk of the lemongrass, rotating to make three incisions while keeping the stalk intact. This will make for a better infusion and allow you to remove the lemongrass more easily when it is ready. Place the prepared lemongrass into a 750-milliliter bottle of rice or barley shōchū at room temperature and infuse for 3 days. I suggest Chiyonosono 8,000 Generations rice shōchū, Takahashi Shuzō's Hakutake Shiro rice shōchū, or their Ginrei Shiro rice shōchū for this infusion. The infusion will last indefinitely.

SHŌCHŪ INGREDIENTS

To make honkaku shōchū, one must follow certain processes (see page 187). Here is a current list of the 54 approved ingredients. Not all are available outside of Japan, and many are rare even there. I have set a personal goal to taste as many as I can! Use this guide in your own search for honkaku shōchū.

米 | kome (rice)

麦 | mugi (barley)

芋 | imo (sweet potato)

黒糖 | kokutō (black sugar)

そば | soba (buckwheat)

あしたば | ashitaba (a type of angelica)

あずき | adzuki (red mung bean)

あまちゃづる | amachazuru (an herb known as southern ginseng)

アロエ | aloé (aloe)

ウーロン茶 | oolongcha (oolong tea)

梅の種 | umé pits (pits from a fruit similar to apricot)

えのきたけ | enokitaké (enoki mushroom)

おたねにんじん | otane ninjin (panax ginseng)

かぼちゃ | kabocha (a squash)

牛乳 | gyūnyū (cow's milk)

ぎんなん | ginnan (gingko seeds)

くず粉 | kudzuko (a starch from the roots of kudzu)

くまざさ | kumazasa (a type of bamboo)

くり | kuri (chestnut)

グリーンピース | gurīnpīsu (peas)

こならの実 | konara no mi (a seed of konara oak)

ごま | goma (sesame seeds)

こんぶ | kombu (a type kelp)

サフラン | safuran (saffron)

サボテン | sabotén (cactus)

しいたけ | shiitake (a mushroom)

しそ | shiso (an herb in the mint family)

大根 | daikon (a radish)

脱脂粉乳 | dasshifun'nyū (skim milk powder)

たまねぎ | tamanégi (onion)

つのまた | tsunomata (a red algae)

つるつる | tsurutsuru (another, rarer red algae)

とちのきの実 | tochinoki no mi (horse chestnuts)

トマト | tomato

なつめやしの実 | natsuméyashi no mi (date)

にんじん | ninjin (carrot)

ネギ | négi (green onion)

のり | nori (seaweed)

ピーマン | pīman (bell pepper)

ひしの実 | hishi no mi (fruit of a water plant)

ひまわりの種 | himawari no tané (sunflower seeds)

ふきのとう | fukinotō (butterbur sprouts)

べにばな | benibana (safflower)

ホエイパウダー | hoeipaudā (whey powder)

ほていあおい | hoteiaoi (water hyacinth)

またたび | matatabi (silvervine, a plant in the kiwifruit family)

抹茶 | matcha (stone-ground green tea)

まてばしいの実 | matebashi no mi (nut of the beech tree)

ゆりね | yuriné (lily root)

よもぎ | yomogi (mugwort)

落花生 | rakkasei (peanut plant)

緑茶 | ryokucha (green tea)

れんこん | renkon (lotus root)

わかめ | wakamé (a type of seaweed)

OPAL MARTINI

(page 221)

SUDACHI SHŌCHŪ SOUR

When sudachi, a citrus fruit grown in Japan's southern prefecture of Tokushima, comes into season, it becomes the star of food and drink in Japanese households and restaurants. Best known for its role in the soy and citrus dipping sauce called ponzu, the fruit also makes a memorable addition to cocktails that call for citrus juice. To highlight the seasonal flavor, I created this Cosmopolitan-like refresher with sudachi liqueur along with grapefruit and lime. The addition of Royal Combier, an orange liqueur enhanced with nutmeg, cardamom, saffron, and aloe, creates a pool of rich citrus notes that engage with the brightness of the shōchū. *Serves one*

2 ounces Awa No Kaori Sudachi Chū

½ ounce fresh lime juice

½ ounce fresh grapefruit juice

¼ ounce Simple Syrup (page 318)

¼ ounce Royal Combier Grande orange liqueur

GARNISH Sudachi or lime wheel

In a shaker tin, combine the Sudachi Chū, lime juice, grapefruit juice, simple syrup, and orange liqueur with ice. This cocktail requires a gentle shake to chill and aerate as the Sudachi Chū is lower in proof, so keep that in mind when mixing. Strain into a chilled cocktail glass. Garnish with a wheel of sudachi (or lime if you cannot find fresh sudachi).

shosho

CHAWARI TODDY

Served cold in a highball or hot in toddy form, the combination of tea and shōchū is a reliable standby for when that first nip in the air hints at the bitter chill to follow. It is the kind of drink I might put together at home—straightforward and light-bodied, demonstrating balance of the mild tannins of the tea and the flavor of the spirit. It is also low-proof, so you can snuggle up with a full pot of tea and a bottle of shōchū for a prolonged and pleasant evening of sipping. I do suggest a shōchū around 25% ABV for this recipe, though a higher proof shōchū will work fine with a slight calibration of the ratios. *Serves one*

5 ounces Hot Bancha (recipe follows)

1½ ounces shōchū

¼ ounce Rich Honey Syrup (page 317)

GARNISH Lemon or orange wheel (optional)

Pour the freshly brewed bancha into a mug. Add the shōchū and honey syrup. Stir briefly to combine. This one doesn't need a garnish, though if you want, you can garnish with a lemon or orange wheel to add a lingering marmalade note over the top of the drink.

HOT BANCHA

In a glass or ceramic brewing vessel, combine 2 teaspoons bancha and 6½ ounces water just off the boil (around 195°F) and steep for 2 to 3 minutes. Bancha may be resteeped up to three times. As you resteep, you may need to raise the temperature of the water incrementally. *Makes 6 ounces*

hakuro

THE GLISTENING WHITE DEW

white dew glistens on the grass,
wagtails sing, swallows leave

It is finally time to pull out the jackets and scarves. The grass gathers condensation in the mornings and evenings as temperatures swing more dramatically throughout the shorter days. Kaki (persimmons) turn from green and yellow to monarch orange, and as soon as they are ripe, I implement them in cocktails like the Kaki Flip (page 230). When the harvest moon arrives, people gather for the Otsukimi festival to celebrate with foods that remind us of the moon, like chestnuts, sunny-side up eggs, and dumplings. In Japan, there is no "man in the moon" as Westerners say; instead we say there is "tsuki no usagi" (the moon's rabbit) who is pounding mochi (glutinous rice cakes). During the harvest moon festival we also eat special omochi.

LINE COCKTAIL

Created by Japanese bartender Yonekichi Maeda, who wrote one of Japan's first cocktail books, *Kokutēru,* in 1924, the Line Cocktail is an obscure treasure that has faded from popularity over time. This could be because the original drink—equal parts gin, sweet vermouth, and Bénédictine with two dashes of Angostura bitters—is a glass of syrupy sweetness rich enough to irk even the most avid sweet tooth. Yet, if you consider the fact that most of Maeda's recipes were intended to be served in very small cordial glasses instead of the larger coupes and cocktail glasses we use today, it makes more sense—it is intended to be finished quickly, at its very coldest, so it remains palatable. Maeda shakes the drink instead of stirring (as contemporary bartending technique would normally instruct) to aerate the cocktail and liven up the texture, which makes the overall experience less cloying. This drink would be great for fans of the Bijou, Hanky Panky, or Martinez cocktails. *Serves one; photo on page 235*

⅓ ounce The Kyōto Distillery Ki No Bi Kyōto dry gin

⅓ ounce Cocchi Vermouth di Torino

⅓ ounce Bénédictine

2 dashes Angostura bitters

GARNISH Pickled rakkyō (see Note, page 234)

In a shaker tin, combine the gin, sweet vermouth, Bénédictine, and Angostura bitters with ice. Shake to chill, then strain into a small cordial glass. Garnish with a gently crushed pickled rakkyō.

FREEZER VERSION

I batch and store a bottle of this cocktail in the freezer for ease of use. For the freezer version, combine 8 ounces each of gin, vermouth, and Bénédictine with 8 dashes of Angostura bitters in a 750-milliliter bottle. (Do not add more bitters at this point because there is a likelihood of ruining the flavor of the drink. You can add more to taste later if needed.) Store in the freezer. To serve, pour a nip over ice, or measure out a few drams and shake to serve up, then garnish. Optionally, add dashes of Angostura to taste.

KAKI FLIP

The stunning display of oranges and reds of the kaki (persimmon) fruits suddenly bursting against the blue sky lifts my spirits this time of the year. The key thing to remember with kaki, as with many things in life, is patience. While the color may indicate a readiness, wait until the fruit feels soft and squishy to the touch before you cut off the tops and eat the insides with a spoon. Or, as in this cocktail, scoop the sweet flesh into your shaker and whip up a tasty treat! For this drink I use a soba (buckwheat) shōchū called Touge, which comes from Kitsukura Brewery in Nagano. Touge shares some of the honeyed notes of persimmon and has a vanilla-tinged buttery tone, which plays beautifully with saffron-scented yellow Chartreuse. To round out the drink, choose an earthy junmai-shu, because the rice and the buckwheat meld together for a smooth flavor profile. The egg brings velvety viscosity to the glass, making it even more comforting to sip. *Serves one*

1½ tablespoons fully ripened Fuyū persimmon flesh

1½ ounces Akashi-Tai Tokubetsu Honjōzo saké

1 ounce Kitsukura Touge soba shōchū

¼ ounce yellow Chartreuse

½ ounce Simple Syrup (page 318)

1 egg

GARNISH Grated nutmeg

In a shaker tin, combine the persimmon, saké, shōchū, Chartreuse, simple syrup, and egg. Dry shake to combine. Add ice, then shake again to chill. Strain into a chilled coupe. Garnish with freshly grated nutmeg.

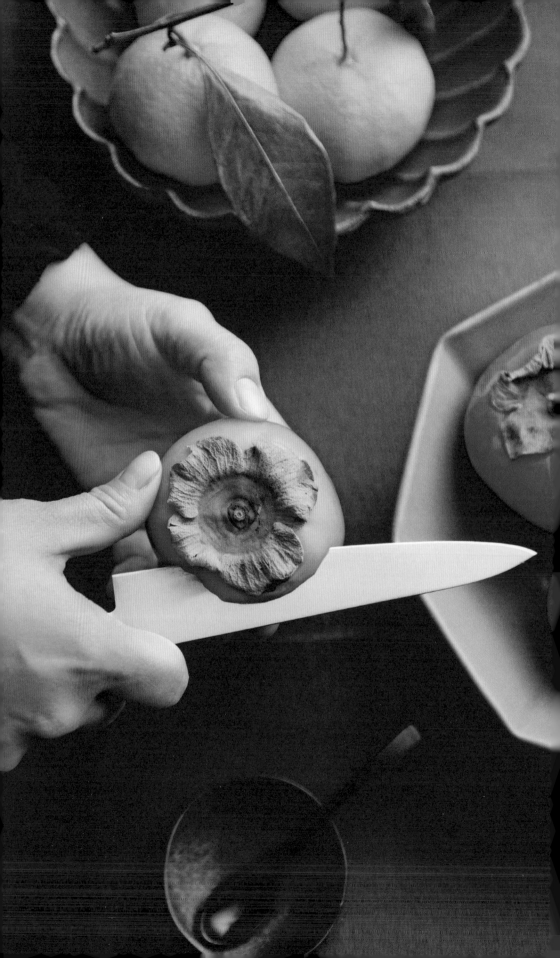

PERSIMMONS

Persimmons, or *kaki* in Japanese, are said to have come over to Japan from China as early as the seventh century. The fruit would then soon be broadly cultivated, resulting in the thousands of different varieties found in Japan today. Aside from being enjoyed as a fresh treat, persimmons are used for their insect repellent capabilities, for dying fabrics, and as a fining agent for nihonshu production.

There are three main classifications of Japanese persimmon: amagaki (sweet persimmon), shibugaki (astringent or tannic persimmons), and fukanzen amagaki (immature sweet persimmons—these only become sweet if seeds grow). Within those classifications, Fuyū is one type of amagaki that is common in the US. They are easily recognizable with their signature shape: squat and round, sort of like a miniature pumpkin. The skins are a saturated harvest orange and the flesh a lighter color similar to orange sherbet. Fuyūgaki are quite popular because they are ready to eat even before they are fully ripe; firm and sweet, with only a hint of bitterness. The other type found in America falls under the shibugaki classification: Hachiya persimmons are oblong and conical in shape, almost like a drop of water just before it falls from the surface onto which it clings. They were developed in the town of Hachiya in Gifu prefecture, just north of Nagoya. Shibugaki persimmons are extremely tannic, so they can only be eaten when fully ripened.

One common ritual in Japan through the fall and winter months is hoshigaki, or the practice of drying persimmons. It can take weeks or months, depending on the temperature and humidity of the environment in which you dry the fruit. But it is worth the wait, and the carefully hung orange orbs swinging like pendulums of old clocks is a joy to behold. Shibugaki persimmons are best suited for hoshigaki as the extra tannins help repel insects as they dry. The drying process neutralizes the tannins, making the final product even sweeter than fully ripened amagaki. To do this at home, first wash the persimmons in water and peel the skin. Dip the fruit in shōchū or neutral spirit to sanitize and then hang the persimmons by the stem in a bright, airy part of the house. After the outer layer begins to harden, massage the persimmons every day, and then every other day as the weeks progress to work the sugars together. Over time you will see a white coating on the outside of the hoshigaki. These are the sugars seeping out, a sign that the dried fruit is just about ready to eat. I like to eat hoshigaki sliced and paired with a mug of brewed matcha, or seasoned with a sprinkle of salt and served alongside sweet potato shōchū mixed with hot water.

VECTOR

For the Vector, my version of the Line Cocktail (page 229), I split French dry with Italian bianco vermouth to flesh out a bouquet of botanicals that play well with the shy tannins from the Ki No Bi dry gin. To the Gibson-like base comes Bénédictine as a honeyed kiss resonating through the glass. The flavor profile is familiar at first, as the juniper and vermouth intertwine, then the sweet nature of the Bénédictine partnered with the savory rakkyō makes this sipper stand apart from the rest. *Serves one*

⅓ ounce The Kyōto Distillery Ki No Bi Kyōto dry gin

⅓ ounce Bénédictine

⅓ ounce Bèrto Aperitiv dla Tradission bianco vermouth

⅓ ounce Noilly Prat Original Dry vermouth

2 dashes Angostura bitters

GARNISH Lemon peel, grapefruit peel, and pickled rakkyō (see Note)

In a shaker tin, combine the dry gin, Bénédictine, bianco vermouth, dry vermouth, and Angostura bitters with ice. Shake to chill, then strain into a small cordial glass. Express the oils of lemon and grapefruit peels over the top of the drink (discard the peels). Garnish with rakkyō.

NOTE | Rakkyō are similar to shallots, with bulbs marginally larger than your typical scallion. When pickled, they have a snappy texture with a sweet onion-like flavor and sour notes coming from the pickling process. A cocktail onion is a potential substitute, but do keep in mind that its flavor is more bitter than a rakkyō.

LINE COCKTAIL

(page 229)

VECTOR

AUTUMN'S JACKET

In the fall and winter months at Kumiko, it often feels like you'll never shake Chicago's eternal chill, so if a guest looks cold we will offer them a silky pashmina to cozy up with during their visit. This drink is all about capturing those snug vibes in cocktail form. A barley-based shōchū provides a roasty shelf upon which the other fall-friendly ingredients land. Cynar, an artichoke-based Italian amaro, bears dry and woodsy notes, a bouquet that mingles perfectly with the deep spice and honey flavors of Bénédictine. From there, luxurious crème de cassis brings in a deep black currant flavor with a wine-like quality—like the moody cousin of the perky cranberry. All together, it's a big bouquet of cashmere and spice. *Serves one*

1½ ounces Kintaro Honkaku barley shōchū

½ ounce crème de cassis

½ ounce Cynar

¼ ounce Bénédictine

¼ ounce Simple Syrup (page 318)

¼ ounce fresh lemon juice

GARNISH Rosemary sprig

In a shaker tin, combine the shōchū, crème de cassis, Cynar, Bénédictine, simple syrup, and lemon juice with ice. Shake to chill, then strain into a rocks glass over ice. Float a burning match around the tip of the rosemary sprig, to warm and awaken the herb, but not burn it. This provides woodsy aromatics without the char. Garnish with the rosemary.

shūbun

AUTUMN EQUINOX

thunder lowers its voice, hibernating creatures
close their doors, farmers drain fields

Just as the shincha harvest heralds spring, when the rice crops are
ready for the taking it means fall has arrived in full force. Shinmai,
the official word for newly harvested rice, is enjoyed and celebrated
as rice is harvested through September and October across Japan.
Prefectures like Hokkaidō, Nīgata, and Akita especially are known for
their rice production. Fresh grains are heavy with more moisture than
rice that's left to age, and once steamed, the grains grow even more
plump and slightly sweet. Shinmai is often enjoyed simply with just a
sprinkle of salt or cooked with chestnuts or matsutaké, a white canvas
to showcase fall's bounty. Later, the rice paddies are drained and
burned to revitalize the soil, and the smoke evokes scent memories of
Japanese whisky—the moment has come to consider drinks like the
Manhattan, picturesque classics which are spirit-forward in nature but
sip like the caress of ginkgo leaves against your skin.

MOMOSÉ MANHATTAN

I delight in a good Manhattan. When you find the right balance of whisk(e)y, vermouth, and bitters, it is one of the most superb cocktails in the world. In Japan, the cocktail is commonly served up with American whiskey, like Old Overholt rye or Wild Turkey bourbon, a detail I was moved to replicate in this recipe. For my personal variation I was inspired by the Perfect Manhattan, which uses both dry and sweet vermouth. I was first introduced to the cocktail in my early days as a bartender, while working for Cornell Catering. I was both taken aback and drawn in by the intensity with which a guest dictated how he wanted the cocktail made. This led me to research more fully classic cocktails and their iterations. To this day, some of my favorite drinks are those made "perfectly," with a split of sweet and dry, or with a split-base spirit. Instead of French dry vermouth, however, I like to use Pineau des Charentes, which has an inherent fruitiness and noticeable acidity that cuts through the lavish texture of the sweet vermouth. From there, the minty alpine botanicals that define Amaro Bràulio stand in for the Angostura bitters, offering a novel layer of bitterness that evokes the flavors of fall in Italy. At the end of the day, it still tastes like a Manhattan, just with a few personal twists and turns in the flavor. *Serves one; photo on page 240*

1½ ounces High West Rendezvous
  rye whiskey

½ ounce Amaro Bràulio

½ ounce Pineau des Charentes

½ ounce Cocchi Vermouth di Torino

GARNISH Lemon peel

In a mixing glass, combine the rye whiskey, amaro, Pineau des Charentes, and sweet vermouth. Add ice and stir to chill. Strain into a chilled coupe. Express the oils of a lemon peel over the top of the drink (discard the peel).

MOMOSÉ MANHATTAN

(page 239)

JAPANESE WHISKY STANDARDS

I am often asked, "What makes Japanese whisky so special?" I could speak to the pure waters of Yamazaki Distillery, the fresh mountain air of Hakushu, the traditions of Yoichi blended with the modernization of Miyagikyo. There is the innovation and passion of Chichibu, the inspiring story and resilience of Hombo, the pedigree of Eigashima and the terroir of Akkeshi. However, the success of Japanese whisky goes beyond the ingredients, the technique, and even the letter of the law. It is the focused intent of the people behind these whiskies that makes them so distinct and of world-renown. There are those who have taken advantage of the prestige of the name "Japanese whisky" and have diluted the reputation. They follow the letter of the law but fail to represent the spirit of monozukuri.

Until recently, the phrase "Japanese whisky" on a label has been a guarantee of quality. However, there are few rules pertaining to what can and cannot be called "Japanese whisky" in Japan. At the time of writing, the current rules state that the spirit must be made from cereal grains (rice koji may not be used) and aged in barrels. There are no minimum age requirements, barrel specifications, or stipulations concerning the origin of the distillate. What this means is that Japanese companies may purchase and bottle 100 percent imported spirit and label and sell it as Japanese whisky. Additionally, they are able to cut aged whisky with new-make whisky.

In order to protect the category, on January 12, 2021, a set of voluntary standards was published by members of the Japan Spirits and Liqueurs Makers Association (JSLMA). The JSLMA is not a government-run organization, so the criteria are based on an honor system. Members include Venture Whisky, Nikka, Suntory, Komasa, Hombo, Hikari, Gaiaflow, Akkeshi, Eigashima, and twenty-five other whisky-license holding establishments (though not all are producing whisky at this time). On top of current standards set forth by the government, here are the requirements for a whisky to qualify for "Japanese whisky" labeling according to the JSLMA:

INGREDIENTS: Malt or grains, and water from Japan. Malted barley must be used.

PRODUCTION: Saccharification, fermentation, and distillation must take place in Japan. The alcohol content at the time of distillation shall be less than 95% ABV.

AGING: Rested in wooden barrels with a content of 700 liters or less, and aged in Japan for at least 3 years.

BOTTLING: Must be bottled in Japan, with an alcohol content of 40% ABV or above.

OTHER: Plain caramel coloring may be used.

I am hopeful that the Japanese government will soon update the current regulations to reflect these standards. Until then, we can continue to sip with confidence from producers who are transparent about their distilling and blending practices.

KINMOKUSEI COCKTAIL

When late fall arrives, most of the world fades into muted tones. Leaves fall to the ground and rustle underfoot, and everything starts to move in slow motion as the kinmokusei (osmanthus) flowers awaken—the buds offer one last bewitching moment of intense drama before winter arrives. To tap into the spirit of that moment, I created this gimlet-inspired cocktail with komé (rice) shōchū, Japanese gin, lime, Galliano, and a syrup made with osmanthus flowers. It is a gin drinker's cocktail, with an added element of botanicals from the Galliano and soft rice notes from the shōchū. *Serves one*

1½ ounces Takahashi Shuzō Hakutake Shiro rice shōchū

½ ounce Nikka Coffey gin

½ ounce Kinmokusei Syrup (page 318)

¾ ounce fresh lime juice

¼ ounce Galliano L'Autentico liqueur

GARNISH Lime peel and rosemary sprig

In a shaker tin, combine the shōchū, gin, kinmokusei syrup, lime juice, and Galliano with ice. Shake to chill, then strain into a cocktail glass. Garnish with a lime peel and a small tuft of rosemary.

SPIRITFREE

GOLDEN ONE

At my childhood home, lining a set of stairs that led up to the house were boulders, all in different sizes and shapes, with some covered in fuzzy patches of moss. Like a cushion meant just for me, I'd sit and listen to the birds sing, and smell the angelic kinmokusei flowers. To capture the essence of the flower in a spiritfree drink, I created this cooler reminiscent of a tall glass of lemonade. Yuzu juice brings a sparkle of citrus to the honey notes of the syrup, reminding me of those moments breathing in the cold air laced with the aroma of the flowers. Green tea adds bones to the otherwise breezy mix, which serves as a sunny contrast to the comforting foods of fall. *Serves one*

2 ounces Cold-Brew Sencha
(page 320)

1 ounce Kinmokusei Syrup
(page 318)

¼ ounce fresh lemon juice

1 ounce yuzu juice

Splash of tonic water, to top

GARNISH Thyme sprig

In a shaker tin, combine the cold-brew sencha, kinmokusei syrup, lemon juice, and yuzu juice with ice. Whip-shake to bring the ingredients together and soften the edges of the citrus. Strain into a chilled highball glass over fresh ice. Top with a splash of tonic water. Garnish with a sprig of thyme.

NOTE | If you can find fresh yuzu juice, that will be best for this cocktail. But you can also use pasteurized juice if that is what is available to you.

kanro

CRISP MORNING CHILL

wild geese return, chrysanthemums
bloom, crickets chirp

Autumn is deepening. The sky feels intensely blue and there's something special about the way the sun shines through the leaves as they change color. Similar to how the sakura blossoms impress in the spring, the way the momiji (Japanese maple) leaves meander through their natural color palette attracts eager onlookers from thousands of miles away. Some trees change color faster than others, so the shift inches like a caterpillar across the landscape. One plant that holds particular significance this time of year is the genteel chrysanthemum, a soulful flower that blooms in shades of white, yellow, and maroon. The kiku, or chysanthemum, is the imperial emblem of Japan, and it represents longevity, goodwill, and the autumnal season, when the flower is celebrated with festivals. As the chrysanthemum's season arrives, we eat the leaves and bulbs, seek out foods made to imitate its shape, and float its flower petals in glasses of saké to lean into the moment.

NEGRONI

Continuing our exploration of classic cocktails that have found a place in Japanese bars, the Negroni is a three-ingredient Italian classic many bartenders strive to perfect. Within its structured framework, even the slightest variation can result in something new and interesting, which is what I aimed for when developing this build behind the bar at GreenRiver. It is still technically equal parts but with a subtle flavor adjustment via a split base of bitters—the addition of Gran Classico, with dried orange peel and woodsy spice flavors like a lush suede, helps temper Campari's aggressive bristles. I also prefer my Negronis on ice, because the richness of the drink can handle a wash of dilution over time and still maintain its integrity. It welcomes the water, just as we welcome the cold that settles in late fall. *Serves one*

1 ounce The Kyōto Distillery Ki No Bi Kyōto dry gin

1 ounce Cocchi Vermouth di Torino

½ ounce Campari

½ ounce Tempus Fugit Gran Classico bitter

GARNISH Lemon peel and orange peel

In a mixing glass, combine the gin, sweet vermouth, Campari, and Gran Classico. Add ice and stir to chill. Strain into a rocks glass over fresh ice. Express the oils of a lemon peel over the top of the drink (discard the peel). With a match, lightly flame an orange peel over the drink (discard the peel).

WHITE NEGRONI

During the chrysanthemum season in the Gion district of Kyōto, flowing strands and meticulously manicured displays of the white, yellow, and maroon flowers show up in front of stores as obeisance to the national flower of Japan. In this Negroni improvisation invented in memory of that moment, the flavor of the flower manifests via a sweet liqueur. Glittering with citrus and a medley of botanicals from Suze, gin, and Cocchi Americano, this drink has amazing complexity when the woodsy notes of gentian play with the green tea tannins in Suntory's Roku gin. A drop of sunshine to lengthen short autumn days. *Serves one*

1 ounce Suntory Roku gin

¼ ounce Suze apéritif

¼ ounce Koval chrysanthemum and honey liqueur

¾ ounce Cocchi Americano dry white vermouth

5 drops Scrappy's cardamom bitters

GARNISH Lemon peel and orange peel

In a mixing glass, combine the gin, Suze, chrysanthemum liqueur, Cocchi Americano, and bitters. Add ice and stir to chill. Strain into a rocks glass over fresh ice. Express the oils of orange and lemon peels over the top of the drink (discard the peels).

SPICED
CHRYSANTHEMUM
LATTE

(page 252)

KIKU
COCKTAIL

KIKU COCKTAIL

A chic and easygoing balance defines this cocktail, which epitomizes the cold morning chill that sweeps in this time of year. Like many Japanese cocktails, great efforts were taken to make the complicated drink appear simple. If you focus, you might notice every sip tastes different based on what you're thinking about in that moment. You can taste the flowers and honey if you concentrate, or revel in the clean vodka that comes through at the finish. With its interplay of sweet honey and opulent saké, this drink would appeal to fans of a classic Bee's Knees cocktail. For those familiar with the Chrysanthemum Cocktail, a classic from *The Savoy Cocktail Book* featuring dry vermouth, Bénédictine, and absinthe, think of this as its sunny cousin. *Serves one*

1 ounce Suntory Haku vodka

1 ounce Dolin Dry Vermouth de Chambéry

1 ounce Chiyonosono Shared Promise junmai saké

½ ounce Koval chrysanthemum and honey liqueur

½ ounce Simple Syrup (page 318)

½ ounce fresh lemon juice

GARNISH 3 spritzes absinthe and a lemon twist

In a shaker tin, combine the vodka, vermouth, saké, liqueur, simple syrup, and lemon juice with ice. Shake to chill, then strain into a cocktail glass. Spritz the drink three times with absinthe and garnish with a lemon twist.

SPICED CHRYSANTHEMUM LATTE

Chrysanthemum tisane illuminates the complexities of the flower splendidly. With a golden sunflower hue, it has a grassy flavor with deep sylvan notes buried underneath a layer of fetching floral aromas. To celebrate the season, I pair the floral brew with cashew milk sweetened with Okinawa black sugar and spiced with star anise, sanshō, and coriander. This brings the spiritfree away from a simple afternoon tea and into the realm of a distinct and complex drink. With a medley of nutty spice and floral overtones, it's a delight suited for sipping any time of the day or night. I suggest snuggling up under a blanket or heated kotatsu to enjoy this spiritfree alongside some wagashi and light reading. *Serves one; photo on page 250*

6 ounces Chrysanthemum Tisane (opposite)

½ ounce Spiced Kuromitsu (opposite)

1 ounce cashew milk

In a teacup, combine the hot chrysanthemum tisane, spiced kuromitsu, and cashew milk. Stir briefly to combine. No garnish.

CHRYSANTHEMUM TISANE

In a glass or ceramic brewing vessel, measure 1 to 1½ teaspoons chrysanthemum herbal tea. Pour 8 ounces just-boiled water over the flowers and steep for 5 to 10 minutes. The flowers may be resteeped over and over again. For the latte recipe (opposite), I suggest using first-steep tea as the flavor is more pronounced. *Makes about 7 ounces*

SPICED KUROMITSU

With a mortar and pestle, crack enough star anise pods to yield 2 tablespoons, and combine with 1 teaspoon dried sanshō berries and 2 teaspoons coriander seeds. In a dry saucepan, toast the cracked spices over medium-low heat until aromatic. Add 1 cup room-temperature water, bring to a boil over medium-high heat, and simmer for 3 minutes. Strain the spiced water over ¾ cup of shaved kokutō in a tempered bowl. Stir until the kokutō dissolves into a homogenous mixture; I recommend doing this over a double boiler as the kokutō can be difficult to dissolve (hence the tempered bowl). Measure in 5 tablespoons honey. Stir until fully incorporated and chill. Store refrigerated for up to 3 weeks. *Makes 10 ounces*

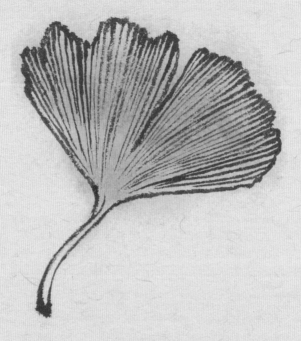

THE FIRST FROST

the first frost comes, light rains fall,
maple leaves and ivy turn yellow

There's always a tinge of sadness when the first frost arrives. It appears without warning, shaking you into the realization that winter no longer lies in wait—it is upon the doorstep. While golden fans of ginkgo leaves still cling to their branches, sweet potatoes emerge in full flush, and other autumnal flavors like walnuts and pomegranates take root in bars and restaurants everywhere. This time of year, we brave the cold to find sublime comfort in intimate drinking dens. There is that brief moment of overheating from the temperature change, and as I teeter on the balance of hot and cold, all I want to drink is a simple classic, like a balanced Vieux Carré (see my version, the Carré Nouveau, page 258). It's time to burrow even further into the standard cocktails—the kind that Japanese bartenders do best.

YAKI-IMO OLD FASHIONED

Fall is satsumaimo season! When a chill hits the air, the street food trucks exchange coolers and kakigōri for a wood-fired grill and bushels of satsumaimo, or Japanese sweet potatoes, destined to become yaki-imo (roasted sweet potatoes). Holding yaki-imo and peeling away the magenta skin to reveal the sweet golden flesh is a tantalizing moment of autumn in Japan that I wanted to bring into the glass. The old fashioned is the perfect template—the spiced kuromitsu brings baking spice and caramel characteristics to the combination of brooding whisky and slow-cooked sweet potato. Each ingredient shines in its own right, but together they create a stunning synergy. *Serves one; photo on page 256*

2 ounces Salt-Roasted Sweet Potato–Infused Japanese Whisky (recipe follows)

½ ounce Spiced Kuromitsu (page 253)

2 dashes Angostura bitters

GARNISH Orange peel and Scrappy's cardamom bitters

In a mixing glass, combine the infused whisky, spiced kuromitsu, and Angostura bitters. Add ice and stir to chill. Strain into a rocks glass over one large piece of ice. Express the oils of a manicured orange peel over the top of the drink and garnish with the manicured peel and one drop of green cardamom bitters.

YAKI-IMO
OLD FASHIONED

(page 255)

SATSUMAIMO
(JAPANESE SWEET POTATOES)

According to Japan's Ministry of Agriculture, Forestry and Fisheries, there are around sixty registered varieties of this tasty root vegetable that grow in Japan. The five most cultivated varieties, making up 72 percent of production, are Koganesengan, Beni Azuma, Kō-kei 14, Shiroyutaka, and Beni Hakura. Koganesengan is typically used in imo shōchū production, Shiroyutaka is used as a raw starch material, and the remaining three are popular for culinary uses. Beni Azuma is loved for the rich, chestnut sweetness it takes on when cooked.

Japanese sweet potato varieties in general have more starch content than American sweet potatoes. They are notable for their magenta skin wrapped around a pale yellow interior, which darkens to daisy yellow when cooked. American sweet potatoes, on the other hand, tend to be a burnt orange hue in and out. Since the Japanese sweet potato has a distinct nutty flavor profile and concentrated sweetness that American sweet potatoes lack, I do not suggest swapping out one for the other. See below for a recipe that infuses Japanese whisky with the rich flavor of this beloved ingredient.

SALT-ROASTED SWEET POTATO-INFUSED
JAPANESE WHISKY

Preheat the oven to 425°F. Wash 2 to 3 medium sweet potatoes and prick a few holes into the skin using a fork. Line a medium baking sheet with foil and cast a thick layer of coarse kosher salt over the foil. Then place the prepared sweet potatoes on the bed of salt and cover with another layer of salt. Wrap the edges of the foil up over the sweet potatoes and cover with another sheet of foil and bake for 1 hour. Remove the top piece of foil and continue to bake for another 15 minutes. Once cool enough to handle, brush the salt from the skin of the sweet potatoes. Peel the sweet potatoes and break them apart into smaller pieces. Place 1½ cups of the roasted sweet potatoes into a large container with a lid and add a 750-milliliter bottle of Japanese whisky (something with an ABV of 45% or higher, such as Ichiro's Malt and Grain, Nikka From The Barrel or Hibiki Japanese Harmony). Set aside to infuse for 2 days, shaking well two or three times a day to break apart the sweet potato. Strain through a coffee filter or cheesecloth and store in an airtight container or sterilized bottle in the refrigerator for up to 1 month. *Makes about 20 ounces*

CARRÉ NOUVEAU

The Vieux Carré is another classic cocktail near and dear to my heart. Invented in New Orleans in the 1930s, it resembles the Manhattan, but offers a more potent layering of flavors with Cognac, bitters, and Bénédictine in addition to rye whiskey. To bring a Japanese essence to the cocktail, iichiko Saiten shōchū steps in place of the rye whiskey, offering notes of jasmine tea and a tinge of funky mustiness from the high percentage of barley kōji used in production. Armagnac appears as a supporting character in lieu of the Cognac, with luxurious chocolate notes and a brawny texture; the stately grape distillate melds into the richly spiced and herbaceous quality of the Bénédictine and bitters. I think of this variation as a more robust, but still refined, take on the Vieux Carré. *Serves one*

¾ ounce Marie Duffau Bas Armagnac Napoléon

¾ ounce iichiko Saiten barley shōchū

½ ounce Bénédictine

2 dashes Peychaud's bitters

2 dashes Angostura bitters

GARNISH Lemon peel

In a mixing glass, combine the Armagnac, shōchū, Bénédictine, and both bitters. Add ice and stir to chill. Strain into a snifter. Express the oils of a lemon peel over the drink (discard the peel).

sōkō

CLARIFIED MEZCAL MILK PUNCH

Bar Trench is one of my favorite modern cocktail bars in Tōkyō, a perfect example of how Japanese bartenders merge elements of Western-style bartending with a century of tradition. The atmosphere may be rambunctious with music and chatter, but the dapper bartenders still float with grace and elegance, making forward-thinking drinks like the Artichoke Julep alongside classics like the Corpse Reviver #2. The last time I was there, they had a mezcal milk punch on the menu—made with mezcal, green tea, and chamomile, which inspired me to create this cocktail.

This milk punch is not your creamy New Orleans–style holiday drink. Instead it's a gentle, wine-like mixture that balances the brightness of lemon and saké with the depth of earthy tea and smoky mezcal. I admire the way the mezcal and the hōjicha play together—there is a smokiness to the tea, which brings out a chocolate quality in the mezcal. Patience is involved in making the drink, as it must be allowed to rest overnight before being slowly strained through a paper coffee filter, but the sumptuous final cocktail is well worth the effort. *Serves ten*

10 ounces whole milk

20 ounces Chilled Hōjicha (page 320)

10 ounces Fidencio Clásico mezcal

8 ounces Fukucho Forgotten Fortune junmai

½ cup granulated sugar

3½ ounces fresh lemon juice

Measure the milk into a large pitcher or bowl and set it aside. In another large pitcher or bowl, combine the hōjicha, mezcal, saké, sugar, and lemon juice. Stir thoroughly until the sugar dissolves. Pour the cocktail mixture into the milk, pouring in soft and slow motions in order to evenly distribute the cocktail without overly agitating the curds that form. Give the mixture a gentle stir and then cover and allow to sit overnight in the refrigerator.

The next day, strain the milk punch through a damp coffee filter. Store the finished milk punch in the refrigerator in a glass bottle. To enjoy, pour straight from the bottle into a wineglass.

WINTER

Many Japanese homes are built to withstand the brutal heat of summer but not the bite of winter's chill, which means families have to get creative with ways to keep warm when temperatures drop. Today, amenities like heated floors and space heaters mostly do the trick, but one of my favorite methods growing up was a traditional Japanese piece of furniture that has been used for generations: the kotatsu. This special seating arrangement dates back to the fourteenth century, when people used to gather around smouldering charcoal burners while cooking.

Horikotatsu, my favorite style, calls for a table set over a hole dug into the ground where a heater rests. A frame is set over the hole and draped with a blanket to trap the heat inside, then a second board is placed on top of the arrangement to provide an eating surface. One of my treasured winter memories is letting my legs warm underneath the blanket while eating dinner—usually a family-style meal cooked in ceramic pots, called nabémono.

The world seems to move more slowly in the winter, allowing room for deliberate and considered rituals like making matcha. From the very first glint of brilliant green powder to the practiced movements of sifting, whisking, and sipping, the ritual of making this revered drink always feels special. The same comforts of ritual may be found in the cocktails I enjoy as snow dusts the ground. Cocktails that don't require too much effort to make, like the classic Vesper (page 265) or Boulevardier, bring peace at home. In cocktail bars, bartenders embrace colorful liqueurs and fresh citrus to contrast the monotonous gray outdoors. Blue Curaçao is a favorite in Japanese bars for its splash of tropical turquoise, and the pineapple-freshness of the Million Dollar (page 313) offers a similarly breezy vibe.

Finally, as the holiday season comes and goes, classics that involve sparkling wines, liqueurs, and creams feel wholly appropriate. I lean into drinks that are lush and creamy like the Grasshopper (see my two favorite versions of the drink on pages 291 and 292), or throw caution to the wind with a bubbly French 75 (page 296) around New Year's Eve. It's time to turn toward traditional drinks that offer warmth, nostalgia, and sometimes even a bit of fun.

THE MICROSEASONS OF WINTER

RITTŌ | *the beginning of winter*

Vesper

Evening Star

Kami Hikōki

Hotto Campari

TŌJI | *winter solstice*

White Grasshopper

Sanshō Grasshopper

Strawberry White Cake

French 75

Holiday Highball

SHŌSETSU | *light snow*

Yuzu Salty Dog

Hōjicha Coconut Daiquiri

Cassis Oolong

SHŌKAN | *small cold*

Spiritfree: Azalea

Warm Note

Sky Diving

TAISETSU | *heavy snow*

Matcha Miruku

Spiritfree: Matcha Miruku

Frosty Mikan

Saké Chai Flip

Neither-Nor

DAIKAN | *great cold*

After Angels

Old Fashioned

Million Dollar

rittō

THE BEGINNING OF WINTER

camellias bloom, the land starts to
freeze, daffodils awaken

Maple leaves hold their ground as the temperatures continue to
dip, and kaki (persimmon) trees hang heavy with fruit, waiting to be
plucked and dried before the holidays arrive. The streets of major
cities like Tōkyō, Kyōto, and Ōsaka light up with twinkling Christmas
lights and pine trees decorated with red and green ornaments. Some
bars decorate for the holidays by putting out poinsettias. Fresh fruit
cocktails bloom with the last of fall's bounty and vividly fresh yuzu
appears on menus everywhere. Nothing feels more comforting than
the hot oshibori when you arrive at a cocktail bar, especially when it
precedes an otōshi like abokado no chīzu-yaki (Avocado Baked with
Cheese, page 46).

VESPER

British author Ian Fleming made the Vesper cocktail famous after including a mention of the drink in his 1953 James Bond novel, *Casino Royale*. With a split base of vodka and gin, and Kina Lillet for balance, the cocktail has inspired countless variations from bartenders around the globe. Japanese bartenders instead aim for the perfect balance in the drink while staying true to the original specifications, so more often than not you will see a bottle of Gordon's Dry Gin pulled from the freezer and shaken briskly with Smirnoff Vodka and Lillet Blanc, finished with a hefty twist of lemon. I fancy a more luxurious iteration, so I turn to Japanese gin and vodka for their softness and subtleties. I also enjoy following Bond's order for this drink to be shaken instead of stirred, so thin chips of ice float upon the surface. Drink it quickly, while it still bites back! *Serves one*

1½ ounces Suntory Roku gin

½ ounce Suntory Haku vodka

½ ounce Lillet Blanc apéritif

GARNISH Lemon twist

In a shaker tin, combine the gin, vodka, and Lillet with ice. Shake to chill, then strain into a coupe. Garnish with a generous lemon twist, expressing the oils before resting it on the side of the glass.

EVENING STAR

An iridescent Champagne shade of gold is not the only thing that sets this Vesper riff apart from the original. I created this variation on the classic for times when I am in the mood for something lower in proof—a drink that will open up and evolve in a pleasant way as you sit and sip. The cocktail tastes deeper in personality than the classic thanks to the apple and honey notes of the pommeau, and demands to be stirred instead of shaken to maintain a perfectly silky texture. Finish the drink with a small shower of lemon oils, for brightness. *Serves one*

½ ounce Nikka Coffey gin

½ ounce Nikka Coffey vodka

1 ounce Rhine Hall La Normande pommeau

1 ounce Koshi no Kanbai Sai junmai ginjō saké

GARNISH Lemon peel, lemon twist

In a mixing glass, combine the gin, vodka, pommeau, and saké. Add ice and stir to chill. Strain into a chilled cocktail glass. Express the oils of a lemon peel over the top of the drink (discard the peel), then garnish with a small lemon twist.

KAMI HIKŌKI

As children, my brothers and I would assemble paper planes and send them flying through the backyard. Sometimes they would get caught in the momiji trees, which in early winter were still graced with a few resilient leaves. Inspired by those playful moments, I created this riff on the Paper Plane, a modern American classic invented by bartender Sam Ross featuring bourbon, Aperol, Amaro Nonino, and fresh lemon juice. I've always loved the cocktail for its precise play of warmth, bitterness, and brightness. To take that model in a distinctly more Japanese direction, I turned to Japanese whisky. Akashi whisky is made of almost all corn, so it serves as a great match for bourbon lovers, and in the drink its sweet grain qualities and hint of peat fit snugly with Cappelletti, the bright red bitter I use in place of Aperol. Made with a base of white wine instead of neutral grain spirit, there is a softness that melds perfectly with the oaky whisky. While the drink itself comprises equal parts, the unaged brandy really pops out in its own right with a lovely roundness. A citrusy cocktail perfect for when the last lingering moments of fall transform into winter. *Serves one*

¾ ounce Copper & Kings Immature brandy

¾ ounce Aperitivo Cappelletti

¾ ounce Akashi Japanese whisky

¼ ounce Simple Syrup (page 318)

GARNISH Lemon peel

In a shaker tin, combine the brandy, Cappelletti, whisky, and simple syrup with ice. Shake to chill, then strain into a chilled coupe. Express the oils of a lemon peel over the top of the drink (discard the peel) and garnish with a manicured twist.

HOTTO CAMPARI

One of the more unexpected hot drinks enjoyed during the winter in Japan is a hot Campari: a mix of lemon, honey, hot water, Campari, and various liqueurs—the choice setting one apart from the other. It is a fantastic cocktail with enticing orange notes that blossom as the Campari warms. With a perky rosy hue, the drink is a playful version of the normally stoic winter toddy—a provocative cocktail that oscillates between a somewhat medicinal bitterness and bountiful bouquets of citrus and spice. Lower in proof, the bitter liqueur with the rich honey makes for a drink that lingers like a comforting embrace long after the last sip. *Serves one*

1 ounce Campari

¾ ounce Awa No Kaori Sudachi Chū

1 barspoon Combier Kümmel liqueur

¼ ounce fresh lemon juice

½ ounce Rich Honey Syrup (page 317)

3 to 4 ounces hot water

GARNISH Lemon peel

In a teacup, combine the Campari, Sudachi Chū, Kümmel, lemon juice, and honey syrup. Add hot water, 3 ounces if you prefer a stronger, more boozy-tasting cocktail or 4 ounces if you like a drink that tastes a little lighter in body and character. Stir briefly to combine. Express lemon oils over the top of the drink and garnish with a manicured twist of lemon.

shōsetsu

LIGHT SNOW

rainbows hide, north wind blows leaves from the trees, tachibana citrus leaves turn yellow

True preparations for winter begin as the last leaves disappear. Some parts of Japan see light snow flurries, but while we would hope for snow when living in Nara and Kyōto it wouldn't always come. The air would grow brisk as temperatures veered toward freezing, but the clouds just held strong as mere whispers in the sky. I am inspired by the hedonistic delicacies of this time, feeling oddly grateful to the cold for making some favorites like oden, rāmen, and gyūdon all the more enjoyable. Sweet potato shōchū continues to find a place in my glass through drinks like the Cassis Oolong (page 278), with its sweet-tart companions crème de cassis and chilled oolong tea.

YUZU

An extremely aromatic citrus, yuzu is a key component in many classic
Japanese condiments such as: ponzu, salad dressing, marmalade, and
pickles. The green yuzu that are harvested in August make their way
into yuzu-koshō, a spicy chile paste soaked in the citrus juice and
zest. Sometimes just the zest will be grated over the top of sashimi or
into chilled soups as summer turns to fall. Once the fruit has turned
fully yellow and the winter solstice is near, people bring yuzu into
their baths to promote health, clear skin, and cure ailments such as
arthritis. The aromas wafting from the hot water are captivating. And
like umé-shu, yuzu-shu is also a popular fruit liqueur in Japan, which
will give you the sensation of a yuzu bath any time of the year.

   Folks in California are fortunate enough to have access to the
fresh citrus, but there are online specialty stores who sell pasteurized
yuzu juice for the rest of the country.

YUZU-KOSHŌ

Yuzu-koshō is a Japanese condiment made with fermented yuzu peel,
salt, and crushed chile peppers. Some people say the hermits of Hidehiko
Mountain first created the pungent condiment as a medicine, while others
place the origins in Hita City of Oita prefecture, or in Soeda, a town in
Fukuoka prefecture. I think it is most likely that families from both regions
harvested yuzu from the mountains between the two prefectures and over time
the condiment grew in popularity.

   What makes yuzu-koshō so indispensable in the kitchen (and my bar) is
its blend of salty, tart, aromatic, umami, and piquant qualities, which bring
a zestiness to dishes like nabemono (Japanese hot pots). It is sometimes used
instead of wasabi alongside sashimi, as well as in dressings or with grilled meats.
A guilty-pleasure treat of mine is to mix 1 tablespoon of Kewpie mayonnaise
with ¼ teaspoon (or more, to taste) of yuzu-koshō to spread onto my grilled
cheese sandwiches. I also incorporate it in a syrup at Kumiko for signature
cocktails and spiritfrees.

   When purchasing yuzu-koshō, seek out brands coming from Kyūshū
and those with the fewest ingredients listed as possible to ensure the purest
unadulterated flavor.

YUZU SALTY DOG

A forgotten or overlooked drink in Western cocktail bars, the Salty Dog cocktail never went out of style in Japan. To add dimension to the classic combo of vodka and grapefruit, I switch the spirit to gin and add a kiss of fresh yuzu juice, which has a balance of floral and bitter qualities. It dovetails perfectly with the tartness of ruby red grapefruit. I also add a layer of matcha to the top of the drink to add a dynamic pop of color and a verdant aroma that leads calmly into the heart of the gin botanicals. It is a great anytime drink, but tastes especially vivacious in early winter when fresh grapefruit comes into season. *Serves one*

Grapefruit wheel and salt, to rim the glass

1½ ounces ruby red grapefruit juice

½ ounce yuzu juice

½ ounce Simple Syrup (page 318)

1¼ ounces The Kyōto Distillery Ki No Bi Kyōto dry gin

1 chashaku of matcha powder (see Note)

Cut a wheel off the grapefruit before juicing and run the wheel along the edge of a rocks glass. Roll the glass immediately through salt for a clean snow-style rim (page 40). In the prepared rocks glass, combine the grapefruit juice, yuzu juice, and simple syrup and add ice. In a shaker tin, combine the matcha and gin with ice. Shake to chill, then strain into the rocks glass so as to layer over the grapefruit base.

NOTE | A chashaku is a traditional utensil for measuring matcha powder; it is the equivalent of about ¼ teaspoon.

HŌJICHA COCONUT DAIQUIRI

The straightforward template of the classic daiquiri lends itself well to seasonal interpretations. In the summer, I enjoy a split base of rhum agricole and aged rum for a light but complex flavor profile (see page 168). In the winter, I experiment with heavier aged rums and rich demerara syrup for a darker, more wintry sweetness. In this variation I combine those elements together with hōjicha, which fans through the drink with a caramel, molasses, and freshly-roasted-coffee-like quality. I think about the story of this cocktail as the story of the seasons: how lively plants like sugarcane and tea start out fresh and green then shift to brown and dry in the winter—there is a beauty in the process because it showcases new and unexpected shades of the familiar ingredients as time goes by. Think of it as wabi-sabi. Finally, in the wintertime we really start to miss the sunshine, so I added a little coconut cream as a reminder of summer. *Serves one*

1½ ounces El Dorado 12-Year rum

1 ounce Chilled Hōjicha (page 320)

¾ ounce Coconut Cream Syrup
  (recipe follows)

¾ ounce fresh lime juice

¼ ounce Rich Demerara Syrup
  (page 318)

GARNISH Powdered genmai
  (Japanese toasted rice)

In a shaker tin, combine the rum, hōjicha, coconut cream syrup, lime juice, and demerara syrup with ice. Shake to chill, then strain into a coupe. Garnish with a dusting of powdered genmai (use a mortar and pestle to gently crush the toasted rice grains into a loose powder).

COCONUT CREAM SYRUP

In a blender, combine 1 (15-ounce) can sweetened coconut cream (such as Coco Lopez), 1 cup granulated sugar, and 1 cup water and blend until smooth. Store in the refrigerator for up to 2 weeks. *Yields 24 ounces*

CASSIS OOLONG

Cassis is a very popular ingredient in Japanese cocktail bars, often paired with soda, tea, or orange juice. I enjoy the mulberry-colored liqueur more in the winter because of the way its intensely dark, lush side contrasts with perky tartness. When paired with oolong tea, the two transform into an enticing tangle of rich tannins, floral notes, and berries, underscored here with the depths of sweet potato shōchū. A simple but satisfying number. *Serves one*

¾ ounce Jacoulot Crème de Cassis de Dijon

1 ounce Nishi Shuzō Satsuma Hozan sweet potato shōchū

Chilled Oolong (recipe follows)

GARNISH Lemon twist

In a mixing glass, combine the crème de cassis, sweet potato shōchū, and oolong tea. Add ice and stir to chill. Strain into a highball glass over fresh ice. Garnish with a manicured lemon twist.

CHILLED OOLONG

In a glass brewing vessel, combine 2 teaspoons oolong tea and 6 ounces hot water (just off the boil, around 195°F) and brew for 3 minutes. Strain, reserve the tea, and resteep the leaves in another 6 ounces hot water for 3 minutes. Strain and combine the two brews. Place the tea in the refrigerator to cool. For a faster chill, you can set up an ice bath and cool it uncovered, on the countertop or in the sink. *Makes about 5 ounces*

HEAVY SNOW

cold sets in, winter begins, bears retreat to their dens, salmon gather and swim upstream

Up in the mountains, snow arrives with vigor, casting thick cloaks across mountain peaks. Sometimes, we would get a light layer of icy diamonds landing gracefully upon dark evergreen trees in our garden. One of my favorite parts of our house in Miyamaki was the engawa, a corridor that ran between the main rooms and the garden. Much like an enclosed hallway, flanked by sliding doors, it stretched along the exterior of the house to provide airflow in the summer and extra warmth in the winter. Our engawa was equipped with a special type of lattice screen covered with translucent paper covering the upper half and a mobile frame on the bottom which would slide up so we could sit at the warm kotatsu and look out into the garden. These lattice screens are called *yukimi shoji,* which means "snow-viewing shoji." Watching the flakes fall while nibbling on mikan and sipping on warm tea would bring much comfort.

MATCHA MIRUKU

When I was a child, my parents would give me warm milk when I had trouble sleeping. Milk isn't a typical ingredient used in food and drink in Japan—at least not in the same abundant way it is in America—but prepackaged milk drinks can be found in Japanese convenience stores and vending machines everywhere, always packaged in happy bright colors with fun fonts. Banana and strawberry are common flavors, as is matcha. Hot matcha in the wintertime paired with milk becomes a hearty drink in modern-day Japanese cafés.

I wanted to capture this feeling in a cocktail, but instead of dairy-based milk I reached for cashew milk, which I enjoy for its depth of nutty goodness. I particularly like the way the earthy notes of the sweet potato shōchū interact with the cashew milk in this drink. This is a nice low-proof nip for under the kotatsu, or to tuck in with before bed. *Serves one*

1½ ounces hot water (202°F)

¼ ounce Rich Honey Syrup (page 317)

1 ounce Nishi Shuzō Tomi no Hozan sweet potato shōchū

1½ ounces cashew milk

3 scoops of matcha powder (about ¾ teaspoon)

In a prewarmed vessel, combine the hot water, syrup, shōchū, and cashew milk. Stir to incorporate. Warm a chawan (Japanese tea bowl) and sift the matcha through a tea strainer into the chawan (this helps prevent clumps). Pour the hot cocktail into the chawan with the matcha and whisk with a chasen (Japanese bamboo matcha whisk) to combine. To get the right level of aeration, start slowly, drawing a wave or W-pattern into the liquid very loosely on the bottom to pull up all the grains of matcha. Then, lift the chasen up and whisk briskly using your wrist until a lovely froth forms all across the surface.

SPIRITFREE
MATCHA MIRUKU

This spiritfree version of the Matcha Miruku (page 281) has an underlying richness thanks to the kinmokusei syrup that takes the place of sweet potato shōchū. Overall, the drink is more floral, and delicate, with the same nutty character and structure from the cashew milk, which offers a fragrant perceived sweetness to this drink while still finishing dry. Because it resembles a hot latte, you can either jumpstart your morning with a mug or settle in with one as a restorative treat in the middle of a long day. *Serves one*

½ ounce Rich Honey Syrup (page 317)

¼ ounce Kinmokusei Syrup (page 318)

3 ounces cashew milk

1½ ounces hot water (202°F)

3 scoops of matcha powder (about ¾ teaspoon)

In a prewarmed vessel, combine the honey syrup, kinmokusei syrup, cashew milk, and hot water. Stir to incorporate evenly. Aim to keep the temperature between 150°F and 160°F. Sift the matcha into a prewarmed chawan. Gently pour the sweetened cashew milk over the matcha and whisk with a chasen to combine. To get the right level of aeration, start slowly, drawing a wave or W into the liquid very loosely on the bottom to pull up all the grains of matcha. Then, lift the whisk up ever so slightly and whisk briskly using your wrist until a lovely froth forms all across the surface of the chawan.

FROSTY MIKAN

Citrus comes into season in the wintertime and my favorite variety is the mikan, a small relative of the mandarin orange, also called satsuma. I used to eat so many my hands would turn a deep orange color from all the snacking sessions. Other times, I'd save them for my favorite wintertime game. When heavy snow hit the mountains, we'd play in the deepest drifts, throwing mikans into fluffy banks of fresh powder and fishing them out the next day to eat frozen. The way the juicy segments snapped with frigid cold felt like tiny fireworks with each bite.

To re-create that memory in a cocktail, I bury satsuma juice beneath a chilly layer of crushed ice and absinthe. As the absinthe seeps into the juice, it louches, creating a cloudy white layer that looks like snow. The first sip is bracingly cold, prickling waves of anisette, with relief from the satsuma juice below offering a sweet contrast. This cocktail brings me joy with each sip when mikan come into season, reminding me of another time and place. *Serves one*

1 ounce satsuma juice (see Note)

¼ ounce Simple Syrup (page 318)

1 ounce absinthe

Club soda, to top

GARNISH Satsuma wheel and ¼ ounce absinthe

In a highball glass, combine the satsuma juice, simple syrup, and 1 ounce absinthe. Stir lightly and fill the glass with crushed ice. Top with club soda. Garnish with a satsuma wheel, and ¼ ounce more of absinthe.

NOTE | I prefer the more intense, fruity, sweet, floral note that satsuma have over regular oranges, but any mandarin orange juice would work in place of satsuma if that is what you have handy.

SAKÉ CHAI FLIP

In Japan, there is a drink called tamagozaké, made with a whole egg whisked with sugar then topped with a slow pour of hot saké. With a soul similar to an American eggnog or the Tom & Jerry cocktail, it is a comforting winter drink with a big, bouncy texture. In my chilled version, a bouquet of baking spice from chai and allspice amps up the holiday aromas while saké adds sweetness and barley shōchū anchors the blend with a solid grain-y backbone. With robust cocktails like this one, seek out an affordable bottle of nihonshu, for its purpose is to meld seamlessly with the other flavors. A more highly polished saké might get lost completely, and that would be a terrible waste. *Serves one*

1½ ounces Akashi-Tai Tokubetsu Honjōzjō saké

1 ounce Mizu Saga barley shōchū

½ ounce Somrus Chai cream liqueur

¼ ounce St. Elizabeth Allspice Dram

½ ounce Kinmokusei Syrup (page 318)

1 egg

GARNISH Black pepper, grated nutmeg, and Angostura bitters

In a Boston shaker (because they're easier to clean), combine the saké, shōchū, chai cream liqueur, allspice dram, and kinmokusei syrup. Crack the egg into the other shaker tin. Bring the two parts together and employ a strong dry shake to fully emulsify. Add three large ice cubes and shake again to chill and build up a nice froth. Fine-strain into a flared cocktail glass or coupe. Garnish with an artistic splattering of Angostura bitters, cracked black pepper, and grated nutmeg.

NEITHER-NOR

A world of opulent flavors exists in the space between the gin-based Negroni and its cousin the whiskey-fueled Boulevardier—both beloved cocktails in Japanese bars. What if, instead of enjoying one or the other, you could enjoy the best characteristics of both cocktails, and with a Japanese angle? That's exactly what I aimed to do in this drink, where Gran Classico and sherry combine in a labyrinth of dark bitter orange and nutty spice, while cranberry gin liqueur adds a piquant tartness reminiscent of Campari. Kintaro Baisen is a roasted barley shōchū, those toasty notes coming through with a unique and long finish, helping click the other ingredients into sync. Compared to the traditional Negroni or Boulevardier, this hybrid offers a lush envelope of beauty that bursts with sheer complexity. *Serves one*

1 ounce Tempus Fugit Gran Classico Bitter

1 ounce Nishiyoshida Shuzō Kintaro Baisen Honkaku barley shōchū

½ ounce Koval Cranberry Gin liqueur

½ ounce Valdespino Contrabandista Medium Dry Amontillado sherry

GARNISH Lemon peel and orange peel

In a mixing glass, combine the Gran Classico, barley shōchū, cranberry gin liqueur, and sherry. Add ice and stir lightly to incorporate the ingredients. It doesn't need as much dilution as the typical Negroni or Boulevardier because the shōchū is lower in proof than gin or whisky, so don't overstir. Strain into a rocks glass over fresh ice. Express the oils of both the lemon peel and orange peel over the drink, then garnish with the manicured peels.

tōji

WINTER SOLSTICE

self-heal herbs sprout, deer and elk shed their horns, wheat sprouts under the snow

Daytime is the shortest, but the excitement of the holidays has come to a head. Japan is not a Christian country, but Christmas found a special home there as certain Western traditions have permeated over time (see page 299). We celebrate with strawberry Christmas cakes, and on winter solstice it is common to take yuzu baths (to prevent illness) and eat delicious squash, lotus roots, and satsuma oranges. On New Year's Eve we decorate with bitter oranges and other symbols of good luck. Drinks are at peak levels of festive, with creamy concoctions like the Strawberry White Cake (page 295) sharing space with bubbly ones like the Holiday Highball (page 298)—anything that brings joy is welcome at home and at the bar alike.

WHITE GRASSHOPPER

The grasshopper is a classic cream-based cocktail that is particularly beloved in Japanese cocktail bars. For my version, I wanted to play up the "green" flavors while tricking the mind with a snowy white appearance. The key ingredient is Munemasa distillery's Mizunomai green tea shōchū. Distilled from barley, black kōji, and freshly steamed green tea, this shōchū brings a distinctly "green" and chocolaty note to the traditional mix of crème de cacao, crème de menthe, and heavy cream. In Japan, most grasshopper cocktails take a spin through the blender with ice for a thick and creamy texture, but I prefer mine shaken because I like how much easier it is to drink without a straw or spoon. Finally, a light dusting of matcha on top tickles the nose, highlights the herbaceousness of the mint, and draws on the green tea shōchū. *Serves one; photo on page 293*

¾ ounce Mizu green tea shōchū

¾ ounce Giffard Crème de Cacao (white) liqueur

¾ ounce Giffard Menthe-Pastille liqueur

1 ounce heavy cream

GARNISH Matcha powder

In a shaker tin, combine the green tea shōchū, crème de cacao, menthe-pastille, and heavy cream with ice. Shake to chill, then strain into your festive glass of choice. Garnish with a light dusting of matcha on the top of the drink.

A NOTE ON THE GLASSWARE ON PAGE 293 | The White Grasshopper, pictured on the right, is featured in a vintage cocktail glass from Central Glass Works, made in the 1920s or '30s. The Sanshō Grasshopper, left, is in a modern-production glass by Kimura Glass Company out of Tōkyō. This is part of their Kikatsu series, fashioned after antique glassware. I wonder if the Central Glass Works glass was the inspiration for Kimura's polka-dot speckled design.

SANSHŌ GRASSHOPPER

For another version of the classic grasshopper, I wanted to highlight one of Japan's most unique spices: sanshō. The zippy botanical has such a radiant quality, which is one of the reasons why it is prominently featured in several Japanese gins—none more so than Nikka Coffey gin. In the drink, sanshō's fierce menthol-like personality pairs brilliantly with the chocolatey notes of crème de cacao. I chose to garnish the cocktail with a sprig of kinomé (leaves of the sanshō tree) on top of the pillowy white canvas. It looks like a small holly leaf on a bed of snow—everything about this drink evokes holiday feelings for me. I hope it will for you, too. *Serves one*

¾ ounce Giffard Crème de Cacao (white)

¾ ounce Giffard Menthe-Pastille

¾ ounce Nikka Coffey gin

1 ounce heavy cream

GARNISH Kinomé sprig

In a shaker tin, combine the crème de cacao, menthe-pastille, gin, and heavy cream with ice. Shake to chill. then strain into a festive glass. Garnish with a sprig of fresh kinomé.

SANSHŌ

The Japanese prickly ash tree, or sanshō, bears leaves, flowers, fruits, and seeds that play an important role in Japanese culinary traditions. Starting in early spring, the small budding leaves called kinomé are used as garnish for their gorgeous aromas, captivating beauty, and bright flavor. They taste both floral and citrusy, and complement dishes such as grilled tofu, braised bamboo shoots, and sashimi. When you bite down on a leaf you can get a tingling sensation alongside a burst of minty freshness.

Midway through spring, *sanshō no mi* (sanshō seeds) are harvested. When enjoyed fresh, they numb and tickle the palate in an incredible way. The pods are also preserved by either drying or curing in a salt or shoyu (soy sauce) solution. Dried pods are sometimes used as a botanical in the emerging category of Japanese gin, and other times ground into a powder and used in Japanese shichimi tōgarashi seasoning.

In early May, seeds that were not harvested blossom into profoundly green flowers, which hold a bright zestiness within their petals. These are often enjoyed fresh atop grilled seafood or in soups.

WHITE
GRASSHOPPER

(page 291)

SANSHŌ
GRASSHOPPER

tōji

STRAWBERRY WHITE CAKE

Every December, dazzling Christmas cakes arrive on the shelves of Japanese stores, tempting everyone's sweet tooth. Made of sponge cake with white whipped cream icing, the cakes are layered with strawberries and topped with powdered white sugar. To harness that personality in a festive holiday cocktail, I reached for strawberry liqueur and soba (buckwheat) shōchū, which has vanilla and almond notes that mirror those found in the sponge cake. A layer of sweet cacao–imbued cream pretends to be frosting, upon which we drizzle a drop of Peychaud's bitters to serve as a visual reminder of the kiss of strawberries that grace the tops of cakes.

Before you mix, notice the smaller proportions of this drink. Like the Line Cocktail (page 234), this recipe falls into the category of short drinks—ones that are meant to be consumed in two or three light, fleeting sips. The format works best for this recipe because it does have a hefty amount of sweetness. I recommend keeping a batch in the refrigerator, or pop a few servings into the freezer for a few minutes before drinking, so it comes out bracingly cold. *Serves one*

¼ ounce Giffard Crème de Fraise des Bois strawberry liqueur

½ ounce Kitsukura soba shōchū

GARNISH Cacao Cream (recipe follows) and 1 drop Peychaud's bitters

In a mixing glass, combine the strawberry liqueur and shōchū and chill in the refrigerator. Prepare the cacao cream, whipping just enough to thicken, but not so much that it hardens into peaks. When ready to drink, pour the drink into a small stemmed cordial glass and gently top with about ¼ ounce of cacao cream to create a layered effect. Garnish with a drop of Peychaud's bitters.

CACAO CREAM

Combine 1 part white crème de cacao with 4 parts heavy whipping cream. Whip lightly, until the mixture thickens but still has enough viscosity to pour smoothly. Use immediately.

FRENCH 75

Roast turkeys are not a common sight at the dinner table in Japan, so in the 1970s the fast-food chain KFC began to market fried chicken to the masses as a special way to mark the holidays (see page 299). Fried chicken and Champagne has since become an annual ritual at many Christmas tables around the country. For me, the only thing better than a glass of good bubbles around the holidays is the classic French 75. You can find well-made ones on Japanese cocktail menus year-round, but the drink takes on extra-special festiveness in December. For this iteration the refined nature of Roku gin weaves seamlessly into the lemon juice and bubbles. *Serves one*

1½ ounces Suntory Roku gin

¾ ounce fresh lemon juice

½ ounce Simple Syrup (page 318)

Champagne, to top

GARNISH Lemon peel, lemon twist

In a shaker tin, combine the gin, lemon juice, and simple syrup with ice. Shake to chill, then strain into a flute and top with Champagne. Express the oils of a lemon peel over the top of the drink (discard the peel) and garnish with a manicured lemon twist.

HOLIDAY
HIGHBALL

(page 298)

FRENCH 75

HOLIDAY HIGHBALL

I prefer my French 75s made with gin instead of Cognac, as is the case in many Japanese bars. There is something marvelous about the way the juniper stands out within the sea of citrus. Thinking about how to make the festive classic even more exciting for the holiday season, I turned to a dose of cranberry gin liqueur from a local Chicago distillery instead of regular gin and took a note from the Japanese tradition of serving the cocktail in a highball glass over a collins spear of ice instead of up in a delicate flute. Not every bar does this, but when they do it's wonderful because it creates a completely different drinking experience. In this variation especially, the ice works wonders as it softens the astringent qualities of the cranberry and lemon and creates a festive visual as the Champagne bubbles dance around the spear. *Serves one; photo page 297*

1 ounce Suntory Roku gin

¾ ounce Koval Cranberry Gin liqueur

¾ ounce fresh lemon juice

½ ounce Simple Syrup (page 318)

Champagne, to top

GARNISH Lime twist

In a shaker tin, combine the gin, cranberry gin liqueur, lemon juice, and simple syrup with ice. Briefly shake to chill, then strain into a tall glass over one large collins spear of ice. Top with Champagne. Garnish with a lime twist.

CHRISTMAS IN JAPAN

From fried chicken to twinkling lights and fluffy, frosted cakes, Christmas in Japan is a prime example of how the influence of the Western world was profound yet cherry-picked to suit the needs of the country. There are a couple of key moments in history that brought us to where we are now—a vibrant display of adopted holiday cheer that quickly gets packed into boxes as preparations are made for an event of more cultural significance: the New Year.

In 1549, Roman Catholic Jesuit missionaries came to Japan via Kagoshima, the prefecture on the southwest tip of the island of Kyushu. Missionaries and influences from the West were quickly cut off, however, and it wasn't until 1868 with the start of the Meiji Restoration that Japan opened its gates to the West. As it stands today 1 percent of the Japanese population claim Christian beliefs. For the other 99 percent, Christmas can be whittled down to romantic dinners and walks beneath sparkling lights, culminating with Christmas cake and KFC.

The strawberry shortcake is not only an emoji on our phones but a staple of the Japanese Christmas celebration. Typically made of a white sponge cake with white frosting and layers of strawberries, it is topped with sugar figurines dusted with a layer of powdery snow-like confectioners' sugar. A look back in time shows that as the country was rising to its feet after WWII, American soldiers would hand out Western sweets to children, a flavor many had never known. In the years following, having the means to make or even buy a cake became a symbol of prosperity, and it is a tradition now ingrained in society.

Another Japanese holiday tradition is "Kurisumasu ni wa Kentakki!" or "Kentucky for Christmas," a slogan that brought a fried chicken franchise from near bankruptcy to great prosperity. There are two different versions to this story. The first, as told by Takeshi Okawara, manager of the first KFC to open in Japan in Nagoya in 1970, involves a white lie told on National Television, stating that the fried chicken was popular for Christmas oversees. Officially, KFC Japan does not align with this tale. Instead, they share that fried chicken was poised to be a great substitution for turkey, which was portrayed in media as the American Christmas tradition, and something that was not available in Japan. Whatever the case may be, Kentucky for Christmas was a wildly successful campaign, and buckets of KFC make their way into homes this time of year.

Christmas is not a national holiday in Japan, and more often than not it is Christmas Eve when people gather to celebrate. Folks go about their typical day, weaving around decorations until the day's end, when they go home to enjoy a bucket of KFC with their family or friends, pouring libations of port wine and Champagne.

No matter the way in which it is celebrated, Christmas is very much a part of Japanese eating and drinking culture—just not in the way that one might expect. That is what makes it so interesting to take a deeper look at the history behind this festive occasion.

shōkan

SMALL COLD

parsley sprouts, spring waters thaw, pheasants start to call

After the abundance of the holidays, food and drink habits take a turn toward quietude. Small happinesses unfurl when the kettle goes on to brew tea or to cut shōchū with hot water. The way the steam curls upward in a tangle of mist looks even more alluring cloaked in January's fleeting rays of soft light. In the kitchen, similar meditations come by making dashimaki tamago (rolled omelet with dashi). It is a dish that requires the gentle technique of folding eggs layer by layer as they cook. In honor of the New Year, we make amazaké, a low-proof (or sometimes zero-proof) drink made from the same ingredients as saké. With a thick texture and pleasing sweetness from the rice, it is delicious in its own right, but some people also count on amazaké for its purported health benefits.

SPIRITFREE

AZALEA

A traditional part of New Year's celebrations in Japan is mochi-tsuki, a communal gathering for mochi pounding. I was seven years old the first time my family went to one in Tomio—there, I tried my first taste of fresh mochi in the form of chewy dumplings dropped into zenzai, a sweet adzuki (red bean) soup. In homage to that delicious dish, I pair koshian (red bean paste) syrup with the creaminess of amazaké (a nonalcoholic rice brew; see page 302) to create a rich base for the drink. Those two lovely flavors fit well together, and even more so when adjusted with the acidity of the verjus and the snappy qualities of the umé-su. A splash of tonic lightens up the otherwise heavy spiritfree and adds a small hint of quinine to temper the sweetness just a touch. Overall, it is a delightful dessert-friendly drink suited for sipping on cold winter nights. *Serves one; photo on page 303*

2 ounces Amazaké (page 302)

¾ ounce Koshian Syrup
(recipe follows)

¾ ounce verjus rouge

¼ ounce Umé-su (page 316)

Indian tonic water, to top

GARNISH Grated nutmeg

In a shaker tin, combine the amazaké, koshian syrup, verjus rouge, and umé-su with ice. Shake briskly to chill, then strain into a cocktail glass using a Hawthorne strainer with a tight coil, or double-strain using a tea strainer, so no ice chips land in the drink. Add the tonic water. Garnish with nutmeg.

KOSHIAN SYRUP

In a blender, combine 2 cups koshian (sweet red bean paste), 1 cup granulated sugar, and 1 cup room-temperature water and blend until smooth. Strain through a fine-mesh sieve and store in an airtight container in the refrigerator for up to 2 weeks. *Makes 25 ounces*

AMAZAKÉ

Originally invented as a medicinal elixir in the Kofun period (approximately 300–538 AD), amazaké is a traditional Japanese drink made from the same ingredients as Japanese saké: fermented rice, water, and kōji. Despite its name (*zaké* is a word for "alcohol"), the beverage is usually alcohol-free or very low-proof. With a restorative nature, amazaké may be enjoyed cold or hot. In the summertime, I enjoy it blended with banana and served cold, or laced with shiozakura for a pleasantly salty refresher. When hot, it is execeptional with green tea—or served with grated ginger, as is customary when people visit temples in the first week of the new year.

To make amazaké, rinse 1 cup of short-grain Japanese rice once to remove any debris. Drain and rinse again, this time raking your fingers through the rice, allowing the grains to gently polish themselves. Continue to rinse and flush until the water runs clear. Add the rice to a rice cooker. Fill with water to the 3 cup line. Cook the rice according to the rice cooker instructions, taking care that the water does not boil over. If your rice cooker has a porridge setting, use that, but with water that comes to the 1 cup line rather than the 3 cup measuring line.

When the rice is cooked, remove the bowl from the rice cooker and use a rice paddle or spoon to make slices through the rice. This allows air flow, turning the rice over so that it releases its heat. To speed up the process, try using a fan to cool. In 10 to 20 minutes, the rice should reach the optimal temperature. Gradually add 1 cup of water to the rice. Stir to even out and let sit until the temperature comes down to 130°F. This takes about 10 minutes.

Once it comes to temperature, crumble in one 200-gram packet of komékōji. It helps to crumble the kōji while it is still in the bag, pressing with your fingers until the pieces are loose. Mix the kōji into the steamed rice, and return the rice bowl to the rice cooker and cover loosely with a clean towel. Set the rice cooker to warm and leave the lid open so that the temperature remains between 130°F and 140°F for 8 hours. Stir occasionally to keep the heat evenly distributed. The amazaké will start to smell sweet with a hint of tang. After 8 hours, remove the bowl from the rice cooker and chill in an ice bath. Blend the rice in a high-powered blender until smooth. Store in the refrigerator. *Makes 8 servings*

AZALEA

(page 301)

WARM NOTE

Once the holidays have come and gone, it is time to turn toward understated flavors that bring nourishment. In the deep winter, I often enjoy a drink called yuzu-cha, made with a scoop of yuzu marmalade and hot water. This hot cocktail was inspired by the curative comfort that such beverages have always offered. Soothing and satisfying, the blend of ginger and green tea shōchū brings flavors of fire and earth together in pristine balance when sweetened with ribbons of honey. The drink hums with a low decibel of earthy spice while staying very clean and bright, the same way a healing brothy soup might taste in the dead of winter. *Serves one*

5½ ounces hot water (195°F)

1½ ounces Mizu green tea shōchū

½ ounce Ochiai Distillery Rihei ginger shōchū

½ ounce Rich Honey Syrup (page 317)

GARNISH Wheel of kumquat or mikan (tangerine)

Measure the hot water into a large teacup. Follow with the green tea shōchū, ginger shōchū, and honey syrup. Garnish with a wheel of kumquat or mikan. For an extra burst of flavor, express the oils of a citrus peel over the cocktail as a final flourish (discard the peel).

SKY DIVING

For as formal and straightlaced as many Japanese bartenders might appear on the surface, most will go to great lengths to make a customer crack a smile. Sometimes that means the use of unexpected flavored liqueurs like blue Curaçao. Ōsaka bartender Yoshiyuki Watanabe won first place in the Nippon Bartenders Association (NBA) cocktail competition in 1967 with this drink, which he named inspired by its bright blue hue. History texts show he used a 3:2:1 ratio of rum to Curaçao and lime cordial. I have adjusted the portions into ounces, thus making the cocktail larger in volume to some degree, but still adhering to the original ratio. I also decided to make a lime cordial from fresh lime peels and juice rather than opting for juice and simple syrup, for a slightly more bitter touch. *Serves one*

¾ ounce Bacardi Superior white rum   ¼ ounce Lime Cordial (page 318)
½ ounce Senior & Co. blue Curaçao

In a shaker tin, combine the rum, blue Curaçao, and lime cordial with ice. Shake to chill, then strain into a small cocktail glass or cordial glass.

daikan

GREAT COLD

butterburs bud, ice thickens on streams in mountains, hens start laying eggs

Midway through January and through the beginning of February is when our house would become the most intensely cold. Doors to unused rooms would be kept closed so smaller areas would hold heat more effectively. My mom would use the engawa like a refrigerator to store cases of mikan for easy snacking. As I reminisce on those times as a child in Japan, I look at myself today and see that little has changed. Food and drink habits still speak to creature comforts. In my case, this means a blend of Japanese and Western traditions—a modest Old Fashioned (page 310) made with Japanese whisky if I am in need of something special, or for nostalgia, a bowl of rice alongside misoshiru (miso soup) and kinpira gobō (sautéed burdock root).

AFTER ANGELS

The comforts of sweet potato help carry me through the wintertime. Nishi Shuzō in Kagoshima makes a sherry cask aged sweet potato shōchū called Tenshi no Yūwaku (the angels, temptation). This is, of course, in reference to the angels share, which wafts from the barrels as the shōchū rests in the hot Kagoshima weather. This shōchū is beguiling, buttery, and bold; so, for a wintery oyuwari serve, I chose to combine it with a purple sweet potato vinegar for tang and nectarous uméshu. The vinegar is powerful, so you only need a small splash, but keep the kettle on, because you may want another round. *Serves one*

3 ounces hot water (195°F)

1½ ounces Nishi Shuzō Tenshi no Yūwaku sweet potato shōchū

½ ounce uméshu

1 (scant) barspoon beni imo-su (purple sweet potato vinegar)

Pour the hot water into a teacup. Measure the sweet potato shōchū, uméshu, and beni imo-su over the water. The heat of the water will help to mix the ingredients.

OLD FASHIONED

Many bartenders in Japan will choose a classic cocktail and dedicate their time and attention to mastering it—for me, that cocktail is the old fashioned. I have spent countless hours working to perfect my preferred build. Spirit-forward and somewhat bitter, this should be a true staple in any bartender's repertoire.
This recipe is my preferred ratio for an old fashioned that skews pretty close to traditional. I would invite you to use it as a jumping-off point to find your perfect blend. *Serves one*

2 ounces Eagle Rare Kentucky Straight Bourbon whiskey

¼ ounce Rich Demerara Syrup (page 318)

2 dashes Angostura bitters

1 dash orange bitters

GARNISH Orange peel

In a mixing glass, combine the bourbon, demerara syrup, and bitters. Add ice and stir to chill. Strain into an old fashioned glass over a tempered ice sphere. Express the oils of a manicured orange peel over the top of the drink, then garnish.

NOTE | The old fashioned is one of the first classic cocktails that I learned how to make, though the recipe that was introduced to me initially was a bit more like a fruit cocktail than a refined mixture of spirit, bitter, sugar, and water. I love the flexibility of the template—within the framework, there are dozens of opportunities for mixing. You could use mezcal and agave nectar with orange bitters, for example, or make a rum old fashioned that uses Japanese curry syrup instead of demerara, and Bràulio Amaro instead of aromatic bitters.

MILLION DOLLAR

The legendary Louis Eppinger created the Million Dollar cocktail while working at the Grand Hotel in Yokohama in 1894. In the original recipe, gin met sweet vermouth, pineapple juice, and grenadine. When Eppinger's protégé Shogo Hamada took the drink with him to Café Raion in Ginza in the early 1920s, it is said he used an Old Tom gin, but the recipe featured in *The Savoy Cocktail Book* (1930) calls specifically for Plymouth. For modern palates I prefer Suntory Roku gin for the soft-handed sophistication it brings to the glass. To create a more even balance, I use dry vermouth instead of sweet, which also takes the fruitiness down a few notches. Consider this a more lithe, somewhat brisk version of the cocktail, suited for year-round sipping. *Serves one*

1½ ounces Suntory Roku gin

½ ounce Cocchi Vermouth di Torino

½ ounce Dolin Dry Vermouth de Chambéry

½ ounce pineapple juice

¼ ounce Grenadine (recipe follows)

1 egg white

GARNISH Lemon peel, pineapple wedge

In a shaker tin, combine the gin, both vermouths, the pineapple juice, grenadine, and egg white. Dry shake, then add ice and shake again to chill. Strain into a coupe. Express lemon oils over the drink (discard the peel) and garnish with a wedge of pineapple.

GRENADINE

Before going out to buy the bright red grenadine of childhood Shirley Temples, consider purchasing BG Reynolds or Small Hand Foods grenadine. Both of those are delicious and reliable products that will bring consistency and richness to a cocktail. If you prefer to make your own batch at home, in a saucepan, combine 2 parts pomegranate molasses to 1 part pomegranate juice and 1 part cane sugar. Warm over low heat and whisk just until the sugar is completely dissolved. If it starts to bubble, remove from the heat and continue to whisk. Store refrigerated for up to 3 weeks.

PART III

CODA

HOUSEMADE INGREDIENTS
Syrups, Infusions, Teas, and More

CASHEW ORGEAT

Crack 5 green cardamom pods and toast in a pan over low heat until aromatic (make sure you agitate the pan so they don't burn). To make via sous vide: Pour 16 fluid ounces cashew milk (such as Elmhurst) in a sous vide bag with the toasted cardamom. Seal the bag and cook sous vide for 1 hour at 180°F.

To make on the stovetop: Combine 16 fluid ounces cashew milk with the cardamom pods in a saucepan and gently warm the mixture. Keep covered on low (just under a simmer) for 30 minutes, and adjusting the heat as necessary to make sure it does not boil over or burn.

Strain the cardamom out of the milk. Weigh the milk and add 2 parts sugar to 1 part spiced cashew milk by weight. Finish with ¼ teaspoon of orange blossom water. Store in the refrigerator. *Makes 32 portions*

Use it:
Japanese Cocktail (page 213)
Japanese Cocktail #2 (page 215)

SHISO NO JYŪSU

Wash 12 ounces of red shiso leaves and set aside. In a large pot, bring 7½ cups (60 fluid ounces) water to a rolling boil. Add the shiso and boil for 5 minutes and then remove from the heat. Scoop out and discard the shiso leaves, leaving the water in the pot. Add 1¾ cups sugar to the shiso water and stir to dissolve. Add 2 teaspoons citric acid (or a scant ½ cup apple cider vinegar) to the pot and stir until the juice turns

magenta. After the juice has cooled, carefully decant into a glass storage container. Keep refrigerated. *Makes 30 portions*

Use it:
Murasaki Sonic (page 191)
Spiritfree: Magenta Cooler (page 193)

SHIOZAKURA SALINE SOLUTION

Remove the shiozakura (salted sakura blossoms) from the packet. For enough garnish for 10 cocktails, I recommend working with at least 20 flowers. Some will fall apart, so it is best to have plenty. (Or alternatively, if you only plan to use a few at a time, only rinse what you will need, as the salt acts as preservative.) Place a bowl on a scale and tare the weight. Add the shiozakura and make a note of the weight, then add two times their weight of warm water and stir until the salt dissolves. Set a sieve over a bowl and separate the flowers from the liquid. Store the saline solution in a sealed container and store the flowers in fresh water in the refrigerator.

Use it:
Spiritfree: Shiozakura Highball (page 135)
Sakura Collins (page 137)
Sakurazuké Martini (page 141)

UMÉ-SU

There are several reliable brands of umé-su you can buy on the commercial market, but please note that there are two distinct types. Uméboshi-su, made from salt-pickled umé and shiso, is extremely salty and sour. Umé-su is sour and sweet. I have had the most luck in the US finding umé-su in Japanese and Korean markets. Look for sugar, not salt, as a key ingredient. It is more common to see the term "extract" used on the Korean-made products. They will have varying levels of sweetness to acidity. To adjust the acidity, I sometimes add rice vinegar. My current easily accessible umé drinking vinegar of choice is Beksul Plum Extract, available from Amazon and H Mart.

If you want to make your own version at home, here is my recipe: Wash 2.2 pounds umé and remove the small round caps at the stem end. Pierce each one 5 or 6 times evenly across the surface with a toothpick. Lay the umé out on a clean towel and pat dry. Once dry, put the umé in a plastic bag and freeze until hard. Sterilize a large lidded jar (with a 5-quart capacity) with boiling water, and set aside 2.2 pounds white rock sugar. Once the jar is ready, place layers of the rock sugar and umé in the jar, beginning and ending with rock sugar. Pour 1 cup rice vinegar over the contents of the jar. Put the lid on rather lightly for the first week to allow the pressure to escape. Swirl the jar once a day for about a week. The syrup will be ready in 2 to 3 weeks. When ready to use, remove the umé and store in a separate jar for snacking or garnish. Store the finished syrup in sterilized jars in the fridge. *Makes 2 quarts*

Use it:
Grey Wolf (page 188)
Spiritfree: Azalea (page 301)

UMÉ-SHU

There are several commercial brands of umé-shu (see page 96),

but if you want to make your own version at home, here is my recipe: Wash 2.2 pounds umé and remove the small round caps at the stem end. Pierce each one 5 or 6 times with a toothpick. Lay the umé out on a clean towel and pat dry. Once dry, put the umé in a plastic bag and freeze until hard. Sterilize a large lidded jar (with a 5-quart capacity) with boiling water, and set aside 2.2 pounds rock sugar. Once the jar is ready, place layers of the rock sugar and umé in the jar, beginning and ending with rock sugar. Pour 6¼ cups (50 fluid ounces) shōchū or vodka (35% to 40% ABV) over the contents of the jar. Seal the container with the lid. Store in a cool, dry place and rotate every week or so. It will take at least 6 months before the umé-shu is ready to drink, though I wait at least 1 year to let the flavors develop. *Makes 45 ounces*

Use it:
Umé Old Fashioned (page 112)
Smoked Umé Margarita (page 115)
Umé Shōchū Sour (page 185)

shiroppu
SYRUPS

RICH HONEY SYRUP

Combine 2 parts honey to 1 part hot water by weight. Stir until the honey has fully dissolved. Store refrigerated for up to 3 weeks.

Use it:
Umé Old Fashioned (page 112)
Umé Shōchū Sour (page 185)
Chawari Toddy (page 226)
Hotto Campari (page 270)
Matcha Miruku (page 281)

Spiritfree: Matcha Miruku (page 283)
Warm Note (page 305)

KINMOKUSEI SYRUP

Combine 1 tablespoon dried kinmokusei (osmanthus) flowers with 1 cup water heated to 205°F (or just boiled) and steep for 6 minutes. Strain. Weigh the liquid and add an equal amount of sugar by weight. Store refrigerated for up to 1 week. *Makes 10 ounces*

Use it:
Kinmokusei Cocktail (page 242)
Spiritfree: Golden One (page 245)
Spiritfree: Matcha Miruku (page 283)
Saké Chai Flip (page 287)

LIME CORDIAL

Using a Y-peeler, strip off the zest of 2 limes, avoiding the pith as much as possible. Set the peeled limes aside for use later. In a bowl, combine the peels and 1 cup sugar and mix thoroughly and vigorously, muddling the peels to express the oils from the zest into the sugar granules. Rest for at least 15 minutes. Transfer to a saucepan. Juice 1 ounce of lime juice and add to the pan, bringing the mixture to a simmer over medium-low heat. Cook for 5 minutes, stirring consistently until the sugar dissolves. Let the lime peels sit in the hot mixture for 10 minutes, then strain and let cool.

Store in the refrigerator. Best if used within 3 days. *Makes 9 ounces*

Use it:
Gimlet (page 153)
Sky Diving (page 306)

RICH CANE SYRUP

Petite Canne sugarcane syrup from Martinique is a great commercial cane syrup to use in cocktails; it is consistent in sweetness and offers a rounder texture than homemade versions. But if you want to make this from scratch, combine 2 parts cane sugar to 1 part hot water by weight. Stir until the cane sugar has fully dissolved. Store refrigerated for up to 2 weeks.

Use it:
Rose Manhattan (page 124)
Washitsu (page 133)

RICH DEMERARA SYRUP

Combine 2 parts demerara sugar to 1 part hot water by weight. Stir until the sugar has fully dissolved. Store refrigerated for up to 2 weeks.

Use It:
Daiquiri (page 168)
Grey Wolf (page 188)
Hōjicha Coconut Daiquiri (page 277)

SIMPLE SYRUP

Combine 1 part granulated sugar to 1 part warm water by weight. Stir until the sugar has fully dissolved. Store refrigerated for up 2 weeks.

Use it:
Smoked Umé Margarita (page 115)
Hishimochi Bitters and Soda
  (page 119)
Sakura Collins (page 137)
Ryūkyū Gimlet (page 155)
Wisteria Cocktail (page 159)
Spindrift (page 167)
Midori Shōchū Sour (page 163)
Elderflower Sour (page 175)
Mojito (page 177)
Kamakiri (page 179)
Kyohō Sour (page 219)
Sudachi Shōchū Sour (page 225)
Autumn's Jacket (page 237)
Kaki Flip (page 230)
Kiku Cocktail (page 251)
Kami Hikōki (page 269)
Yuzu Salty Dog (page 274)
Frosty Mikan (page 284)

French 75 (page 296)
Holiday Highball (page 298)

STRAWBERRY SYRUP

Hull 1 pound strawberries: To hull a strawberry, place the tip of the knife just under the green leafy cap and cut a small cone out of the top of the strawberry, removing the hard white core underneath. Rinse the strawberries and pat them dry. Halve lengthwise. Place a bowl on a scale and weigh the strawberries. Add an equal weight of granulated sugar to the bowl. Stir well until each strawberry half is coated in sugar. Cover with plastic wrap and allow to rest in the refrigerator for 24 hours. At this point the juices of the strawberries will have leached out into the sugar. Weigh the batch, transfer strawberries and juice into a pot, and add half of the weight in water. Bring up to a simmer over medium-low heat, allowing it to bubble away for 15 minutes. Remove from the heat and allow it to cool. Strain out strawberries (and discard, or save for other uses) and store refrigerated for up to 2 weeks.
Makes about 20 ounces

Use It:
Ichigo Sour (page 127)

infyūjon
INFUSIONS

GINGER-INFUSED SHŌCHŪ

In a large glass jar, combine 3 tablespoons grated fresh ginger and one 750-milliliter bottle rice shōchū and let infuse at room temperature for 24 hours. Strain through a fine-mesh sieve (or for a smoother finish through a coffee filter). I suggest Chiyonosono 8,000 Generations rice shōchū or Takahashi Shuzō's Hakutake Shiro rice shōchū for this infusion. The infusion will last indefinitely.

Use it:
Kamakiri (page 179)
Warm Note (page 305)

GREEN TEA-INFUSED SHŌCHŪ

In a large glass jar, combine 5 tablespoons loose-leaf Japanese green tea and one 750-milliliter bottle rice or barley shōchū and let infuse at room temperature for 3 hours. Strain and store in a cool, dark place. I suggest Chiyonosono

ON SHŌCHŪ INFUSIONS I use commercial brands of green tea and lemongrass shōchū to make the cocktails in this book, because they will be consistent every time, but that doesn't mean you shouldn't make your own seasonal infusions at home if the spirit moves you. When made commercially, the primary flavor contributors to shōchū are usually added at the second stage of the fermentation process just before the moromi (mash) is distilled, so the flavors of the ginger, lemongrass, or other ingredients will be expressed differently in the commercial products versus home infusions. That said, it is not uncommon for bars to create their own shōchū infusions with fresh fruits and vegetables—a wonderful way to capture shun (seasonality) in a bottle. The infusion times suggested here are just that: suggestions. Depending on which shōchū you choose, how finely the ingredients are cut, and the general temperature of the room in which you are infusing, these factors will change the rate and intensity of the infusion. Trust yourself and taste as you go.

8,000 Generations rice shōchū, Takahashi Shuzō's Ginrei Shiro rice shōchū, or The Yanagita Koma Honkaku barley shōchū for this infusion. The infusion will last indefinitely.

Use it:
Ryūkyū Gimlet (page 155)
Midori Shōchū Sour (page 163)
White Grasshopper (page 291)
Warm Note (page 305)

SPICE-INFUSED VODKA

In a suribachi (mortar and pestle), lightly crack 1 tablespoon pink peppercorns. Add the cracked pink peppercorns, 1 tablespoon dried hibiscus, ¼ teaspoon salt, and 1 tablespoon grated fresh wasabi* to a large glass jar. Pour in a 750-milliliter bottle of Suntory Haku vodka. Allow to infuse at room temperature for 48 hours. Strain through a coffee filter and store refrigerated for up to 3 weeks. *Makes about 24 ounces*

*If you do not have fresh wasabi, you can use wasabi paste—just be sure to seek a brand that uses actual wasabi and not horseradish. The label will say "hon-wasabi."

Use it:
Kumiko Bloody Mary (page 150)

ocha
—
TEA

CHILLED HŌJICHA

In a glass or ceramic brewing vessel, combine 3 grams hōjicha and 10 ounces hot water (195°F) and steep

for 2 minutes. Strain into a glass vessel and place in the refrigerator to cool. For a faster chill, you can set up an ice bath and cool it, uncovered, on the countertop or in the sink. *Makes about 9 ounces*

Use it:
Clarified Mezcal Milk Punch
  (page 261)
Hōjicha Coconut Daiquiri (page 277)

CHILLED MUGI-CHA

In a saucepan, bring 1 quart water to a boil. Add 1 sachet mugi-cha to the water, lower the heat, and simmer for 5 minutes. Remove from the heat and allow to steep for 10 minutes. Strain off the brewed mugi-cha and cool in an ice bath. Store in the refrigerator for up to 1 week. *Makes about 30 ounces*

Use it:
Mugi Gin and Tonic (page 180)
Spiritfree: Mugi Tonic (page 182)

COLD-BREW SENCHA

In a glass jar, combine 10 tablespoons sencha leaves and 3 cups room temperature filtered water and steep for 3 hours. Strain out the leaves and keep the tea. I enjoy steeping the leftover leaves for a personal cup or two of tea after cold-brewing. There is still flavor in the leaves and I hate to waste such goodness. *Makes about 24 ounces*

Use it:
Ryokucha-Hi (page 156)
Spiritfree: Magenta Cooler
  (page 193)
Spiritfree: Golden One (page 245)

RESOURCES

bā yōhin to garasu

BARWARE AND GLASSWARE

Bar Times Store: *bar-times-store.tokyo*
Cocktail Kingdom: *cocktailkingdom.com*
Etsy: *etsy.com*
Kimura Glass: *kimuraglass.net*
Korin: *Korin.com*
Koto Tea: *kototea.com*
MTC Kitchen: *mtckitchen.com*
Nalata Nalata: *nalatanalata.com*
Nihon Ichiban: *anything-from-japan.com*
SoKichi: *sokichi.co.jp*
Toiro: *toirokitchen.com*
Umami Mart: *umamimart.com*

zairyō

INGREDIENTS

Amazon: *amazon.com*
Asian Food Grocer: *asianfoodgrocer.com*
H Mart: *hmart.com*
Kettl Tea: *kettl.co*
Koto Tea: *kototea.com*
MTC Kitchen: *mtckitchen.com*
Rare Tea Cellar: *rareteacellar.com*
Spirit Tea: *spirittea.co*
Yunomi: *yunomi.life*

supirittsu

SPIRITS

Astor Wines & Spirits: *astorwines.com*
Binny's Beverage Depot: *binnys.com*
K&L Wine Merchants: *klwines.com*
Total Wine: *totalwine.com*

BARS OF NOTE

FUKUOKA

Bar Oscar

Hakata Yatai Bar Ebi-chan

KYŌTO

Bar Bunkyu: *barbunkyu.jimdofree.com*

Bar Ixey: *facebook.com/ixey26*

Bar Rocking chair: *bar-rockingchair.jp*

Bee's Knees: *bees-knees-Kyōto.jp*

Cinematik Saloon: *cinematiksaloon.com*

L'Escamoteur: *facebook.com/ LEscamoteur-1392735951033939*

nokishita711: *nokishita.net*

ŌSAKA

Bar Juniper: *facebook.com/bar.juniper*

Tom & Jerry Bar: *tom-and-jerry-bar.com*

SAPPORO

Bar Yamazaki: *bar-yamazaki.com/english.html*

TŌKYŌ

Bar BenFiddich: *facebook.com/BarBenfiddich*

Bar Four Seasons: *bar-fourseasons.jp/*

Bar High Five: *barhighfive.com*

Bar Hoshi: *facebook.com/Bar-89F-1554652388099013*

Bar Ishinohana: *ishinohana.com*

Bar l'Osier at Shiseido Parlor: *losier.shiseido.co.jp*

Bar Lupin: *lupin.co.jp*

Bar Orchard Ginza: *facebook.com/barorchardginza*

Bar Shake: *barshake.jp*

Bar Tram: *small-axe.net/bar-tram*

Bar Trench: *small-axe.net /bar-trench*

Bar Triad: *small-axe.net/bar-triad*

Bar Tsubomi

Gen Yamamoto: *genyamamoto.jp*

JBA Bar Suzuki: *jba-barsuzuki.owst.jp/*

Kamiya Bar: *kamiya-bar.com*

Le Parrain

Little Smith: *littlesmith.net*

Main Bar at Tōkyō Kaikan: *kaikan. co.jp/en/restaurant/main_bar*

Mixology Experience: *spirits-sharing.com*

Mōri Bar

Nikka Blender's Bar: *nikkabar.wixsite.com/nikka*

Old Imperial Bar at Imperial Hotel Tōkyō: *imperialhotel.co.jp/e/tokyo/ restaurant/old_imperialbar*

The SG Club: *sg-management.jp*

Star Bar Ginza: *starbar.jp*

Tender

Y&M Bar Kisling

YOKOHAMA

The Bar Casablanca: *casablanca.yokohama*

Bar Noble: *noble-aqua.com/bar_noble*

Bar Sea Guardian II at Hotel New Grand: *hotel-newgrand.co.jp/ english/restaurant/sea-guardian-2*

Cocktail Bar Nemanja: *bar-nemanja.com*

BIBLIOGRAPHY AND RECOMMENDED READING

Alexander, Jeffrey W. *Brewed in Japan: The Evolution of the Japanese Beer Industry*. UBC Press, 2013.

Arnold, Dave. *Liquid Intelligence: The Art and Science of the Perfect Cocktail*. W. W. Norton & Company, 2014.

Boothby, William. *The World's Drinks and How to Mix Them*. Palace Hotel, 1900.

Brekell, Per Oscar. *The Book of Japanese Tea*. Tankosha Publishing, 2018.

Broom, Dave. *The Way of Whisky: A Journey Around Japanese Whisky*. Mitchell Beazley, 2017.

Chong, Doryun, et al. *Tokyo 1955–1970: A New Avant-Garde*. The Museum of Modern Art, New York, 2012.

Craddock, Harry. *The Savoy Cocktail Book*. Constable & Company, LTD, 1930.

Fitts, Robert K. *Issei Baseball: The Story of the First Japanese American Ballplayers*. University of Nebraska Press, 2020.

Fuller, Hector. *Getting Into Port Arthur*. The Reader Magazine: Volume 4, Number 6, November 1904.

García, Héctor, and Francesc Miralles. *The Book of Ichigo Ichie: The Art of Making the Most of Every Moment, the Japanese Way*. Penguin Books, 2019.

Hachisu, Nancy Singleton. *Japan: The Cookbook*. Phaidon Press, 2018.

Hachisu, Nancy Singleton. *Preserving the Japanese Way: Traditions of Salting, Fermenting, and Pickling for the Modern Kitchen*. Andrews McMeel Publishing, 2015.

Higuchi, Susumi et al. "Japan: Alcohol Today," *Addiction*, 2007; 102:1849–62.

Howard, A.C. *A.C. Howard's Directory, for the City of Indianapolis*. A.C. Howard, 1857.

Hughson, David. *The New Family Receipt-book, Or, Universal Repository of Domestic Economy: Including a Fund of Useful Knowledge and Experience in All the Various Branches of Cookery, Medicine, Confectionery, Pastry, Brewing, Distilling, Pickling, Preserving, Perfumery, Dyeing, Gilding, Painting, Varnishing, Agriculture, Farriery, Gardening, Hunting, Fishing, Fowling*. United Kingdom: W. Pritchard and J. Bysh, 1817.

Karan, Pradyumna P., and Kristen Stapleton. *The Japanese City*. University Press of Kentucky, 1997.

Kaze, Yoshimura. "The Rise of Cocktail Culture in Japan Observed in Cocktail Books from the Meiji and the Early Showa Era." *Journal of Liberal Arts and Sciences at Tokyo City University*, Vol. 8, 2015.

King, Joseph L. *History of the San Francisco Stock and Exchange Board*. Joseph L. King, 1910.

Lippit, Seiji M. *Topographies of Japanese Modernism*. Columbia University Press, 2002.

Lyman, Stephen, and Chris Bunting. *The Complete Guide to Japanese Drinks: Sake, Shochu, Japanese Whisky, Beer, Wine, Cocktails and Other Beverages*. Tuttle Publishing, 2019.

MacElhone, Harry. *Harry's ABC of Mixing Cocktails*. Dean & Son, Limited, 1923.

Mansfield, Stephen. *Tokyo: A Cultural and Literary History*. Signal Books, 2009.

Meehan, Jim. *The PDT Cocktail Book: The Complete Bartender's Guide from the Celebrated Speakeasy*. Sterling Epicure, 2011.

Neff, Robert. *Letters from Joseon: 19th Century Korea Through the Eyes of an American Ambassador's Wife*. Seoul Selection, 2012.

Niehaus, Andreas, and Tine Walravens. *Feeding Japan: The Cultural and Political Issues of Dependency and Risk*. Palgrave Macmillan, 2017.

Pellegrini, Christopher. *The Shochu Handbook: An Introduction to Japan's Indigenous Distilled Drink*. Telemachus Press, LLC, 2014.

Sand, Jordan. *House and Home in Modern Japan: Architecture, Domestic Space, and Bourgeois Culture, 1880–1930*. Harvard University Press, 2003.

Sanmi, Sasaki. *Chado the Way of Tea: A Japanese Tea Master's Almanac*. Tuttle Publishing, 2005.

San Francisco Call. Volume 104, Number 17, June 17, 1908.

Society for Nada Sake Research (SNSR); nada-ken.com/main/en/.

Sorby, Karol. *Asian and African Studies*. Slovak Academic Press, 1997 (Vol. 6–2, 151).

Stalker, Nancy K. *Devouring Japan: Global Perspectives on Japanese Culinary Identity*. Oxford University Press, 2018.

Stevens, Carolyn S. *On the Margins of Japanese Society: Volunteers and the Welfare of the Urban Underclass*. Routledge, 1997.

Teitelbaum, James. *Destination Cocktails: The Traveler's Guide to Superior Libations*. Santa Monica Press, 2012.

Thomas, Jerry. *How to Mix Drinks, or the Bon Vivant's Companion*. Dick & Fitzgerald, 1862.

Tipton, Elise K., and John Clark. *Being Modern in Japan: Culture and Society from the 1910s to the 1930s*. University of Hawaii Press, 2000.

Tsuji, Shizuo. *Japanese Cooking: A Simple Art*. Kodansha USA, 1980.

Urushido, Masahiro, and Michael Anstendig. *The Japanese Art of the Cocktail*. Houghton Mifflin Harcourt, 2021.

Utsukushii Kurashikata Institute. (2020). 72 Seasons (1.3.1) [Mobile App] App Store. apps.apple.com/us/app/72-seasons/id1059622777.

Uyeda, Kazuo. *Cocktail Techniques*. Mud Puddle Books, 2010.

Wondrich, David. *Imbibe! Updated and Revised Edition: From Absinthe Cocktail to Whiskey Smash, a Salute in Stories and Drinks to "Professor" Jerry Thomas, Pioneer of the American Bar*. TarcherPerigee, 2015.

ACKNOWLEDGMENTS

As with the best things in life, the path traversed to write this book was not walked alone. I am indebted to my co-writer, Emma Janzen, who brought her expertise as a spirits journalist, editor, and book author to bring clarity and life to my story.

This book would not have come into existence if it weren't for Jennifer Sit, Executive Editor at Clarkson Potter, who saw the need for a book on Japanese culture and cocktails. I must extend my deepest thanks to Talia Baiocchi, Editor in Chief of PUNCH, who recommended me as the author for such a book and another expression of gratitude to Jennifer for her trust and guidance along the way.

Thank you, Kevin Miyazaki, for photographs that capture the essence words cannot express.

My thanks to the people who graciously shared their time, knowledge, and expertise, including Greg Boehm of Cocktail Kingdom, Master Sommelier Ken Frederickson of High Road Spirits, Eric Swanson of Tokiwa Imports, and brand ambassadors like Gardner Dunn of Suntory, Emiko Kaji and Naoki Tomoyoshi of Nikka, Yumi Yoshikawa of Chichibu Distillery, Jonathon Edwards of Vine Connections, Maxwell Leer of MTC Sake, and the countless others who have offered sips, stories, and peeks into the lives of some of the world's greatest saké breweries and Japanese spirits and shōchū distillers.

Emma said writing a book is a family affair, and she was right. Her partner, Zach, my friend and bartender at Kumiko, Kayla, and my husband, Sammy, all lent their time and support. My deepest gratitude goes to my parents, Nancy and Chris Momosé, who taught me to live as a multicultural woman, how to make people feel at home, and for sharing some family recipes.

—JULIA

A million thanks to the two extraordinary women who brought me on board for this project. Julia, it's been a distinct honor and pure joy to help bring your vision to fruition. Thank you for opening my eyes to such a beautiful world and for trusting me with your stories. Jennifer Sit at Clarkson Potter, thank you for believing I was a good fit for this project, and for your patient guidance through this process!

Thanks also to the teachers, guides, and counselors who spared their time, knowledge, advice, and connections to us—Eric Swanson, Maxwell Leer, Greg Boehm, Shingo Gokan, Matthew Rowley, Maggie Hoffman, Hanna Lee—and to Kana Wahizu and Stephen Lyman for their kindness and expert tours of southern Japan.

Finally, thanks to my family for "the time away," and to my Zach for being the best partner in crime a girl could ask for—from our wild adventures on the ground in Japan to the smallest brainstorming sessions (ahem, interruptions to your daily routine), as usual I couldn't have done this without you by my side.

—EMMA

SUBJECT INDEX

RECIPE INDEX

Library of Congress Cataloging-in-Publication Data
Names: Momosé, Julia, author.
Title: The way of the cocktail / Julia Momosé;
    photographs by Kevin Miyazaki.
Description: New York: Clarkson Potter/Publishers,
    2021. | Includes bibliographical references and index.
Identifiers: LCCN 2020042679 (print) | LCCN
    2020042680 (ebook) | ISBN 9780593135372
    (hardcover) | ISBN 9780593135389 (ebook)
Subjects: LCSH: Cocktails—Japan. | Cocktails.
Classification: LCC TX950.59.J3 M67 2021 (print) | LCC
    TX950.59.J3 (ebook) | DDC 641.87/40952—dc23
LC record available at https://lccn.loc.gov/2020042679
LC ebook record available at https://lccn.loc
    .gov/2020042680

ISBN 978-0-593-13537-2
Ebook ISBN 978-0-593-13538-9

Printed in China

Photographer: Kevin Miyazaki
Illustrator: Yuko Shimizu
Editor: Jennifer Sit
Designer: Ian Dingman
Production editor: Mark McCauslin
Copy editor: Kate Slate
Production manager: Jessica Heim
Compositors: Merri Ann Morrell and Hannah Hunt
Indexer: Elizabeth T. Parson

10 9 8 7 6 5 4 3 2 1

First Edition